Russia at the Twenty-First Century

NEW HORIZONS IN
COMPARATIVE POLITICS

Russia at the Twenty-First Century

Politics and Social Change in the Post-Soviet Era

STEVE D. BOILARD
Western Kentucky University

Harcourt Brace College Publishers
Fort Worth Philadelphia San Diego Orlando Austin San Antonio
Toronto Montreal London Sydney Tokyo

Publisher: Christopher P. Klein
Senior Acquisitions Editor: David C. Tatom
Senior Product Manager: Steve Drummond
Project Editor: Denise Netardus
Art Director: Garry Harman
Senior Production Manager: Kathleen Ferguson
Cover Photograph: Charlie Steiner, International Stock

ISBN: 0-15-505317-5
Library of Congress Catalog Card Number: 96-78842

Address for orders:
Harcourt Brace College Publishers
6277 Sea Harbor Drive
Orlando, FL 32887-6777
1-800-782-4479

Address for editorial correspondence:
Harcourt Brace College Publishers
301 Commerce Street, Suite 3700
Fort Worth, TX 76102

Website address:
http://www.hbcollege.com

Printed in the United States of America

7890123456 066 987654321

To the memory of Wolfram F. Hanrieder

Scholar, Flyfisherman, Friend

Contents

Foreword

The extraordinary events of 1989–1991—the fall of the Berlin Wall, the disintegration of the Warsaw Pact, the collapse of the Soviet Union, and the end of the Cold War—force us to rethink older assumptions, not only in the realm of foreign policy and international relations but also in the field of comparative politics. For just as at the international level the world of bipolar superpowers (the United States and the Soviet Union) competing in a cold war struggle for influence and domination has ended, so too at the domestic level can Russia no longer be understood in terms of the models used in the past: as a monolithic, totalitarian, Marxist-Leninist state.

Steve Boilard's book *Russia at the Twenty-First Century* recognizes and comes to grips with these new realities. Unfortunately for students and scholars alike, most books available on Russia still focus on the earlier Soviet experience with an epilogue added purporting to bring the analysis up to date.

Professor Boilard recognized the need for a whole new approach and an entirely new text. Rather than just adding a postscript to an already-dated book, he started from scratch. The result is an original, conceptually innovative, and fresh approach freed from the burden of older paradigms. As Professor Boilard states in his Preface, his teaching on Russian government and politics had been "hindered by the virtual absence of broadly drawn texts that treated the post-Soviet Russian Federation as a country in its own right, rather than as little more than the epilogue to the grand story of the Soviet Union." The models and pedagogical devices of the past have outlived their usefulness.

Professor Boilard set out to reconceptualize post-Soviet Russia as a new, emerging, developing country rather than through the lenses of old-fashioned, outdated models. The result is a beautifully written, well-integrated, and conceptually fresh approach that represents a quantum improvement over earlier texts. The book not only clearly, fairly, and succinctly presents Russia as it is today but also does so with cohesiveness and flair, and within a logical framework that helps us understand where Russia may be heading at the beginning of the new millennium.

Following a stimulating introduction on how to interpret present-day Russia, Professor Boilard devotes two chapters to historical background. He then analyzes Russian society and politics in the next three chapters, focusing on living and social conditions, political parties and political groups, and the changing Russian political culture and values. The next part of the book discusses changing institutional arrangements and the Russian state. Four more chapters are devoted to public policy issues: social and economic policy, ethnicity and federalism, law and order, and religion. Finally, Professor Boilard analyzes Russian foreign policy and the country's new place in the world, and concludes with an assessment of where the country may be heading as it enters the twenty-first century.

I believe this is the best book available on Russian politics. It is well organized, nicely written, and easy to understand. Moreover, it is written using a comparative framework that instructors and students alike will find useful in placing Russia in a broader comparative context. I am pleased to be able to introduce this book and to recommend it to you.

HOWARD J. WIARDA
Professor of Political Science
The Leonard J. Horwitz Professor of
Iberian and Latin American Politics
Editor, the Harcourt Brace New Horizons
in Comparative Politics Series

Preface

This book was inspired by the need to construct a suitable analytical framework for my course on contemporary Russian government and politics. I was hindered by the virtual absence of broadly drawn texts that treated the post-Soviet Russian Federation as a country in its own right, rather than as little more than the epilogue to the grand story of the Soviet Union. No one can expect a definitive and comprehensive treatment of so tumultuous a society as contemporary Russia, but any attempt to understand a subject requires a structure for analysis. The pedagogical frameworks that seemed to serve so well during the Soviet period, with their emphases on totalitarian control, Marxist-Leninist ideology, and a bipolar international environment, have outlived their usefulness. They seem as quaint as my Studebaker's radio-dial markings designed to facilitate quick tuning to civil defense frequencies.

I therefore have sought to reconceptualize post-Soviet Russia as a new, emerging country rather than as the remains of an old, defeated empire. For the past two years I have sought to build from this conception a narrative that describes contemporary Russian government and politics with some degree of cohesiveness and context. It has been a matter of shooting at a moving target if ever there was one. I nevertheless believe that this book fairly, clearly, and succinctly describes Russia as it is today and offers sound reflections on where Russia may be headed at the dawn of the twenty-first century.

I am indebted to many people for their help in making this book possible. In particular I wish to thank the following persons who offered helpful suggestions or information on parts of the manuscript: Georg Bluhm, Jeffrey Gedmin, Joseph Hines, Vladimir Kompaniets, Bessic Matchavariani, Ross Miller, Anthony O'Regan, Robin Remington, Michael Rigg, and Wendy Shelburne. Harcourt Brace's acquisitions editor, David Tatom, lent support to this project in its critical, early stages. His assistant Katherine Clayton, and the project editor, Denise Netardus, ably shepherded the book through the more frenetic stages of production. The series editor, Howard Wiarda, was especially supportive, helping to conceptualize the project during a transatlantic phone call and offering crucial assistance throughout the writing of the manuscript. Most of all, I offer my heartfelt appreciation to my wife, Christine, without whose endless patience and boundless faith I could not have undertaken this project.

STEVE D. BOILARD

1
—

Overview and Introduction

For centuries Russia has figured prominently in the collective consciousness of Western civilization and the policies of its political leaders. The West's perception of Russia has stemmed from an admixture of fascination and disdain, pragmatic acceptance and ideological enmity, tentative hope and manifest fear. Among this range of emotions has seldom appeared fraternal affection or cavalier indifference.

Understanding Russia

The shifting balance of attitudes about Russia and the turbulence of its relations with the West stem partly from the difficulties in understanding the country. Its Byzantine politics and convoluted history lend to its inscrutability. Winston Churchill described Russia in 1939 as a "riddle wrapped in a mystery inside an enigma." The entity to which Churchill referred technically was the Union of Soviet Socialist Republics, of which the Russian Soviet Federative Socialist Republic (RSFSR) was only one (very large) part. But most understood the USSR to be a new incarnation of the Russian empire, albeit with unprecedented ideological foundations. Its

1

mystifying layers were deliberately preserved by the country's Communist rulers—the Soviet Union's latter-day tsars and commissars. The business of divining Soviet geopolitical intentions became increasingly urgent with the advent of nuclear weapons in the 1940s and 1950s. Over time, however, the West and Moscow settled into an uneasy "peaceful coexistence." The conservatism of Leonid Brezhnev's leadership in the 1960s and 1970s, coupled with the conciliatory international atmosphere of détente, lent for a time a sense of stability and consistency to the West's understanding of the Soviet Union. It was "the other superpower," and it came to be regarded as a permanent, integral part of the international environment. The country's domestic politics were popularly assumed to be under the virtually omnipotent, unswerving control of Communist Party bureaucrats.

The Soviet Union's leadership transitions of the early 1980s reinvigorated academic and political debates concerning the nature of the USSR. A few years later, Mikhail Gorbachev's ascension to power infused Soviet studies with a new urgency and vitality. The economic, political, and foreign policy reforms, initiated by Gorbachev under the rubrics of *perestroika* (restructuring), *demokratizatsiya* (democratization), and *novoye mushleniye* (new thinking), so altered the domestic policies and external behavior of the Soviet Union that even the most widely accepted verities about the eastern superpower were thrown into question. The nature and scale of developments in the Soviet Union took even the United States' Central Intelligence Agency by surprise— although CIA Director Robert Gates hastened to point out that some of the agency's data were superior to that even of the Soviets themselves.

In addition to the more tangible transformations (both intended and otherwise) that resulted from Gorbachev's reform efforts, the quantity and quality of information available to analysts of the Soviet Union also increased dramatically. Throughout the Cold War period, even the most tenacious Western researcher was faced with a serious shortage of pertinent information. Access to reliable domestic data was hampered by numerous institutional and political constraints, including adherence to "democratic" centralism in the Kremlin; rigid state-imposed restrictions upon news reporting; censorship of published material; deliberate falsification of data and disinformation; severe travel restrictions upon foreign visitors; an (at times justified) unwillingness of Soviet citizens to speak freely with strangers; and assorted other obstacles. Official Soviet statistical information, especially economic data, was problematic for a number of reasons, including intentional distortions and unavoidable difficulties arising from the unusual role of prices and money in the Soviet economy. In order to overcome those obstacles, "Sovietologists" devised various methods for extracting, extrapolating, and correcting data. They deciphered the arcane language of Soviet Cold War communiqués, divined Moscow's geopolitical intentions from grainy satellite photographs, and untangled the skein of the country's political hierarchy by officials' relative proximity to the General Secretary at May Day parades. They were not always wrong.

Then Gorbachev's reforms, and the unintended demise of the Soviet Union itself, reduced the need for the Sovietologists' services. A torrent of data—loosed by the easing of censorship under *glasnost*, the unaccustomed garrulity of Soviet (and former Soviet) officials freed from the threat of political reprisals, the nascent development of investigative journalism in the country, the dramatic lifting of restrictions upon Westerners conducting field and survey research—all of these inundated those who studied the Soviet Union. To some analysts this abundance of raw material was like an answered prayer, providing rich, unprecedented opportunities to explore important questions about the world's largest country. For others, over-whelmed with volumes of information which invalidated earlier "certain-ties" or, even worse, obfuscated them, the opening of the Soviet Union represented another illustration of the dictum: When God wants to punish, He answers our prayers.

But to truly understand modern Russia requires more than access to Soviet archives. The difficulty in understanding Russia is exacerbated by the fact that Russia periodically undergoes monumental changes: territorially, politically, and ideologically. And in what might possibly be interpreted as a macropolit-ical variation on Heisenberg's uncertainty principle (which asserts that the process of measuring alters the system being measured), the Soviet Union changed—in fact, it disintegrated—just as the West was coming to under-stand it.

Russia has now shed its Soviet trappings and has emerged as a separate country, along with the fourteen other former Soviet republics. Once again the Russians are reinventing their country, but toward what goal remains to be seen. Is it developing into a Western-style democracy? A nationalistic Slavic state? A fractured empire? Even Russians lack a defined, common per-ception of their country's current identity, let alone a sense of its destiny. Russia is a country in transition. Describing and analyzing it is therefore a tentative, potentially frustrating business.

The attempt is nevertheless rewarding. Despite the collapse of the Soviet Union, Russia remains one of the most important players, at least potentially so, in world politics. It covers more territory than any other country in the world, outweighing the geographically largest European country—Germany—with over 47 times the territory and almost twice the population. It possesses enormous reserves of oil, coal, natural gas, gold, and strategic minerals. Russia shares its 12,500-mile border with some strategically important countries, including China and North Korea, and has access to several major bodies of water, including the Pacific Ocean, the Caspian Sea, the Black Sea, the Baltic Sea, and the Barents Sea. It is a country that has made tremendous contribu-tions to science, space exploration, music, and literature. It also possesses the capacity, in the form of thermonuclear weapons, to destroy the world. Russia is an important country indeed.

Misdevelopment and Modernity

A central question about Russia's development concerns its modernization during the Soviet period. In its 75 years under Communist rule, Russia developed from an agrarian, backward country to an industrialized, urbanized, powerful state. The Soviet leadership modernized entire sectors of the country's economic base, established a far-reaching bureaucratic apparatus, and created a fearsome military machine. But not all growth is salubrious. It is not as though the Soviets succeeded in building a functioning, cohesive, civil society whose only flaw was a severe constraint of economic and political choices. If that were the case, post-Soviet Russia could indeed be quickly and effectively transformed by holding democratic elections and freeing market forces.

Instead, the Soviets' modernization of Russia might be viewed as *mis*development—the constructing of inappropriate or inefficient infrastructure, the maldistribution of resources, the decimation of agriculture, and most egregiously, the grotesque malformation of societal values and political culture. Worse perhaps than even underdevelopment—itself a burden at one point overcome by all "developed" countries, and surmounted in a matter of decades by the high-profile "Asian tigers" and other success stories—overcoming misdevelopment requires first the eradication of malignant growth and the exorcism of malevolent humors. For Russia the physical costs alone are enormous, as the country seeks to repair environmental damage, replace a disintegrating housing stock, break up monopolistic firms, and otherwise reverse the misshapen legacy of the Soviet past. But in addition to these physical costs, the psychosocial costs are incalculable. Addressing that part of the Soviet legacy that lies within the Russian people will require more than heavy lifting and careful budgeting.

Reinventing Russia

What is the new Russia to become? Now relieved of the Bolshevik fiction that it was destined to lead the entire world toward a Marxian utopia in which states, and even national groups, would be obsolete, Russia today must define a new identity, a new raison d'être. In the heady first days of post-Soviet independence, President Boris Yeltsin's leadership seemed to define Russia in such a way that it belonged in what the Americans had called the "First World." This not only meant that Yeltsin was committing his country to democracy and capitalism; it also suggested that Russia's relations with the West would finally be normalized. In this case normalization meant more than the "peaceful coexistence" touted by Soviet leader Nikita Khrushchev in the 1950s. It was to move beyond the détente forged in the 1960s and 1970s by Brezhnev and U.S. President Richard Nixon. It even was to surpass the "Common European Home" sought by Gorbachev in the 1980s. More than any of these earlier efforts to secure an equal footing with the West, and perhaps even to gain the West's acceptance, Yeltsin's initial vision for Russia interpreted the entire Soviet era, beginning with the Bolshevik revolution, as an unnatural break in Russia's relations with the world. Whereas Khrushchev (in power from 1957 to 1964) sought to mitigate the likelihood of nuclear confrontation with West; whereas Brezhnev (1964–1982) sought to secure the West's acceptance of its sphere of influence in Eastern Europe; whereas Gorbachev (1985–1991) sought a partnership *with* the West; Yeltsin sought membership *in* the West—or, more precisely, he sought to make the concept of "West" obsolete by eliminating the geopolitical distinction between East and West.

In Russia's first five years of post-Soviet independence Yeltsin found that creating a Western identity for Russia requires much more than freeing market forces, adopting the appropriate constitution, and holding elections. Although Yeltsin made the necessary professions of faith on behalf of his country, many of his countrymen have refused to be baptized in the waters of Westernism. Identity is a psychological quality, influenced, of course, by physical reality. Without the fruits of Western-style prosperity readily available, Russians' commitment to the path plotted by Yeltsin flagged. As the years of post-Soviet independence wore on, Yeltsin found that the zealousness of the recently converted had worn off.

By the mid-1990s, a large segment of the population, as well as many of Russia's elected representatives, questioned Yeltsin's (and most Westerners') assumption that the failure of the Soviet Union must naturally trigger Russia's enlightened (or repentant) adoption of a Western liberal identity. Why Western? Why democratic? Why indeed should this particular amalgam of territories and peoples constitute a unified state at all? The sovereign state known as the Russian Federation that emerged from the rubble of the Soviet Union is the product of a variety of circumstances: its borders were defined by earlier administrative decisions by the Soviet authorities (such as the decision to transfer the Crimea from the RSFSR to the Ukraine in 1956), its culture has been influenced by decades of Communist indoctrination, and its demographics derive in large part from massive relocation programs dictated by Stalin. Should the disintegration of the Soviet empire that began with the collapse of the Warsaw Pact and spread to the dissolution of the Soviet Union into its 15 constituent republics necessarily stop there? The claims of independence by regions of Russia shortly after Russia achieved its own independence—particularly by Tatarstan and Chechnya—speak against the notion of Russian cohesion and unity.

About This Book

This book focuses upon the politics and government of post-Soviet Russia. To the extent that the Russian Federation is a new country, there is a danger of ascribing to contemporary events a significance they may not deserve. And to the extent that Russian politics is still undergoing profound turbulence, there is a danger of fundamentally misreading likely development scenarios. Like Churchill, I cannot forecast the actions of Russia. Nevertheless, a study such as this must resist the temptation to focus on the closed chapter of the Gorbachev years as a way of minimizing the risk of embarrassing misinterpretations and failed predictions that accompanies analysis of the open-ended post-Soviet period. Instead, this book confines the recitation of Soviet history to a single chapter (Chapter 2) and offers additional reflections on events from Soviet history when warranted in subsequent chapters. It is hoped that the reader will take advantage of some of the countless books and studies that focus on Russian and Soviet history.

The remainder of the book focuses on the contemporary political environment and governmental structures of the Russian Federation. The risks associated with analysis from such a contemporary perspective are slightly attenuated by limiting detailed analysis of specific policies, governmental processes, and personalities—all of which are quite transitory. Even with these precautions, obsolescence of analysis has doubtless crept in. Nevertheless, with the passage of over five years since the creation of the post-Soviet Russian Federation, Russia's government, society, and economy have developed to a point where a reasonably durable analytical framework can be constructed.

Structure

After a concise review of Russia's historical background, this book examines four major subjects: Russian society and its political environment; the formal constitutional structure and political institutions of the Russian Federation; salient issues and policy responses; and Russia's role in the international system. Along the way the reader will encounter important questions about the country, many of which have intrigued students of Russia for many years, and few of which can be settled with any finality here. The reader is encouraged to keep these and other questions in mind, particularly when relating the discussions in this book with knowledge of unfolding current events:

- Is Russia returning to a development path that was interrupted by the Communist Revolution? How permanently has the Soviet experience affected Russia? Why did the Soviet Union collapse?

- Is democratic government a viable institution for the Russian people? Can democratic institutions be created by authoritarian means?

- How can the multi-national character of Russia's population best be accommodated by political and social structures? What role does religion play in Russia? Does a civic culture bridge ethno-national divisions?

- What is the relationship between patriotism and nationalism? How can the principle of self-determination that justified Russia's post-Soviet independence be reconciled with the need to preserve the Federation's multi-national unity?

- Is capitalism a viable economic basis for post-Soviet Russia? What should be the relationship between political and economic reform? How can a centralized, command economy be privatized? How much patience do Russians have for the process of reform?

- What are the proper geographical boundaries for Russia?

- What are Russia's foreign-policy interests? How do they conflict and coincide with America's?

- Is Russia part of Europe? Is it part of the West?

This book examines contemporary developments within Russia that may suggest answers to some of these questions. It also offers reflections and opinions. But it should be borne in mind that Russia, like the post–Cold War world itself, is in the midst of a transformation whose final result is not only unknowable, but subject to influence. And that, in the final analysis, provides a compelling reason for the study of contemporary politics.

Part I

Historical Background

2

Antecedents to the Russian Federation

As a geographical concept, Russia has existed for well over a thousand years. Its history has been epical, often tragic with periodic triumphs. By dint of its length and intensity, Russia's history is said to be deeply etched into the souls of its people. Even today, as Russia struggles to define itself in the so-called New World Order, many Russians harbor a somewhat fatalistic sense of their country's developmental trajectory, which has gained the momentum of a millennium. Knowing Russia's past may not facilitate the prediction of its future, but it eases the task of understanding its present.

Beginnings

From prehistoric times, the Slavic peoples occupying the area of modern Russia were subject to successive waves of invasion. These invasions and occupations influenced the cultural and economic development of the Slavs. Sometimes these foreign influences worked to the Slavs' long-term benefit, introducing agricultural techniques, administrative mechanisms, and other skills and technologies. But many raids were characterized by a murderous cruelty, which became a recurrent theme of Russia's past. The country's early history is filled with stories of gruesome tortures including a drinking cup fashioned from the skull of a conquered ruler. Although the Slavs attempted to establish defenses, invaders were largely unimpeded by natural geographic barriers. This helps account for Russians' preoccupation with security.

The early Eastern Slavs came under the control of Scandinavian Vikings ("Varangians"). Rurik, a Varangian leader, seized the city of Novgorod (about 100 miles south of present-day St. Petersburg) in A.D. 862. After successive conquests, Rurik's successor, Oleg, established a capital at Kiev (the capital of modern Ukraine). The result was Kievan Rus—a united Russian state. Subsequent rulers expanded the borders of Rus, adopted a written language based on the Cyrillic alphabet, and established the Russian Orthodox Church—a variant of Christianity linked to Constantinople and intentionally separate from Rome. By the eleventh century the state had developed a distinct identity and boasted considerable commercial, cultural, and religious importance.

After its zenith in the eleventh century Kievan Rus steadily declined, falling victim to a combination of internecine battles, disrupted trade, and periodic raids by marauding armies. Its people began to migrate northward—a trend that would have long-term implications for Russia's development. In the thirteenth century Kievan Rus fell to the Mongols ("Tatars" in Russian parlance). Kiev was destroyed, and Moscow steadily grew in importance. For two centuries the Mongols maintained domination over the Russians and exacted annual tribute. Although the Mongols generally allowed Russians to continue their day-to-day lives, the "Mongol Yoke" was economically and politically oppressive. When Russians would periodically rise up against the Mongols, they encountered savage counterforce and retribution.

Tsarist Russia

The Russians, led by Ivan III ("the Great"), eventually overthrew their Mongol oppressors, terminating the savage Mongol Conquest in 1480. Ivan III also seized control of the cities of Tver and Novgorod, consolidating Muscovite Russia. With Constantinople's fall to the Turks in 1453, Moscow assumed itself to be the "Third Rome," strengthening the concept of Russia as a united Christian empire. Ivan III adopted the title "Tsar" (a Russian variation on Caesar), and Russia's Tsarist era began.

The powers of the tsar were consolidated and increased under Ivan III's grandson, Ivan IV ("The Terrible"). But with Ivan IV's death in 1584, Russia's ruling circle became plagued with conspiratorial regents, foreign intrigue, and a series of false pretenders to the throne. The "Time of Troubles" had descended upon Russia, and embattled rivals called upon foreign powers, including Sweden and Poland, to intervene. This condition of domestic turmoil and foreign occupation continued until 1613. With the Poles driven from Moscow the year before, the Russian Assembly (*Zemsky Sobor*) elevated Mikhail Romanov to tsar and made the title hereditary. The House of Romanov would rule Russia for the next three centuries, until the revolution of 1917.

The Russian Empire

Russia became a European power of significance and took on a more Western identity under Tsar Peter I ("the Great"), the Romanov who ruled the country from 1689 to 1725. Peter's Russia, continually at war, secured a number of impressive victories over other powers. It was Peter who developed Russia's navy and more effectively organized its army. And it was he who reoriented the country's focus to the West.

Peter traveled extensively in Europe, and he was eager to transplant large features of its culture to Russia. His interest in the West was perhaps best symbolized by his moving of Russia's capital city from Moscow to St. Petersburg (on the shore of the Baltic Sea) in 1712. Peter's affection for the West also manifested itself in "Westernizing" policies, whereby arts and sciences, court customs, and even Russians' affinity for long beards were modified to conform with Western trends. Peter developed a reputation as a modernizer and social reformer, which contrasted sharply with many of his predecessors (and not a small number of his successors).

A successor who did share Peter's penchant for Western ways was Catherine II ("the Great"), who ruled Russia from 1762 until her death in 1796. Formerly a German princess, Catherine considered herself a great ruler and a philosopher of the Enlightenment era. In the latter self-defined capacity, she engaged in correspondence with several liberal French thinkers, including Voltaire. Despite her familiarity with liberal ideas, however, Catherine did little to attenuate the autocratic nature of the Russian court. She is frequently described as an "enlightened despot" by Russian and Western historians alike. In fact, Catherine's despotism, her distrust of and ambivalence toward the peasantry, was symptomatic of the Russian monarchy. Whatever the particulars of the various "Great," "Terrible," and "Bloody" tsars and emperors, the imperial edifice sat atop an oppressed, sometimes restive, population. Its worsening precariousness under Catherine II was clearly illustrated by a yearlong uprising in 1773 and 1774. The rebellion, led by a Don Cossack named Emelian Pugachev, united Cossacks, Tatars, serfs, and others against the aristocracy. Although ultimately quelled by force, the rebellion revealed the growing tension between the elites and the masses.

Russia's international position under the tsars swung between strength and weakness. Russia emerged as a Great Power in the eighteenth century, and at one point in the early nineteenth century it and France were the two major powers on the Continent. Napoleon's invasion of Russia and occupation of Moscow, followed by Tsar Alexander I's pursuit of Napoleon's retreating army and subsequent occupation of Paris, are illustrative of the shifting balance of power. Russia participated as one of the four Great Powers at the subsequent Congress of Vienna, but its fortunes continued to shift with the dynastic and imperial wars so characteristic of nineteenth century Europe's international relations and diplomacy.

Domestically, a pattern of alternating reform and repression had taken root in Russia. After Pugachev's uprising, almost a century would pass before the tsar at the time, Alexander II, finally removed a significant cause of popular unrest by abolishing serfdom in 1861—the year before Abraham Lincoln's Emancipation Proclamation. By this time, however, even the freeing of the serfs could not appease radical groups opposed to the regime. Intellectuals, nationalists, populists, and revolutionaries advocated a variety of visions for their country. A pronounced cleavage divided the regime's opponents between "Slavophiles," who advocated an ethnically distinct Slavic state grounded in Orthodoxy, and "Westernizers" who sought to resurrect and expand Russia's European identity and politics, which had begun under Peter I. The discontinuity of the two visions was nevertheless papered over as the radicals found common cause in their disdain for the current regime. The government unwittingly helped to unite its opponents through the imposition of widespread censorship, the practice of religious and political persecution, and its involvement in unpopular (and sometimes disastrous) foreign wars.

Repression and Revolution

Public unrest was exacerbated with the onset of Russia's industrial revolution in the last decades of the nineteenth century. Exploitive and unsafe working conditions, food shortages, and urban overcrowding composed a new category of grievances beyond the now familiar authoritarianism of the regime. By the time the final tsar, Nicholas II, assumed power in 1894, living conditions in the cities were so intolerable that the burgeoning urban population became a fertile recruiting ground for the growing reformist and revolutionary groups. This "proletariat," as the Marxist revolutionaries called it, assumed a pivotal role in the revolutionary events which were to transpire. It was in the proletariat's interest that a growing revolutionary group, the Social Democratic Labor Party, putatively would fight.

Founded in 1903, the Social Democrats increasingly became divided over the issue of how to proceed along the revolutionary path. The Menshevik (minority) group sought to develop a broad-based party acting according to the ideal of workers' democracy. For them, the revolution itself remained an eventuality beyond the immediate future, requiring first the full development of capitalism. The Bolshevik (majority) group, headed by V. I. Lenin, preferred to create an elite party that would guide the revolution without the direct participation of the workers. For the Bolsheviks (and Lenin in particular), the workers could not rise above their "trade union consciousness" and required an intellectual "vanguard"—the Bolsheviks—to act on their behalf. The Bolsheviks believed that the capitalist stage of development could be bypassed, and they sought an immediate transition to socialism.

On "Bloody Sunday" in 1905 the slaughter of more than a hundred unarmed petitioners by guards at the tsar's Winter Palace knocked out one of the regime's few remaining props: the popular belief that it was governmental underlings and renegades—not the tsar himself—who were responsible for the people's privations. In the following months strikes, demonstrations, riots, and assassinations would collectively constitute the 1905 Revolution, and by October Nicholas conceded to establish the trappings of a constitutional monarchy. Within a year, however, the tsar had reneged on most of his promised reforms. General public dissatisfaction with the regime continued, and increasingly radical revolutionary groups continued to agitate against the government.

Then, in 1914, Russia was drawn into war against Germany in defense of its Slavic ally, Serbia. The resultant First World War created conditions for a successful coup de grâce against the tsarist regime. Simultaneously weakening the country and galvanizing public opposition, the war cut the tsar's power base, including his own armies, from under him. In March 1917 Nicholas abdicated the throne in favor of his brother, Michael. Refusing that poisoned chalice, Michael turned sovereign power over to a "Provisional Government" headed by Prince Georgii Lvov. Lvov's government refused to remove Russia from the war—perhaps the most important and immediate demand of the disaffected population. Meanwhile, Lenin's Bolsheviks, who were not part of the Provisional Government, established a power base in the Petrograd (née St. Petersburg) Soviet, as the local revolutionary council was known. With the promise of "land, bread, and peace," the Bolsheviks gained popular support. Emboldened by the government's disarray as well as their own successes, the Bolsheviks overthrew the Provisional Government on November 7, 1917. The following July they adopted a constitution for the newly formed Russian Soviet Federated Socialist Republic (RSFSR).

Although Lenin was successful in overthrowing the Provisional Government, it would be three more years before the Bolsheviks (now calling themselves Communists) would consolidate power. During that time a civil war would rage, pitting the Communists against the "White" armies—a motley combination of monarchists, Mensheviks, and other groups. To gain the necessary *peredyshka* (breathing space) to contend with these domestic opponents, Lenin's new regime signed an armistice with Germany at Brest-Litovsk in 1918. The terms were harsh for Russia. The Russians transferred gold and other wealth to Berlin, and the transfer of western territory to Germany forced a moving of Russia's capital to Moscow. But Lenin presumed that the protagonists of the "imperialists' war" would ultimately destroy one another, so he considered it expedient to make short-term deals with and concessions to the imperialists in Berlin. True to this Machiavellian logic, Lenin would abrogate the Brest-Litovsk treaty after Germany was defeated several months later.

Far from freeing Russia from battles with foreign armies, however, the Brest-Litovsk treaty prompted tsarist Russia's allies, including the United States, Britian, Japan, and others to enter Russian territory with the declared intention of re-establishing an eastern front against Germany. Not at all enamored with the new regime in Russia, the western forces gave succor to the White armies—a fact that in later years was not neglected in official Soviet history. After Germany's defeat, the Allied forces were largely withdrawn, and the Communists went on to secure their victory over the Whites. In the process the Communists proceeded to establish Soviet Socialist Republics in neighboring Armenia, Azerbaijan, Belorussia, Georgia, and the Ukraine. Communist Russia initially maintained that these new republics should be considered independent countries, but by the end of 1922 they had all been absorbed into the new Union of Soviet Socialist Republics. The USSR was born.

The Soviet Union

Lenin maintained that the Russian Revolution was fought in the interests of *all* the world's workers—not just the Russian proletariat. The Bolsheviks had expected that their revolution would trigger uprisings throughout Europe and North America, fulfilling Marx's injunction: "Workers of the world, unite!" Expecting the imminent arrival of world revolution and the consequent Marxist utopia, Trotsky announced that his duties as the People's Commissar for Foreign Affairs would comprise issuing "a few proclamations," after which he would "shut up shop." Yet with a few short-lived exceptions, the companion revolutions did not materialize. Until the Second World War, Russia's sole companion in the Communist "world" was Outer Mongolia—hardly an auspicious beginning for the Communist Millennium. As a further disappointment (or perhaps not) for the Bolsheviks, the Marxian principle that the state should wither away had become stalled somewhere between the revolution and the civil war. But Lenin and other seraphs of the revolution were seldom burdened by any compulsive desire for ideological consistency; they were nothing if not flexible, pragmatic, and opportunistic. Perceiving no immediate danger of their regime giving way to the utopian statelessness of Communism, the Soviet leadership prepared for a somewhat longer interregnum. (It would be Stalin, not a successful world Communist revolution, who in 1925 would relieve Trotsky of his duties.)

The Soviet Union was thus established as a repository of the world's revolutionary flame, to be turned loose at such a time as would be warranted. With the founding of the Soviet Union the revolutionary zeal that had motivated the Bolsheviks was diluted by the more conservative desire to ensure the survival of the Soviet state. The revolutionary goal of fundamentally transforming world civilization could be achieved, according to Lenin's logic, only by securing the shorter-term, but essential, objective of maintaining the integrity (such as it was) of the Communists' new state. Once the business of ensuring the Soviet Union's security and viability was complete, Moscow could lead the way to the world Communist (or Socialist) revolution, which had missed its appointment with the First World War. This logic reversed the order of Trotsky's formulation, which perceived the survival of Russian socialism to depend upon world revolution. But Trotsky and his "left" allies were soon silenced by Stalin.

Thus the Soviet Union emerged as a country whose leadership was at once conservative (in its desire to stabilize its rule) and revolutionary (in its declared goal of eventually fomenting world revolution). The established governments of the world were therefore not inclined to extend friendly relations with a country that sought their ultimate demise, and the USSR spent its first years in diplomatic purgatory.

The Stalinshchina

As the political order began to coalesce after the First World War, the new and old great powers of Europe began to construct new relationships. Germany resumed its critical role in the development of the Slavic power in the east. With the signing of the Rapallo treaty in 1922, the two countries—one ostracized as illegitimate and ideologically noxious, the other branded as the defeated instigator of the world war—committed to economic, trade, and even military cooperation as a form of mutual support in a hostile world. Within a decade, the power of both countries was rapidly increasing at the hands of ruthlessly ambitious men. In Germany it was the Austrian, Hitler; in the Soviet Union it was the Georgian, Stalin.

After Lenin's death in 1924, Josef Stalin had contrived a successful path to supreme power using a combination of political manipulation and ideological contortion. Stalin's machinations surpassed even his predecessor's "salami tactics," whereby Lenin systematically divided his opposition like a butcher slicing meats. During the time of Stalin's rule (the *Stalinshchina*), the Soviet Union pursued a range of effective, frequently harsh modernization and militarization policies. Stalin was anxious about the international weakness of the backward, largely rural country over which he had established power, especially when compared with competitors such as Germany. In 1931 Stalin proclaimed that his country would have to make up a century's worth of modernization in ten years. A decade later he had in many ways succeeded. The country's production, investment, and development were dictated by "five-year plans," a testament to the Communists' hubris in harnessing the economy but nevertheless brutally effective. The progress achieved by the interwar Soviet Union is remarkable by a variety of standards: industrialization, mechanization, and urbanization; the building of infrastructure, the creation of a world-class army, the establishment of a complex bureaucracy; progress in science and technology; increases in literacy and life expectancy. All this, while simultaneously consolidating and centralizing power over a population that could never be considered wholly, or even largely, accepting of the Communist regime.

This last feat reflects the core of what would come to be known as Stalinism: the domination of the population, even of most of the governmental bureaucrats, by a pervasive system of ideological indoctrination, omnipresent surveillance, and political punishment (including exile, imprisonment, and execution). At its peak, this system became a destructive orgy of self-saving betrayal, societal anomie, and state-conducted torture—known later simply as the Terror. The Second World War's demands upon Soviet manpower and patriotism would require the mitigation of the worst of these excesses, and Stalin's death in 1953 would pave the way for Khrushchev's "de-Stalinization." Yet the core of the Soviet political system continued to rest—indeed, had to rest—upon the political neutralization and physical restriction of the hapless population. Without these, the Communist Party could not retain control of the country.

Stalin's success in strengthening the Soviet Union in the 1930s, coupled with Hitler's concurrent success in remilitarizing Germany, militated against the nonrecognition policy of most Western countries. Moscow came to be viewed as a useful counterweight to the Third Reich, and the Roosevelt administration in Washington extended formal diplomatic recognition in 1934. Another Soviet-German treaty (this time a nonaggression pact and a secret plan to divide Poland) in 1939 somewhat enervated Moscow's anti-German credentials. But Hitler's invasion of the Soviet Union in 1941 instantly restored Moscow's availability as an anti-German ally. Another audacious attack—this time at Pearl Harbor by the Japanese—brought the United States into the conflict, and soon the United States and the United Kingdom were working in an uneasy alliance with the Soviet Union against the Axis forces: Germany, Japan, and Italy.

By the time of Germany's defeat, itself a testament to Soviet strength and perseverance, the Soviet Union had seized or reclaimed most of the territory between Stalingrad and Berlin. The borders of the Soviet Union itself had been pushed to the Baltic Sea and into eastern Poland and Romania, and the Red Army occupied most of Eastern Europe. British and American forces, now with the assistance of liberated France, occupied the Continent's western territory. Efforts to create a mutually amenable European political order upon the ruins of the German Reich were unsuccessful. The ideological antipathy and politicomilitary suspicion between the Soviet Union and the West—only submerged, never eliminated during the wartime alliance—returned with a vengeance. Geopolitical disagreements became strategic conflicts, and the war-ravaged Continent was divided between the nascent "superpowers" which resided at its eastern and western flanks.

The Cold War

For the next four decades there ensued the Cold War, whose fundamental logic of bipolar competition would largely direct the Soviet Union's development until its demise in 1991. The immediate postwar years saw a geographical expansion of the Communist world—what the West called the "Second World"—to include such countries as Czechoslovakia, Hungary, and Poland. By 1949 the territory from which Nazism had sprung—or at least an eastern portion of it—had been transformed into a socialist state: the German Democratic Republic (GDR). The creation of the GDR was a partial fulfillment of Stalin's prophecy that fascism was the final stage of capitalism, upon which socialism would be built. The fulfillment was only partial because simultaneously upon the Reich's western territory was established a capitalist democracy allied with the United States (the Federal Republic of Germany).

Even more significantly, the fulfillment of Stalin's prophecy about socialism's triumph must be further discounted because Moscow's new socialist partners did not develop as the result of indigenous popular revolutions. With the exception of Yugoslavia and possibly Albania, the communist states of Eastern Europe were created at Moscow's instigation and maintained by the constant threat of Soviet military power. That threat was translated into lethal military action on at least three occasions in the 1950s and 1960s under the ex post facto justification of the "Brezhnev Doctrine." The Brezhnev Doctrine essentially proclaimed that the Soviet Union had the right, even the obligation, to defend the gains of socialism.

As the Cold War continued, the Second World grew beyond the Soviet Union and Eastern Europe. Often backed by Soviet power, and in some cases enjoying genuine indigenous support, revolutionary groups established communist regimes in Vietnam, Cuba, China, and in parts of Africa and Latin America. Communist parties also became institutionalized in the multiparty systems of West European democracies, although Soviet satraps never seized power in these countries.

For the Soviet Union, the expansion of the Communist world required revisions to Party doctrine. The interwar precept of "socialism in one country" no longer applied, as Moscow exploited the expansionist opportunities which the postwar world afforded. In its place the Kremlin now claimed that the "correlation of forces" in the world permitted a more active world role. The Soviet Union sought to control the growing number of Second World states through socialist international institutions such as the Warsaw Treaty Organization (a military alliance), the Council for Mutual Economic Assistance (for facilitating intrabloc trade), and the Communist Information Bureau (for directing East and West European Communist parties).

More importantly, the proliferation of nuclear weapons in the East and the West required that Moscow revise its doctrine asserting the inevitability of war. Sensing the undesirability of a nuclear exchange, Khrushchev resurrected the Leninist notion of "peaceful coexistence" in 1956. The two superpowers were nevertheless locked in an arms race, and by degrees the Soviet Union began to achieve rough parity with the United States. Shortly after Brezhnev assumed power in 1964, the Soviet Union's relationship with the United States finally stabilized, and an era of "détente" began.

To a large extent, détente sprang from the recognition that the arms race had produced a situation of "mutual assured destruction" (MAD), whereby neither country could avoid a devastating retaliatory nuclear attack in the event of a nuclear war. The recognition of MAD prompted the two countries to sign the Strategic Arms Limitation Treaty (SALT I) in 1972 and a number of other treaties over the next two decades. Most significantly for the Soviet Union, détente marked the high-water mark of Soviet prestige in the world. Moscow's top leaders were meeting face-to-face with American presidents; arms control treaties that acknowledged and preserved the Soviet Union's military parity were coming into force; and the Second World was reaching into almost all the world's continents.

The Irony of Détente

Experiencing for the first time a solid sense of international security, the post-Stalin leadership saw less need for the bunker mentality of the *Stalinshchina*. Compared with Stalin's time, Soviet domestic politics thawed somewhat. The regime permitted greater movement of its citizens around the country, allowed some access to Western media and visitors, and even initiated new economic reforms. The Soviet Union progressively adopted the societal and political trappings of other industrialized states. But notwithstanding these post-Stalin reforms, there always remained a political threshold that could not be breached: the supremacy of the Party.

The Soviet leadership by the time of détente had become highly conservative in its foreign and domestic policies. Although failing to achieve Marx's Communist stage, and even Brezhnev's "real developed socialism," the Soviet Union had established itself as a superpower, with the world's largest military force, an enormous sphere of influence, and a relatively docile population. It was a status quo that the Kremlin sought to preserve.

Yet a modern nation's health requires more than a geopolitical balance of power and internal political acquiescence. A nation—or an empire—must also tend to its economic and spiritual health. And that points to the irony of détente's achievements. Although Moscow finally secured its primary international goal of Western acceptance and recognition of its sphere of influence, almost at the same moment the Soviet Union was losing stability from within. After Stalin's death in 1953, the regime had purchased the compliance of the masses largely through a guarantee of employment, housing, health care, and other necessities. This "contract" is summarized in the sardonic saying, "we pretend to work, and they pretend to pay us."

But by the 1970s the regime encountered mounting difficulty in fulfilling its side of the bargain. Partly this was due to the rising expectations of workers who learned of Western standards of living through the increased media exposure allowed by détente. More worryingly it was also due to the slowing efficiency of the Soviet economy. This stemmed from a variety of causes. The easy, extensive gains of industrialization had largely been achieved, and the economic system foundered as it sought to make the transition to a post-industrial age. The central planners struggled in vain to keep up with the myriad decisions a complex economic system demands. Workers and managers lacked the motivation to perform adequately, and entrepreneurship could hardly be fostered without adequate incentives. The system bred corruption, sloth, and alienation.

Neither could Moscow's external empire in Eastern Europe be considered internally secure merely because the West had recognized the reality of Soviet power. The economic systems in Eastern Europe had not had as long to develop the insalubrious effects of centralization, but opposition to Communism in Eastern Europe did not especially require economic grievances. East Europeans opposed their Communist governments as instruments of Moscow's domination. This had changed little since the Second World War. Despite scattered instances of genuine support for the Communist parties, for socialist ideology, and even for Soviet patronage in Eastern Europe, the Soviet bloc had been forged amid obstinate internal opposition. While most of that opposition was quickly brought under control—even eventually concealed—it could not be eliminated. Indeed, it would not be an exaggeration to say that the Soviet Union never entirely managed to consolidate its control over Eastern Europe. Because of the enduring, if largely passive, resistance in Eastern Europe, the Soviet Union could maintain the cohesion of its bloc only with constant effort. Moscow's success depended upon its ability to keep the East Europeans politically neutralized, if not indoctrinated; spiritually docile, if not pacified; physically obedient, if not cooperative. Western recognition of the Soviet sphere of influence could not create support for Moscow in Eastern Europe.

By the beginning of the 1980s, the declining cohesion of Moscow's empire was witnessed by the rise of the Solidarity movement in Poland and the civil war in Afghanistan. At the same time Soviet society was displaying signs of social, economic, and environmental decline through such indicators as decreasing life expectancy and decreasing agricultural yields. Brezhnev's own ill health and advanced age prevented his making any substantial course corrections, and the Soviet system was still on its path of decline when he succumbed to a heart attack in 1982. Brezhnev's successor, Yuri Andropov, briefly raised hopes that he might be able to steer the country toward a more promising future. But although he managed some tentative reforms, Andropov's health failed and he died within fifteen months. The next leader, Konstantin Chernenko, was dying when he took power in February 1984. No one was surprised by his death scarcely a year later. For the first five years of the decade, the health of the Soviet leadership was a metaphor for the health of the country itself.

The Gorbachev Era

Such was the setting when Mikhail Gorbachev took the post of General Secretary in 1985. Healthy and only 54 years old, Gorbachev was from a younger generation of Soviet leaders. He had come through the Party ranks after the death of Stalin, and thus was less tainted by and invested in the Stalinist system. He also had been a protégé of Andropov. In short, Gorbachev possessed the health, political background, and connections that permitted a more energetic approach to reform. Gorbachev immediately acknowledged that all was not well with the USSR, and before long he was calling for radical reforms. He strengthened his power base by moving ideological conservatives out of the Politburo and other positions of power, and appointing persons who shared his desire for reform. Before long Gorbachev had stabilized his power base and set out to correct the Soviet Union's "drift" away from the "proper policies."

During his seven years in power, Gorbachev undertook the most far-reaching reforms in Soviet history. He did not initially conceive them as such; Gorbachev developed his reform program gradually and improvisationally. In retrospect, it is clear that Gorbachev did not realize the scale and intractability of the diseases from which his country suffered. Indeed, if the disease is understood to be socialism itself, clearly Gorbachev never grasped the root cause of the Soviet Union's decline. For all his commitment to reform, Gorbachev remained a socialist to the end.

Gorbachev began his efforts to reverse his country's decline by calling upon the people to work harder, better, and soberly—in a word, to repent. One is reminded of the charge in Nike advertisements to "just do it." Using a combination of moral appeals and restrictions on alcohol consumption (for which he was widely disliked), he sought the *uskoreniye* ("acceleration") of the economy. When little improvement was observed, Gorbachev tried to enlist the support of the intelligentsia and others with his policy of *glasnost* (openness). Through glasnost, Gorbachev eased censorship of various publications and encouraged the criticism of governmental corruption and inefficiency. This unleashed an outpouring of grievances and anti-government tirades, but it did not have the desired effect of shaming or forcing bureaucrats and managers into behaving more professionally.

By 1987 Gorbachev's umbrella program of *perestroika* ("restructuring") was in full swing. Perestroika entailed numerous decrees and laws to decentralize economic decisionmaking and otherwise to make the economy work more efficiently. It tapped into limited market forces, permitting some "cooperative" (semiprivate) enterprises and small business ventures. But most enterprise managers and bureaucrats in the government ministries resisted the reforms, seeking to retain the privileges they had secured for themselves within the corrupt system. Gorbachev found that even as General Secretary of the Communist Party, he could not impose his will on the enormous network of Soviet elites who had become ensconced during the Brezhnev period. He then turned to more drastic measures still: he sought to unleash the political power of the masses.

In a dramatic break from the Soviet past, Gorbachev moved to partially separate the functions of the Party and the state. He established a directly elected legislature (the Congress of People's Deputies), which in turn elected a full-time Supreme Soviet. The post of Chairman of the Supreme Soviet was established to serve as the head of state. Secret, multicandidate elections to the Congress of People's Deputies were held in March 1989. Gorbachev's *demokratizatsiya* ("democratization") was not an effort to transform the Soviet Union into a true republic, however. Instead, it allowed the people limited (though frequently real) choice in selecting their leaders. Candidates appearing on the ballots had been approved by the government, no parties other than the Communist party could run, and a third of the 2,250 seats were chosen not by the people but by various organizations and institutions. Party members won almost 88 percent of the seats (the rest were independents). But even this was an embarrassment to the Party. After members were elected to the Supreme Soviet, it elected Gorbachev as its Chairman. Gorbachev now held separate bases of power at the top of the government and at the top of the Party.

The elections brought some dedicated reformers to power. A group of about 200 reformists formed an "Inter-regional Group" within the legislature, eventually pushing the pace of Gorbachev's reforms. Even more importantly, the elections gave the Soviet Union's legislature a degree of legitimacy that it had always lacked. Meanwhile, the population had warmed to its newfound political voice, pressing for freer local elections, engaging in strikes, and staging protests. Criticism of the Communist Party and of official ideological precepts grew. This presented Gorbachev with a stark dilemma: the Soviet leadership's legitimacy—such as it was—stemmed from the doctrine of Marxism-Leninism that justified one-party rule. To the extent that Gorbachev's reforms attacked this doctrine, Gorbachev and the reformers undercut their own position. It became evident that anti-authoritarian reforms might require authoritarian control to maintain the power necessary for conducting the reforms. (In later years, Boris Yeltsin, the first post-Soviet leader of Russia, would face this same dilemma.) When encountering difficulties, Gorbachev vacillated between further decentralization and retrenchment. But finally, in February 1990, he agreed to the removal of the Party's constitutional monopoly on political power. The following month, the Congress of People's Deputies formally removed Article 6 from the Constitution, allowing opposition parties to form and challenge the Communist Party of the Soviet Union. In a free market of competing ideologies, the Party's days were numbered.

Meanwhile, demokratizatsiya and glasnost were dissolving the glue that held together Moscow's internal and external empires. East European peoples interpreted Gorbachev's reforms as a tacit endorsement of reform in their own countries. They suspected that the feared Brezhnev Doctrine was finally defunct—a suspicion eventually confirmed by Gorbachev himself. By the fall of 1989, virtually all of the East European countries had overthrown their Communist governments while Moscow merely looked on.

Within the Soviet Union itself, elections at the republic and local levels did boost reformist voices in the government, as Gorbachev had wished. But they also provided a political base for the resurgent nationalist forces in many of the republics. In a kind of feedback phenomenon, the East European revolutions unwittingly inspired by Gorbachev now provided powerful inspiration for the nationalist forces within the USSR. By allowing the countries of Eastern Europe to break away from the Soviet sphere of influence, Gorbachev lent credibility to the growing belief that Moscow was unwilling to use military force against secessionists.

In reality, the Soviet leadership was deeply divided over the question of using force to protect central power, let alone the very assumption that central power should be preserved. In late 1989 and early 1990, one republic after another issued declarations of autonomy, sovereignty, or their intent to achieve independence. Lithuania was among the first to act, declaring its independence in March 1990. Gorbachev and his allies came under increasing pressure from conservatives within the Party to act. But Gorbachev seemed to believe that the union could be preserved only by allowing greater freedom for the republics. Then the RSFSR itself adopted a Declaration of State Sovereignty on June 12, 1990.

Three months earlier the RSFSR, like other republics, had held democratic elections to its republican legislature. The newly elected Russian Congress of People's Deputies selected Boris Yeltsin, a former member of the

Soviet Politburo, as its leader. Now Gorbachev and Yeltsin competed for control over the republic, which comprised three-quarters of the USSR's territory. There were in effect two Moscows: one Soviet and one Russian.

There ensued a "war of laws" in which Russia and the other republics that had declared sovereignty passed laws that deliberately conflicted with federal laws. Gorbachev responded in August with a decree that Russia's declaration of sovereignty was "null and void." But at the same time he sought to develop a new union treaty that would placate the nationalists. Most republics were skeptical. Tensions between the increasingly assertive republics and the besieged Gorbachev regime moved rapidly toward a breaking point.

In the first days of 1991, the Soviet government finally used military force against the Baltic republics, which had been among the first to declare independence from Moscow. On January 2 elite "Black Beret" troops seized Latvia's press headquarters in Riga. During the next two weeks more Soviet troops entered Lithuania, seizing the national guard headquarters and the radio and television stations in Vilnius. Fourteen people were killed, and more than 150 were injured. Four more people were killed on January 20, when Black Berets seized the Latvian Interior Ministry. The fighting over the Soviet Union's fate had begun.

Suggested Readings

Acton, Edward. *Russia: The Tsarist and Soviet Legacy.* 2nd ed. London: Longman, 1995.

Dobrynin, Anatoly. *In Confidence: Moscow's Ambassador to America's Six Cold War Presidents.* New York: Random House, 1996.

McAuley, Mary. *Soviet Politics 1917–1991.* Oxford: Oxford University Press, 1992.

Neville, Peter. *A Traveller's History of Russia and the USSR.* New York: Interlink Books, 1990.

Ragsdale, Hugh. *The Russian Tragedy: The Burden of History.* Armonk, N.Y.: M. E. Sharpe, 1996.

Riasanovsky, Nicholas V. *A History of Russia.* 5th ed. New York: Oxford University Press, 1993.

Thompson, John M. *Russia and the Soviet Union: An Historical Introduction from the Kievan State to the Present.* 3rd ed. Boulder, Colo.: Westview Press, 1994.

Treadgold, Donald W. *Twentieth Century Russia.* 8th ed. Boulder, Colo.: Westview Press, 1995.

3
——

The Re-Emergence of Russia

Mikhail Gorbachev could perhaps as well as anyone understand the defiant determination of Winston Churchill in 1942: "I have not become the King's First Minister to preside over the liquidation of the British Empire." But a half century after Churchill, Gorbachev's understanding of his mission was not borne out by events. Presiding over the dismantling of the Soviet empire is precisely what Gorbachev did, with a speed and completeness that mocked his declared intentions. Less than seven years after he assumed power, the country forged by Lenin and Stalin at such awful cost would pass into history. In its place would emerge 15 newly independent countries, of varying size, ethnic makeup, military strength, and international orientation. But it would be Russia, whose imperial namesake the Bolsheviks overthrew in 1917, that assumed the USSR's place in international institutions, diplomatic treaties, and above all in the minds of many Russians.

The Collapse of the Soviet Union

The precise date of the Soviet Union's demise is difficult to identify. In December 1991 the Russian legislature invalidated the 1922 treaty that had established the Soviet Union, and in the same month Gorbachev resigned as the Soviet Union's last leader. But these were formalities that officially acknowledged the Soviet Union's nonexistence; they were, in effect, the signing of the Communist state's death certificate. Earlier events indicated the de facto demise of the regime, or at least its transition to terminal status. Foreign Minister Eduard Shevardnadze's admission in 1989 that the Molotov-Ribbentrop pact did in fact include a secret protocol facilitating Moscow's seizure of the Baltic states and Bessarabia (Moldavia), as well as the partition of Poland, can be interpreted as a watershed in the progressive weakening of Moscow's grasp on its dominion. By officially affirming the open secret that at least parts of the Soviet Union had been forcibly annexed, Shevardnadze and Gorbachev abandoned the Party's tattered, sacred myth that the peoples of the constituent republics had joined the union voluntarily.

The nationalist defections that followed destroyed the other myth, received with somewhat less skepticism in the West, that however the Soviet Union had been cobbled together, Russian and socialist indoctrination had taken root sufficiently to make the "union" viable. The revolutions of 1989–1991 demonstrated that Moscow's efforts to create a Soviet nation, exemplified by the New Soviet Man, were in vain. Like its East European empire, the Soviet Union had been held together by force, threats, and official lies—lies about the role of the Party, about the invidiousness of capitalism, and about the wisdom and effectiveness of Stalin and his successors (and even Stalin's immediate predecessor, Lenin). Once those tools of control had been weakened, foregone, or destroyed, the veneer of "Soviet nationalism" disintegrated. What remained was a motley collection of peoples spread across much of Eurasia who, for all their differences of race, ethnicity, religion, and language, did share a recent history of oppression and deprivation at the hands of a Leninist system that came ultimately to work against the interests even of many of the heretofore "elites."

The August Coup Attempt

Having abandoned such central precepts as the Brezhnev Doctrine and the unity of Party and State, Gorbachev encountered increasingly hostile opposition from other Party elites who thought Gorbachev foolishly defeatist. These so-called conservatives rejected Gorbachev's argument that his reform path was the only way to avoid economic and societal breakdown. While sometimes conceding the desirability of modifying some policies, the conservatives insisted that the Soviet Union could be preserved only by refusing to give in to demands for popular sovereignty and national self-determination.

The conservatives' argument held true for the short term. Neither the timing nor the nature of Gorbachev's reforms was inevitable. Had Gorbachev not set out on the path of glasnost and perestroika, the fiction that the Soviet people already enjoyed democracy and freedom could have been officially maintained. Secure in the perception that the Soviet people comprised a population of socially anomic and politically emasculated subjects, official indifference to the privations of the masses could have continued. The bipolar order of the Cold War could have remained, with Washington not disabused of its misunderstandings about Soviet power and prestige. In short, the Soviet leadership could have chosen to attempt maintaining the status quo.

The status quo could not be maintained forever, of course. The shortcomings of central planning would manifest themselves in ever-greater ways. Eventually the country's economic decline would slip further to economic collapse. The people's chafing under political oppression and economic privation would eventually push them in desperation to challenge their state—an ironic fulfillment of Marx's dialectical materialism. The overextension of the Soviet empire would eventually force a territorial contraction, with the Red Army pulling out from Afghanistan, or perhaps abandoning Poland, or perhaps elsewhere. In short, the Soviet Union could not exist with its most basic elements—political neutralization of the people and central direction of the economy—in perpetuity. But beyond recognizing that the Leninist system's congenital flaws were ultimately fatal, predicting its lifespan—70 years? 100?—would be arbitrary prophecy.

Motivated by the belief that the Soviet Union's natural life span should be something longer than the 74 years already achieved, a small group of conservative party and military leaders staged an attempted coup against Gorbachev in August 1991. Their move was precipitated by the imminent signing of a "new union treaty," which would grant a large measure of autonomy to the remaining constituent republics of the Soviet Union. For the conservatives, the new union treaty was tantamount to a declaration of independence for the Soviet republics. For Gorbachev, the treaty was a necessary concession to the nationalist pressures in the republics. Nationalism among the various peoples of the USSR was not created by Gorbachev, but his reforms facilitated, and perhaps provoked, their resurrection. For Russia, the new union treaty would help realize the fulfillment of its sovereignty declaration in 1990.

On August 18, the day before the treaty was to be signed, the coup leaders made their move. They informed Gorbachev, who was vacationing in his dacha in the Crimea, that they were responding to a crisis and required that he sign a document turning over power to them. When Gorbachev refused, the coup plotters had him placed under house arrest. Undaunted by so small a thing as the lack of formal authority, Gorbachev's captors then assumed emergency executive powers. In a throwback to past Soviet practice, the alleged change in leadership was not immediately announced over television and radio, but instead was prefaced with the now-ominous broadcast of unscheduled classical music. Then, early in the morning of August 19, the

Soviet press agency revealed that Gorbachev had an "illness" and announced that Vice President Gennady Yanayev had assumed presidential powers. Yanayev led the eight-member "State Committee for the State of Emergency in the USSR," which issued decrees suspending various civil freedoms.

For all its drama, the coup collapsed after three days. A variety of factors contributed to its failure. Boris Yeltsin, who had not been detained by the coup plotters, rallied the anticoup forces. He proclaimed his own control of the RSFSR and called for general strikes and public resistance. Meanwhile, the glasnost-liberated media continued to operate, informing and uniting the citizens. And most reassuringly for the anticoup forces, military units refused to follow the Committee's orders to move on the Russian parliament building, known as the White House. Thousands of Muscovites had surrounded the building and pleaded with soldiers not to attack it. This building became a symbol of democratic resistance in the Soviet Union and, especially, in Russia.

The coup was the climax of the Soviet Union's demise, and the dénouement would be over in only four more months. The life-and-death emergency created by the coup forced military and political leaders from across the Soviet Union to choose sides. Whereas it had been possible for a time during Gorbachev's incremental reforms to await further developments passively, the coup eliminated the choice of procrastination. All too clear was Harvey Cox's dictum, "Not to decide is to decide." It was not so much a question of siding with Gorbachev or not, but rather a matter of supporting or rejecting the Soviet Union's political and social institutions. The reformist image of the Party nurtured by Gorbachev was now destroyed, and even Gorbachev himself was ultimately forced to abandon it. The military had proven to be an unreliable ally, for both sides. It was largely sidelined during the Soviet Union's last days. In short, the ideological "middle ground" of socialist reform constantly sought by Gorbachev finally dissolved, erased by the exposure of "reform Leninism" as a chimera.

In practical terms, the coup attempt catapulted to completion the disaggregation of the union. Republics that only days earlier were prepared to voluntarily sign a treaty proclaiming their ultimate allegiance to Moscow in exchange for greater latitude under that tutelage now balked at such a weak offer. The coup attempt showcased the Soviet Union's imperial side, which was not so far different from the tsars' empire. Now was the time to break free of the Soviets' deadly embrace. Before the end of the year, all the Soviet republics—including even Russia—would be reconstituted as sovereign states.

Two Revolutions

The breakup of the Soviet Union was occasioned by two revolutions. National revolutions, fought on behalf of the republics' titular nationalities, caused the

Soviet Union to divide along its internal provincial boundaries. This can be seen as a dismantling of the Soviet empire—a reversal of the annexations and conquests that had been effected by Stalin, Lenin, and the tsars before them. At the same time, a democratic revolution destroyed the Soviet state itself. The demands for popular sovereignty and multiparty government could not be reconciled with the essential characteristics of the Party regime. The two revolutions are connected; it was the supremacy of the Party and the imposition of authoritarian control that kept the residents of each republic politically neutralized and that bound the republics together. The Party also purported to transcend ethnonational interests. Given the nature of the Soviet Union, it would be difficult to imagine one revolution without the other.

The effect of the revolutions could be seen in the "two Moscows." Gorbachev's Moscow, as the seat of the Soviet government, was quickly fading into irrelevancy. The coup attempt had struck a powerful blow to Moscow's claim of reform socialism. Yeltsin's Moscow, on the other hand, took on a new importance and relevance. It symbolized Russian national self-determination, as well as anti-Communism and popular sovereignty. The second revolution came to its conclusion as 1991 reached its final month. Boris Yeltsin and other republican leaders affirmed the sovereignty of their emergent countries, declaring the Soviet Union to be a dead letter. A decision by the RSFSR Supreme Soviet on December 12, 1991, dissolved the 1922 treaty establishing the USSR. But dissolving the union could not erase the economic, military, and societal bonds that had been forged over decades and even centuries, prompting the leaders to fashion a post-Soviet relationship with each other. By December 21, all but four of them (the three Baltic republics and Georgia) had joined to form the Commonwealth of Independent States (CIS) to help structure their transition to independence. The founders took pains to make clear, however, that the CIS should not be construed as a substitute for the USSR and that the members of the CIS retained full sovereignty.

All that remained were a few formalities. On Christmas Day Mikhail Gorbachev delivered a speech announcing his resignation from the post of president of the Soviet Union—a country that now had no territory and no population. If Gorbachev earlier sounded like a determined Churchill, he now sounded like a defeated and rueful Thatcher, whose removal by her own party in 1990 caused her to puzzle over the "funny old world." Gorbachev's final reflections on his seven-year program were poignant:

> Addressing you for the last time in the capacity of a president of the USSR, I consider it necessary to express my evaluation of the road we have traveled since 1985, especially as there are a lot of contradictory, superficial, and subjective judgments on the matter. . . . This society has acquired freedom, liberated itself politically and spiritually, and this is the foremost achievement. . . . All these changes demand immense strain. They were

carried out with sharp struggle, with growing resistance from the old, the obsolete forces; the former party-state structures, the economic elite, as well as our habits, ideological superstitions, the psychology of sponging and leveling everyone out.

They stumbled on our intolerance, low level of political culture, fear of change. That is why we lost so much time. The old system collapsed before the new one had time to begin working, and the crisis in the society became even more acute. I am aware of the dissatisfaction with the present hard situation, of the sharp criticism of authorities at all levels including my personal activities.

But once again I'd like to stress: Radical changes in such a vast country, and a country with such a heritage, cannot pass painlessly without difficulties and shake-up.[1]

Then, after thanking his friends and allies, Gorbachev pronounced his final public words as president of the USSR: "I wish everyone all the best." That evening the Soviet flag was lowered from the Kremlin for the last time, and minutes later it was replaced by the Russian tricolor. The next day the RSFSR was renamed the Russian Federation.

The Soviet Union had succumbed to both aspects of revolution—territorial secession and political rejection. But the 15 new countries now faced the task of recreating territorial and political states.

Evaluation

Had Gorbachev's reforms destroyed the Soviet Union? It has been observed that the Soviet Union was almost constantly undergoing reform from its conception in 1917. Significant economic reforms were implemented by every Soviet leader with the possible exception of Chernenko, whose shortness of tenure (13 months) might permit forgiveness on this point. Politically, the Soviet Union spent most of the Khrushchev years trying to de-Stalinize itself, and some of the Brezhnev years re-introducing some of the less murderous aspects of Stalinism. Ideologically, the country gradually scaled back its radical raison d'être as the crucible of world revolution until, during the détente era, it became a conservative superpower trying desperately to maintain the geopolitical status quo.

The Gorbachev-era reforms (with the exception of repealing Article 6) were remarkable in their degree rather than their substance. Neither the

---

1. Gorbachev, Mikhail, "Text of Gorbachev's Resignation Speech," *Facts on File* 51:2666 (Dec. 31, 1991): 970.

introduction of market mechanisms through perestroika nor the loosening of censorship under glasnost altered the essence of the Soviet Union as a Party state, any more than Nicholas II's granting of a consultative assembly changed the reality of authoritarian monarchy. Only with the abandonment of the Communist Party's supremacy was the regime organically altered, facilitating the final demise of the Soviet system.

Of course, the disintegration of the Soviet Union and its empire did not take place in a geopolitical vacuum. Other world powers—in particular the United States—played a weighty, though largely passive, role in the Second World's collapse. That is, it was in part the strength and resolve of the United States and NATO that contributed to Moscow's costs in maintaining its external empire. It was in part the information provided by the West at international human rights conferences and broadcast by Radio Free Europe, Voice of America, and other media outlets that kept the custodians of Marxist-Leninist ideology on the defensive. It was in part the material success and political freedom of western societies that caused the performance—and therefore the legitimacy—of the Second World to suffer by comparison.

More than this, though, the United States and the Federal Republic of Germany lent crucial support to Gorbachev in the form of diplomacy. German Chancellor Helmut Kohl and U.S. Presidents Reagan and Bush displayed political support for Gorbachev in the face of his domestic opponents. The Western allies extended economic aid as a reward for Moscow's concessions on arms control and German unification. Perhaps most important, the Western powers did not seek to exploit the Soviet Union at the time of its worst turmoil and weakness in 1989–1991, allowing the Cold War to end with the (relatively) nonviolent collapse of the Second World rather than with an eastern expansion of victorious Western military power and an imposition of punitive treaties upon the "evil empire" that once had threatened to "bury" the West.

The West's role in the Soviet Union's demise thus was more passive than active. By its policies and diplomacy the West perhaps influenced the timing and nature of the Soviet collapse. But the root cause of the Soviet Union's eventual demise sprang from domestic, not international, causes.

The Russian Federation

Russia emerged from the Soviet Union as an old and a new country simultaneously. The return to Russia's historical basis was symbolically manifested in the names of its cities. The Soviets changed place names to honor their own leaders and to emphasize the break with the past: Leningrad (from St. Petersburg); Stalingrad (from Tsaritsyn); Sverdlovsk (from Yekaterinburg); and Gorky (from Nizhny Novgorod). The leaders of post-Soviet Russia in turn resurrected the old names. It was a fulfillment of the Soviet-era joke about two elderly men sitting on a park bench. "Where were you born?" the first asks. "In St. Petersburg," replies the second. "Where did you grow up?" "In Petrograd." "Where do you live now?" "In Leningrad." Sensing a look of displeasure, the first inquires "Where would you like to live?" "St. Petersburg," the second sighs. (Stalingrad already had been changed to Volgograd in 1961 as part of the Soviet Union's de-Stalinization campaign. So far the new Russian leadership has not seen fit to restore its pre-Soviet name.) After the Soviet Union's collapse, even historical names of governmental institutions were brought back. The lower house of the Russian parliament, for example, is named after the late-nineteenth century Duma.

But the Russian Federation is not a restoration of prerevolutionary Russia. Its territory, government, economy, and people have changed dramatically. What exists today as Russia is a unique entity. None of the earlier conceptions of Russia were defined by its current borders. None contained this particular amalgam of nations (in large measure the result of Stalin's deportation policies). Borders are still under some dispute. Border regions such as Primorsk krai have challenged the constitutionality of Soviet-era border agreements, such as one signed in 1991 that allocates about 1,500 hectares of long-disputed territory to China. Similarly, the long-running dispute between the Soviet Union and Japan over the Kuril Islands has been inherited and exacerbated by the Russian Federation. Just as important, the international environment in which Russia now finds itself has itself undergone monumental changes. Russia today is as new as it is old.

Rebuilding Russia

At the time of the Soviet Union's formal dissolution in December 1991, Russia emerged as something less than a functioning democracy. Yeltsin was ruling the country by emergency powers granted by the Russian Congress of People's Deputies after the August 1991 coup. The country's bureaucracy and economic institutions were largely under the control of Soviet-era apparatchiks. Serving as the country's constitution was the heavily amended version of the RSFSR's 1978 constitution. And only the most rudimentary forms of political parties and interest groups sought to aggregate and articulate the people's post-Soviet interests. Although the second revolution's goal of state sovereignty had been secured, achieving the first revolution's objective of popular sovereignty was only beginning.

The business of rebuilding Russia can be divided into two large tasks: state-building and nation-building. The first involves the establishment of governmental authority and the development of political institutions. The second entails the fostering of a cohesive national identity. As conceived by Yeltsin, the first task required that the authority of the new Russian government be founded upon democratic legitimacy, rather than one-party rule. The demise of the Soviet Union's political foundation—the Party and the state ideology of Communism—made this task especially urgent. The second task, nation-building, required that the citizens of Russia, of whatever ethnic background, be made to identify in some way with the Russian nation. At the very least, it required that the disparate ethnonational groups that comprised the Russian population be made to accept the territorial integrity of the newly sovereign country. In the first months after independence, Yeltsin and his lieutenants undertook these two tasks with mixed results.

Questions still lingered among the post-Soviet peoples as to their political and national status. Not everyone had desired the Soviet Union's demise. As recently as March 1991 three-quarters of those voting in an all-union referendum supported the preservation of the USSR "as a renewed federation of equal sovereign republics." In the RSFSR, seven out of 10 voters supported the referendum. So when the Soviet Union formally expired at the end of 1991, there were those who wondered if Russia might establish some new structure that tied together the old Soviet territories.

An obvious candidate was the CIS, notwithstanding claims by its founders to the contrary. With these considerations in mind, the Russian leadership was slow to adopt all the institutions of independent statehood, perhaps leaving the door open for some renewed confederation among the former Soviet republics. For example, Russia was the last of these countries to create its own defense ministry, instead trying to establish a unified military structure under the aegis of the CIS. Russia also hesitated in withdrawing its troops from other former Soviet republics, ostensibly waiting to ensure the safety of ethnic Russians living in those territories.

Gradually, however, Russia made substantial progress in the process of state-building. In the first five years after formal independence, the country held two democratic parliamentary elections and one national presidential election; adopted a new constitution; clarified the relationship between the federal and republican governments; fashioned an official statement of foreign-policy interests and an official military doctrine; stabilized its currency and privatized much of its economy; and adopted numerous federal laws to re-establish the relationship between state and society. The Russian people began to overcome their identity crisis, which had been brought on by the loss of empire. And confidence in Russia's democratic transition and stability was expressed by the West in the form of summits with Russian leaders, substantial loans from the International Monetary Fund and membership in the Council of Europe and NATO's Partnership for Peace.

That Russia had made the transition to independence and international recognition is no small feat. In its first months of independence, the country faced numerous obstacles, from hyperinflation and unemployment to threats of coups and civil wars. Russia's constitution came under repeated attacks, and some factions even launched efforts to restore the Romanov dynasty. Yet by the time of the country's first post-Soviet presidential elections in June 1996, the basic foundation of Russian politics and government had begun to take shape. Considerably less progress had been achieved, however, in nation-building: developing a cohesive Russian national identity.

Prospects

The question of Russia's meaning—as a people, as a nation, as a world power, even as a territory—reopened with the removal of the "Soviet" layer from Moscow. No longer conflated with the Soviet Union, Russia now has to be defined in its own right. Its history must once again be reinterpreted. Should Russia's development as a state be viewed in its pre-Soviet context—a development path "hijacked" by the Bolshevik revolution? If so, it is to tsarist times that Russians must now look for the answers to their identity. Alternatively, should the Soviet period be seen as a constituent part of Russia's development—a natural consequence of Russia's essential character? If so, perhaps the democratic results of Russia's post-Soviet revolution will prove less permanent than the reformists might wish. Even considering that the territorial disintegration was facilitated in large measure by a quasi-democratization of the political system, this does not promise continued democracy on the part of the new states. Indeed, the lesson of the February and October revolutions in 1917 should serve as an adequate warning that an anti-authoritarian revolution may not guarantee the establishment of a nonauthoritarian regime.

Put differently, these questions turn on two main themes: the universality of democracy and liberalism (as a direct contrast to the universality of Marx's dialectical materialism), and the role of nationalism. Put in yet another way, how much of Soviet Russia—its political system, its ideology, its society and culture—should be considered "Soviet," and how much historically and culturally "Russian"? These questions further turn on the matter of understanding the relationship between "Russian," "Slavic," "authoritarian," and "non-Western."

There had always been much discussion about the extent to which the non-Russian republics of the Soviet Union were being "Russified." But surely this cut both ways; during most of its years under Communist control Russia was being "Sovietized." This question has practical implications: Is it possible to remove the legacies of the Soviet period without altering Russian culture? Is Russian culture compatible with democracy? To what extent is altering the Russian culture even possible? One quickly comes to appreciate how Russia's future may be uncertain.

Russia has entered a new stage of its development with little consensus on any of these questions. It arrives at the twenty-first century much as it entered the twentieth—seeking stability, purpose, and identity.

Suggested Readings

Bonnell, Victoria E., et al. (eds.) *Russia at the Barricades: Eyewitness Accounts of the August 1991 Coup*. Armonk, N.Y.: M. E. Sharpe, 1994.

Fish, M. Steven. *Democracy from Scratch: Opposition and Regime in the New Russian Revolution*. Princeton: Princeton University Press, 1995.

Grachev, Andrei. *Final Days: The Inside Story of the Collapse of the Soviet Union*. Boulder, Colo.: Westview Press, 1996.

Löwenhardt, John. *The Reincarnation of Russia: Struggling with the Legacy of Communism, 1990–1994*. Durham: Duke University Press, 1995.

Matlock, Jack. *Autopsy of an Empire*. New York: Random House, 1996.

Remnick, David. *Lenin's Tomb: The Last Days of the Soviet Empire*. New York: Random House, 1993.

Steele, Jonathan. *Eternal Russia: Yeltsin, Gorbachev, and the Mirage of Democracy*. Cambridge: Harvard University Press, 1994.

Tolz, Vera. *The USSR in 1991: A Record of Events*. Boulder, Colo.: Westview Press, 1993.

Part II

Russian Society and Politics

4
—

Living Conditions

"War to the palaces, peace to the huts!" read a common Bolshevik placard on the eve of revolution. Perhaps more than any other factor, living conditions directly affect popular attitudes about governmental performance. If the government claims legitimacy on the basis of its works, then living conditions broadly defined—including personal and national security, as well as diet, health, leisure activity, and other factors—must meet minimal expectations to make that claim of legitimacy credible. And even more important than absolute living conditions are relative living conditions: relative to the conditions of other societies, and relative to the same society in earlier times (that is, have conditions improved or worsened under the government?). Favorable comparisons reinforce the government's policies and beget "conservatism," if that term is defined as a general commitment to the status quo. Unfavorable comparisons foster demands for change in governmental policy—and perhaps in the government itself. It cannot be far from the minds of the current leaders of the Russian Federation that the wretchedness of urban life under Tsar Nicholas II was at least as responsible as Lenin's rhetoric in agitating the people against the regime.

Like the overthrowing of the Romanov dynasty in 1917, the breakup of the Soviet Union in 1991 was driven by a powerful combination of ideological fervor and less selfless expectations for a better life. After 1917, the people's decreasing commitment to the former and growing disappointment in the latter required that the regime adopt a garrison orientation toward society. But Russia's post-Soviet leadership largely denied itself the brutal force and merciless determination used so effectively by the Bolsheviks. As the population's anti-Soviet ideological fervor wears off, Russian leaders are increasingly pressed to deliver on the implied promise of improved living conditions.

The Soviet Record

Once having consolidated power after winning the civil war, the new Soviet regime pronounced that the people's misery under tsarism was as good as over, insofar as the country was now ruled by a "dictatorship of the proletariat." With a hubris that was characteristic of Leninism, the Kremlin officially abolished homelessness and unemployment and proclaimed instant equality among its people. Of course, the life of the average Russian peasant or worker at the beginning of the twentieth century was so wretched that improving it hardly required heroic effort or imagination. But although the Soviets' proclamations deserve a measure of skepticism, there is no denying their accomplishments as reflected in the more pedestrian measures of societal progress.

By seizing control of virtually all areas of public life and dictating the country's development through Five-Year Plans, the Soviets were able to industrialize the economy, electrify towns, provide jobs and housing to the masses, ensure the affordability of food and other necessities, and guarantee a level of medical care. Life expectancy more than doubled from 32 years at the time of the revolution to its peak of about 65 in the mid-1960s. By that time infant mortality had dropped to 25 deaths per 1,000—about a tenth of its rate in 1913. Universal education was instituted and literacy neared 100 percent.[1] Enormous strides were made in the political and social equality of women. And literature, theater, music, and other arts were made more accessible to the general public. By a variety of standards, the living conditions of Russians improved substantially under Soviet rule.

As the decades passed, however, the growth in absolute living standards slowed. It was one thing to split up palatial tsarist-era apartments to provide housing for poor families; constructing new, adequate apartments was another.

---

1. Official statistical data from the Soviet period is not entirely reliable; these figures represent typical Western estimates. The official life expectancy, at birth, in the Soviet Union in the 1960s was 70 years.

Opening free health clinics to the entire society (in 1919) provided easy gains, but improving the quality of health care was another matter. Promoting the political equality of women did not ensure the political efficacy of the population generally. In short, the redistributive gains experienced by the masses in the early Soviet period did not ensure absolute gains by the country as a whole. And even where absolute gains were made, they seldom kept pace with those in Western countries.

The period of Leonid Brezhnev's rule in he 1960s and 1970s has been called the era of stagnation, pointing to the plateau of social and economic conditions experienced in the Soviet Union. No amount of cajoling could produce more than superficial improvements in these areas. Worse, living standards as a whole were slipping.

The Crisis

The country over which Mikhail Gorbachev assumed leadership in 1985 was suffering an ominous reversal in a number of measures of living conditions: life expectancy was dropping, infant mortality was rising, and alcohol-related illnesses were increasing alarmingly. Still, little of the restiveness that characterized Nicholas II's Russia was evident among the RSFSR's population. Indeed, a survey of former Soviet citizens who emigrated shortly before Gorbachev came to power indicated that well over half were "very satisfied" or "somewhat satisfied" with their standard of living in the Soviet Union, including their housing, jobs, and medical care. Only in the category of "goods" did a majority of the émigrés express dissatisfaction in their Soviet living conditions.[2] Even among the people who made them, Soviet consumer goods were considered poorly designed and shoddily made. The young and urban segments of the population in particular desired access to high-status Western goods, and some of this demand was met through the black market.

Dissatisfaction with overall living conditions thus does not appear to have created insuperable demands for change in the early 1980s. There were no demonstrations led by a latter-day Father Gapon, whose peaceful march for societal and political reform was cut down by the tsar's palace guard on Bloody Sunday in 1905, an act that galvanized and expanded opposition to the regime. Rather, the agitation for reform in Gorbachev's Soviet Union came from Gorbachev himself. And the popular forces he unleashed were at least as concerned about achieving the more abstract goals of national self-determination and popular sovereignty as material living conditions. At the

---

2. James R. Millar and Elizabeth Clayton, "Quality of Life: Subjective Measures of Relative Satisfaction," in James R. Millar, ed., *Politics, Work, and Daily Life in the USSR: A Survey of Former Soviet Citizens* (Cambridge University Press, 1987): 31–57.

time of the Soviet Union's collapse, the forces of radical reform seemed enchanted by the arrival of political and national liberation. Before long, however, the novelty of liberation would wear off, and Russians' workaday life would again become centered on more prosaic concerns. At this point living conditions assumed a critical role in affecting Russia's political and economic development.

Living Conditions under Yeltsin

Since extricating itself from the Soviet Union in 1991, Russia has seen a decided slip in the living conditions of its citizens. Most dramatically, the basic amenities constitutionally guaranteed under Soviet rule have been left largely at the mercy of the market, and this has meant increases in homelessness, unemployment, and other privations. (Not until the summer of 1991 did the Soviet authorities officially acknowledge the very existence of unemployment.) Russian society is undergoing the socioeconomic variegation lauded by free-market economic theory for providing the necessary incentive for hard work and entrepreneurship. It is experiencing the widespread unemployment necessary to move the workers out of inefficient jobs and into productive employment. However, many perceive that the new market forces' shuffling of the population into different strata (classes?) has not been especially fair or just. In many cases those perceptions were understandable.

Housing

The housing situation provides a particularly clear example. Even more than during the Soviet era, decent housing is a scarce commodity in many parts of Russia. Partly this is a result of privatization and conversion of use. Partly it is exacerbated by the demand produced by ethnic Russian immigrants, as well as the return of ethnic Russian Soviet soldiers previously stationed in Eastern Europe and the Near Abroad. And of course, partly it is a result of the shoddy construction which is characteristic of Soviet-era apartments. Dilapidated five-story 1950s-era apartments in Moscow are known as *khrushcheby*, combining Khrushchev (who ruled while the apartments were constructed) and *trushcheby* (the Russian word for slums).

Society's response to these new problems and opportunities has not followed the script written by the new Russian government's economists, who in turn have borrowed from the theories of Adam Smith and Friedrich Hayek. The problems of supply and demand are not addressed simply through competitive pricing and entrepreneurship. In some areas society's response has been one of despair, with severe overcrowding seen as the only mid-term "solution" to the housing shortage. In others, the predatory ruthlessness exhibited by some Russians crosses the line into criminality. Contracts in which apartment owners are offered cash for the right to inherit the apartment are not unknown in the United States and Europe. But in Russia the number of these apartment owners found dead or missing shortly after signing the contracts is symptomatic of something especially noxious.

The renewed popularity of Soviet-era dachas provides an alternative. These small country houses were seldom luxurious, but they housed single families and thus provided an escape from the travails of communal living. Although dachas were usually considered a luxury, owning one was not out of the question. Then the RSFSR land reform law of 1990 allocated land for individuals to construct dachas—a type of homestead act. Unfortunately, control of the land was quickly infused with crime, corruption, and gangs. Land prices escalated. Not only private speculators benefited from these new opportunities. "Dacha cities" sprang up outside the main cities, and local authorities found ways to extract money through fees, utility hookups, inspections, and the like. In some ways, the housing situation in the Russian Federation is as corrupt and bureaucratic as it had been under the Soviets.

Nonetheless, Russia's housing situation shows some signs of improvement. Less than 20 percent of urban Russian families now live in Soviet-style communal apartments. Private houses now account for almost a quarter of Russia's urban housing stock. (Russia's current efforts to address its housing shortage are addressed in Chapter 8.)

Homelessness

One immediate effect of Russia's housing crisis is homelessness, a problem associated with many of Russia's cities, particularly Moscow. During Moscow's cold spells—which can last for months—it is not uncommon for several people to die of exposure in a single night. Yet not all of these widely publicized deaths are a direct result of homelessness. Some of these victims simply pass out on the street from drunkenness. Further, a number of Russia's new homeless have lost their apartments for reasons other than economics. For example, some lost their residency permits while serving prison sentences. Although this underscores a major problem with Russia's administration of housing—the continued use of residency permits in urban areas—Russians are not especially sympathetic to the plight of the homeless.

Nonetheless, homelessness is a real problem in Russia. Police estimates place the number of homeless persons in Moscow alone as high as 300,000. Local authorities have been slow to respond to the problem. At the beginning of 1996, Moscow had only one "night shelter," with 24 beds. City officials announced plans to open one shelter in each of Moscow's 10 districts by the end of the year, but funding was still in question. Generally local governments have taken a fairly tough line toward homelessness. Some have adopted penalties for begging and vagrancy. (In Soviet times these were criminal acts.) There also have been reports the police beat homeless persons in Moscow and other cities.

Various international organizations have addressed some of these problems. The Salvation Army now operates in Moscow, serving meals at railway stations and distributing religious literature. Doctors Without Borders provides free medical assistance. Habitat for Humanity has begun investigating the possibility of building homes in Moscow and St. Petersburg. But the causes of Russia's homeless problem, like those in other countries, spring from deep-rooted societal conditions whose correction requires more than merely providing beds, food, and medicine.

Goods and Purchasing Power

The range and quality of consumer goods—a constant source of grievance in the Soviet Union—has improved dramatically in post-Soviet Russia. The initial improvement in this regard has been facilitated through renewed trade. French wines, Italian shoes, American compact discs, German automobiles— all are readily available for purchase in Russia. Yet whereas yesterday's shoddy goods could be obtained at the annoying but affordable price of waiting in line for at least an hour a day on average, today's high-quality goods require hard currency, which for a Russian is considerably less plentiful than time.

In 1996 the average Russian monthly wage was 77,300 rubles, or about $150. Hyperinflation, currency devaluation, and price liberalization make a comparison of Soviet-era and modern wages virtually meaningless. But in terms of buying power, the salary of the average Soviet citizen has dropped dramatically with the demise of Communism and, more to the point, the lifting of price controls. (See Table 4–1 for a comparison of Russian and American purchasing power.) The proportion of an urban family's income spent on food alone rose from about a third in 1989 to well over half in 1994. As a cost-cutting measure, many families grow their own food—not on farms, but on small plots of land in urban areas. The average Russian's diet has also suffered with the rise in food costs, thus adding to health problems.

Although access to basic creature comforts and amenities has improved since the Soviet era, most Russian families still lag far behind the West. Russia has about 12 phone lines available for every 100 citizens—less than a quarter of the rate in the United States. Answering machines are rarely encountered. Major appliances such as clothes washers, dryers, and dishwashers are owned only by the upper class. Automobiles are even more difficult to obtain (although they are increasingly considered more necessary than home appliances). On the other hand, well over 90 percent of Russian households have a refrigerator, and televisions have been standard equipment for Russian apartments since the late Soviet period.

Table 4–1   Amount of Time Required for the Average Worker in Russia and in the United States to Earn Enough Money to Purchase Selected Goods in 1994

Source: *New York Times*, October 16, 1994

	Russia	U.S.
Sugar, 1 lb.	29 minutes	3 minutes
Bread, 1 lb.	14 minutes	5 minutes
Milk, 0.5 gal.	1 hr., 10 min.	9 minutes
Sausage, 1 lb.	2 hr., 27 min.	12 minutes
Gasoline, 1 gal.	1 hr., 16 min.	8 minutes
Television	71 days	6 days

Various services provided for free (or close to it) by the Soviet state have largely been curtailed. Many employers have stopped providing such services as child care and medical care free of charge to their employees. Where free or subsidized services are still available, they are often of intolerably substandard quality. In late 1996 the Finance Ministry was urging that even more medical services become fee based. Private businesses offer quality services, but the cost can be prohibitive. Russians have not adapted well to the expectation that they pay for such services. There have even been reports of families abandoning the corpses of their departed for lack of money to pay funeral costs. (Russian President Boris Yeltsin subsequently issued a decree guaranteeing free burial or cremation to Russian citizens.)

By 1996 the drop in living standards appeared to have slowed. According to official Russian data, average real income fell less than 1 percent in the first three quarters of 1996 compared with the same period in 1995. In addition, the proportion of families existing beneath the poverty line fell from 26 percent to 22 percent during the same period. Although Russia's standard of living continues to compare unfavorably with much of the rest of Europe, the direction of change seemed to have improved.

Drug Addiction and Prostitution

Soviet authorities had insisted that prostitution developed as a tragic but logical result of capitalism; the Soviet Union thus was considered immune to such socioeconomic ills. But in the 1980s Gorbachev's glasnost revealed the errors in that logic. Prostitution, like AIDS and alcoholism, was not solely the execrable inheritance of Western capitalism. Nevertheless, the economic pressures that pushed some women into prostitution came into greater prominence in the post-Soviet Russian Federation. A 1992 survey asked 15- to 17-year-old Russian girls to rank the 20 most lucrative professions. Prostitution tied for ninth place with director and sales clerk.

Widespread prostitution poses a number of hazards for Russian society, not the least of which are borne by the prostitutes themselves. The spread of sexually transmitted diseases, the links to drugs and crime, and the birth (or abortion) of unwanted babies take their toll on society. Rarely have Soviet women had access to means of birth control, and this situation has not significantly improved in post-Soviet Russia. A severe shortage of prophylactics has driven some local health networks to wash used condoms for reuse. As they did in the Soviet era, frequent abortions serve as a substitute for birth control. Russian abortion laws are fairly liberal, and, as a consequence, the number of abortions is roughly equal to the number of live births. This is about three times America's abortion rate. The health effects, both psychological and physical, are taking their toll. Partly Russian medical care is the culprit: In the mid-1990s, the mortality rate of Russian mothers during childbirth was about five times that of mothers in the United States.[3]

Drug abuse in Russia is rampant. The Soviet authorities had steadfastly denied that drug abuse existed in their country, once again defining the problem as a symptom of capitalist debauchery. Glasnost in Gorbachev's Soviet Union chipped away at that fiction. In 1985 the government admitted that 3,000 drug addicts lived in the country. Five years later government figures had increased more than tenfold. Unofficial estimates ran into the millions. In post-Soviet Russia, authorities now estimate that 2 million Russians regularly use illegal drugs. Only about 50,000 of them are estimated to be receiving treatment. Marijuana is the drug of choice (cannabis grows wild in the country), although the demand for opium and heroin from Central Asia has been rising rapidly.

Poor living conditions and social alienation can literally drive Russians to drink. Russians' propensity for drinking is storied, but recent trends show that alcoholism is increasing. A 1996 report by the Alcohol Policy Center in Russia found that 30 percent of Russian women between 30 and 50 years old show effects of chronic heavy drinking: liver conditions, heart problems, or alcohol poisoning. Half of the men in this age group were similarly afflicted. Russia's Interior Ministry estimated in 1995 that more than 100,000 Russians die each year from the direct effects of alcohol. In 1996 the Anti-Alchoholism Center in Moscow estimated the figure to be 400,000. In addition, the number of

---

3. On reproductive issues in Russia, see V. Perevedentsev, "Women, the Family, and Reproduction," in Vitalina Koval, ed., *Women in Contemporary Russia* (Providence: Berghahn Books, 1995): 73–86.

babies showing the effects of fetal alcohol syndrome has been rising alarmingly. Other indirect effects of alcoholism include absenteeism in the workplace and accidental fires and automobile accidents caused by drunkenness. Drinking among the young remains common, offering little hope that generational change will soon deliver an abatement of the problem. And the increasing availability of trendy Western drinks adds to alcohol's allure.

Environment

An especially costly legacy of the Soviet period is environmental damage. Notwithstanding a rise in public awareness and activity (a Russian branch of Greenpeace has been established, for example), Russians' living conditions will be adversely affected by this legacy for generations to come.

The "extensive" production gains obtained in Stalin's time relied on the lowest of technology, boosting production by increasing use of raw materials (including slave labor). Enormous waste and environmental damage is frequently characteristic of such extensive production gains. Even with the gradual introduction of technology, Soviet industry remained inefficient and wasteful. Without economic incentives (in the form of real prices, or competition), Soviet factory managers preferred the easier, low-tech methods. Highly polluting soft brown coal was preferred to the more efficient varieties, which are harder to extract. Toxic wastes were stored or dumped with few environmental protection measures and without particular regard for the proximity of drinking water supplies. Environmental regulations, where they existed, were commonly ignored. The enormous Soviet steel-making complex at Magnitogorsk, for example, exemplified the penchant for size and scale without efficiency.

Military bases all around the former Soviet Union are notorious sources of nuclear contamination. For decades the Soviet navy disposed of radioactive waste in open fields near major bodies of water and sank decommissioned nuclear submarines in shallow water as a matter of policy. The other military services committed similar sins.

The scale of the environmental damage effected by the Soviets can be breathtaking. They diverted water to irrigate cotton fields in Turkmenistan and Uzbekistan, causing the Aral Sea to shrink to a third its original size. This development also concentrated the level of pollutants in the Aral Sea. At the same time, the Caspian Sea has been rising. In Russia's republic of Dagestan, 120,000 acres of coastal land have been submerged. A particularly striking and tragic effect of Soviet industrial pollution has been the tainting of Lake Baikal, once among the clearest, purest large bodies of water in the Soviet Union (and the world's largest lake). The Baikalsk pulp and paper factory has continuously dumped untreated waste into the lake since the 1950s. Today, the lake is a recognized monument to Soviet environmental negligence. In the mid-1990s the United States and Russia were establishing joint efforts to protect the lake's ecology. The Russian government also has devoted funds, including $38 million for conservation work in 1996, to help clean up the various environmental legacies of the Soviet Union. But this only scratches the surface of the task that lies ahead.

Atomic power is one of the most dangerous legacies of the Soviet Union's lax environmental policies. The Soviet Union's nuclear carelessness is shocking. Not only has nuclear weapons testing taken its toll, but under Brezhnev the country even experimented with nuclear devices for excavation. A 1971 blast to divert rivers in Perm formed a radioactive lake that even today is considered unsafe. There are even rumors that the excavation program has left an unexploded nuclear device buried in Siberia.[4]

Storage of nuclear waste from power plants also has posed a serious problem. Under Soviet rule numerous dump sites were established with inadequate protections and many have become filled beyond safe capacity. Since the demise of the USSR, Russia has been enticed by the promise of hard currency to store the nuclear waste of other countries. Notwithstanding a 1991 environmental protection law that prohibits bringing radioactive materials into Russia for burial or storage, Yeltsin issued a decree allowing the import of nuclear waste. Shortly thereafter work began on a nuclear waste disposal plant in Siberia. Although the Russian Supreme Court scaled back Yeltsin's decree in 1996, the government was poised to secure the necessary international agreements to permit the continued importation of waste. In addition, the promise of high profits has spurred some local governments and private individuals to seek contracts for accepting spent nuclear fuel from countries such as Hungary. Illegal dumps accepting Russian-produced radioactive waste have also been discovered in Russia.

As of 1996, Russia operated 29 reactors at nine sites. Nuclear power only accounts for about 12 percent of the power in the country, whose energy sources largely are drawn from its enormous oil reserves. The design of many of Russia's nuclear reactors is patently unsafe. Reactors of the type that melted down at Chernobyl, Ukraine, in 1986 continue to operate today. Not only are Soviet-era nuclear reactors considered unsafe by design, but they also lack security and safety measures. Accidents and intentional sabotage remain real threats. In 1995 protesting workers at the Kola nuclear power station in northern Russia threatened to set the plant afire if their wage arrears were not paid. (The workers were at least temporarily placated with partial payment of their back wages.) Responding to safety and environmental concerns, Russian authorities have

---

4. See Aleksandr Pashkov, "Is Site of 1971 Peaceful Nuclear Blast Still Hazardous?" *Izvestia*, September 28, 1994: 4, in *The Current Digest of the Post-Soviet Press* 46:39 (October 9, 1994): 7–9.

stated that they will not build any new nuclear power plants. However, by this they do not include adding or replacing reactors at existing power plants. The country was building four new lightwater reactors in the mid-1990s.

There are some bright spots. The Russian government has acknowledged most of the dangers listed here and has undertaken efforts to protect against nuclear dangers. In 1993 the government created the Ministry for the Environment and the Rational Use of Natural Resources. The ministry's head, Viktor Danilov-Danilyan, promised to seek a substantial increase in the fines for violating environmental laws. He also was working with the president to establish an "environmental police force" to enforce those laws. Russia has also taken high-profile actions toward international cooperation, including the hosting of a nuclear safety summit with the Group of Seven countries in 1996. In the same year Russia also signed an agreement with the United States and Norway to address the radioactive hazards from decommissioned Russian nuclear submarines in the Arctic. Further, nuclear weapons testing has abated considerably since the last major nuclear arms race in the early 1980s. Still, with half-lives measured in thousands of years, nuclear legacies do not quickly fade.

Health

Although the Soviet Union established a universal (if inefficient) health care system, much of this system disintegrated along with the Communist regime. Today Russian health care suffers from severe shortages of funding, workers, and the most rudimentary supplies. Russian doctors, like their Soviet predecessors, do not work in an especially prestigious profession, and they are paid less than bus drivers. All but emergency care is difficult to come by and often is of unsatisfactory quality. Over a third of Russia's hospitals still lack such basic amenities as hot water. As in a Third World country, many of Russia's health care programs and disease control efforts rely on outside assistance. International organizations and foreign aid provide training, funding, and supplies. But distribution problems persist, and many Russian hospitals and clinics operate catch-as-catch-can. It is not uncommon for Russians returning from abroad, as well as benevolent foreign visitors, to carry in (often illegally) such simple medical supplies as latex gloves, syringes, and catheters. Many medical tools and procedures are improvised. Surgeries are delayed, sometimes with fatal consequences, for want of anesthetics.

Largely as a result of these shortages in health care, Russians' health has declined since independence in 1991. Polio and cholera, which had been almost banished from the First World (and even the Soviet Union), became increasingly common in post-Soviet Russia. Infectious diseases have spread at alarming rates, with cases of diphtheria increasing almost threefold in 1993 and nearly doubling again in 1994. Russians are dying of cancer at twice the rate of Americans, due partly to Russians' widespread addiction to smoking

(Russia has one of the highest rates in the developed world) and exacerbated by inadequate monitoring and treatments. Cases of hepatitis have been rising, partly as a consequence of the severe shortage of sterile syringes, unsanitary conditions in many clinics, and even the introduction of fluorine waste into water supplies. Widespread drug abuse also assists the spread of the disease. Seventy percent of 1,000 new cases of HIV infection in 1996 were attributed to intravenous drug use. The incidence of measles and infectious respiratory diseases such as whooping cough have increased across Russia since 1991. Worsening atmospheric pollution has also led to a sharp increase in respiratory problems.

Some of the new outbreaks of disease have direct economic links. Malaria reappeared after the termination of mosquito abatement programs, an unaffordable luxury in many regions. Hygiene and sanitation also are at fault. Incidences of food poisoning are common, and cases of scabies have tripled since 1985. Inadequate sewage treatment in many regions has resulted in alarming levels of E. coli bacteria in drinking water. Because of the rudimentary level of Russian medical care, tuberculosis, which has reached epidemic proportions, is 17 times more likely to prove fatal than in the United States. Factory vaccination programs—vigorously enforced by the old Communist Party—have been suspended. An immunization rate of less than 50 percent has allowed the number of diphtheria cases to double annually since 1990.

But a large part of Russia's health crisis results from a widespread public distrust of the health care authorities. Although emergency treatment and most regular care is free, many Russians will refuse surgery or other medical treatments out of fear of the doctors' level of competence or intentions. No doubt Soviet medical care during the reigns of Stalin and Brezhnev helped to create these fears. Soviet hospitals never threatened to surpass their Western counterparts in terms of quality, and Russians' perceptions about state-provided medical care may well be a manifestation of their broader attitudes about the state. But access to health care for the bottom rungs of society was perhaps less bad in the Soviet Union than in many Western countries. Although Russia retains the governmental promise of free health care, private clinics and extralegal "moonlighting" operations are available for hard currency. True to the old ways, many Russians will resort to bribery in the quest for better medical care. Simple amenities like a change of bedclothes might be available only to those who grease the palms of orderlies. Like housing, access to high-quality medical care depends on one's ability to pay.

Some of the public's fears are grounded in less understandable, more fantastic beliefs. For example, rumors are spread among some ethnic minorities that outbreaks of disease are the result of Russian chemical weapons being used against them. And many Russians today are turning to faith healers, who purport to transmit their healing powers over television and radio. (A 1993 law making "mass healing events" illegal has not significantly mitigated this activity.)

Cumulatively, these continuing problems in terms of Russia's public health have kept Russia's mortality statistics at uncomfortable levels. In 1996 life expectancy for men was only 57 years. In that same year the country's death rate was 14.5 per thousand, compared with less than 8.6 in the United States. Russia's "natural" rate of population growth (births minus deaths) is negative; in 1996 it was about −5.4 percent. Still, these figures were an improvement over 1995.

Human Rights

Some of the most dramatic progress in living conditions since the fall of the Soviet Union has been in the area of human rights. The Russian population enjoys freedoms unknown to virtually all its predecessors: freedom of worship, assembly, and speech; freedom to travel and to emigrate; freedom to elect its own leaders and to run for political office. Virtually all remaining political prisoners who had been convicted during the Soviet era were released during the late Gorbachev and early Yeltsin periods. Russia signed the European Human Rights Convention in early 1996 as part of its obligations for being admitted to the Council of Europe. The Duma also passed a constitutional law creating the post of Russian Human Rights Commissioner, with substantial powers to investigate charges of human rights abuses. Russia's progress in these areas cannot be underestimated. For the first time in their country's history, Russians possess many of the basic freedoms enjoyed for years by citizens in the West. By some accounting, human freedom and dignity are among the most important facets of living conditions.

The post-Soviet Russian government has nevertheless come under internal and external criticism for an uneven human rights record. International organizations such as Amnesty International have issued formal reports and statements cataloging a series of abuses in Yeltsin's Russia. In addition to human rights abuses connected with the war in Chechnya (see Chapter 9), the government has been accused of permitting arbitrary searches and detention as method of control; tolerating severe overcrowding in federal prisons and the occasional torture of inmates; and allowing the at times fatal hazing of military conscripts. The plight of Russia's homeless and impoverished can also be viewed as a human rights issue. Clearly, while Russia has made enormous strides, it still has a long way to go to overcome the legacy and habits of its thousand-year past.

Living Conditions, Freedom, and Security

Whereas Russians' access to goods and services remains clearly substandard by the standards of the developed world, their enjoyment of various freedoms has clearly improved in comparison to the Soviet period. Indeed, these might be seen as two sides of the same coin. Political philosophy has long been preoccupied with the tension between liberty and equality. If the Soviet Union was able to achieve greater equality in its society, it came largely at the cost of limiting economic freedom. (It will be recalled, however, that members of the *nomenklatura* class within the Communist Party enjoyed a significantly higher status and material standard of living than the masses. And many of these have used their Soviet-era advantages to seize special opportunities in post-Soviet Russia.) Further, holding the Soviet system together against what might be seen as a more natural inequality required strict limits on political freedom. That Gorbachev naively underestimated this necessity may have been the Soviet Union's undoing.

Suggested Readings

Adelman, Deborah. *The "Children of Perestroika" Come of Age: Young People of Moscow Talk About Life in the New Russia*. Armonk, N.Y.: M.E. Sharpe, 1994.

Dutkina, Galina. *Moscow Days: Life and Hard Times in the New Russia*. New York: Kodansha, 1996.

Feshbach, Murray. *Ecological Disaster: Cleaning up the Hidden Legacy of the Soviet Regime*. New York: Twentieth Century Fund Press, 1995.

Koval, Vitalina, ed. *Women in Contemporary Russia*. Providence: Berghahn Books, 1995.

Peterson, D. J. *Troubled Lands: The Legacy of Soviet Environmental Destruction*. Boulder, Colo.: Westview Press, 1993.

Samorodov, Alexander T. "Transition, Poverty and Inequality in Russia," *International Labour Review* 13:3 (Spring 1992): 335–353.

5

Political Parties and Elections

"**S**ome comrades," General Secretary Mikhail Gorbachev complained in 1987, "apparently find it hard to understand that democracy is just a slogan."

The efforts to develop democracy in Russia build upon a past of frustration and disappointment. The country's absolutist tendencies are evident throughout its history. Until the last few years before the 1917 Revolution, the tsarist monarchy forewent even the symbolic pretenses of democracy. In contrast, the Soviet Union undertook great efforts to hide its authoritarian nature, relying heavily upon periodic elections to justify the regime's authority. That the elections offered no real choice and that one party—the Communist Party of the Soviet Union (CPSU)—possessed a monopoly of power provided only two of many reasons that invalidated Moscow's claim that the country was therefore democratic. So long as one-party rule remained the sine qua non of Soviet rule, honest evaluators could dismiss the mechanical trappings of democracy such as elections as so much window dressing. Then came Gorbachev's reforms and the subsequent collapse of the Soviet Union.

Real electoral choice is the heart of genuine democracy, and well-defined, responsible

53

parties are especially well suited for facilitating that choice. The success of Russia's transition from authoritarianism to liberal democracy will depend in no small measure upon the creation of viable, distinct parties and the conducting of periodic, fair elections.

Parties and Political Groups

The Communist Party of the Soviet Union—*the* Party—was never a political party in the Western sense of the term. The 1977 Constitution called the CPSU "the nucleus of [the Soviet] political system," and post-Soviet Russian critics have labeled it a quasi-state organization.[1] Its contrast with the democratic ideal of a party is stark. The CPSU did not so much aggregate group interests as it sought to indoctrinate Soviet subjects. Rather than contesting elections to acquire governmental power, the Party was practically indistinguishable from the government. It did not offer alternatives to governmental programs; it dictated those programs. The Party sought above all to mobilize, co-opt, and control the 10 percent of the population that joined its ranks often in search of the concomitant privileges that a party state afforded.

After three-quarters of a century under such a system, Russians can be forgiven some hesitation in warming to the practice of multiparty democracy. Thus the sardonic reply to Gorbachev's unprecedented introduction of multiparty elections in 1989: "Isn't one Party bad enough?" Like the founders of the United States two centuries earlier, the leaders of post-Soviet Russia initially eschewed political parties as distasteful, divisive, and even antidemocratic institutions. During his first five years as Russia's president, Boris Yeltsin would not formally associate himself with any political group. He conceived of the presidency as properly above the squalid business of party politics—a sentiment earlier held by such notable figures as George Washington and France's Charles De Gaulle. Although the virtue of the Russian presidency has nevertheless suffered without the connivance of party affiliation, it is clear that the development of parties in Russia has indeed been a chaotic affair that has enmeshed many of its perpetrators.

The End of One-Party Dominance

The CPSU lost its constitutional monopoly in March 1990, and the subsequent Law on Public Associations permitted the growing number of informal political groups to register and participate in the political process. The law defined "public associations" broadly, allowing the creation of both explicitly

---

1. Vyacheslav Nikonov, *Nezavisimaya gazeta*, August 7, 1992.

political groups (what amounted to nascent political parties) and more socially and economically oriented organizations such as sporting societies and trade unions. In effect, the Law on Public Associations provided for a broad range of organizations that collectively could serve the myriad functions once carried out by the CPSU.

Once one-party rule was broken, thousands of new groups sprang up to fill the void. Yet few if any of these groups could immediately be considered parties. They were too small and amorphous, and they lacked any clear role in the political system. They were given to factionalism, and many were geographically isolated. In Gorbachev's final year, the Soviet Union was transformed from a one-party system not to a multiparty state, but to a partyless state.

The political landscape was constructed of loose, nascent associations. Some of the early political groupings adopted the title "popular front," although the connection of this term with revolutionary activity might not be entirely appropriate. Sometimes analysts refer to these groups as "proto-parties," suggesting that eventually more mature parties will emerge. But the implication that there is some linear evolutionary development toward "real" parties can be misleading. The term "surrogate party" might be more precise, given that the groupings do not meet the criteria of parties, but might serve as substitutes until the political environment is able to spawn and support the genuine article. For this book, the term "party" is used for the sake of simplicity, although with the understanding that this not be confused with the Western variant.

"The Infantile Stage of Multipartyism"

Even after the collapse of the Soviet Union and the establishment of the Russian Federation as a sovereign country, Russia's political landscape was fractious and anomic. For the first several years of Russia's independence, nascent party organizations were short-lived—dividing, combining, dissolving altogether, and re-emerging with new ideological foundations. Their development and behavior more closely resembled narrowly defined interest groups than political parties. Indeed, to return to the analogy of America's founding, many of Russia's political parties bore a resemblance to the "factions" discussed by James Madison in *The Federalist* papers. The smallest of these have been labeled "divan parties," for their entire memberships supposedly could sit comfortably on a sofa. (The alternative moniker, "taxicab party," expresses the same idea.) And most Russian parties, large and small, were dominated by individual personalities, to which the parties' fortunes were mortally tied.

Not only have Russia's political groupings been narrowly segmented along functional or interest lines, but they also tend to be defined along regional lines. The issue of whether the Russian Federation is a viable political entity will be discussed later, but for now it is enough to note that the vast geographical and cultural differences among Russia's disparate peoples provide fertile ground for regional parties. Article 13 of the 1993 Russian Constitution commits the country to "multipartyism." But it makes an enormous difference whether this means the type found in the United Kingdom, say, or in Italy.

Finally, Russia's parties are not the only groups carrying out political functions. Political activity in Russia is channeled through clans, ethnic associations, and myriad other groupings. More than party structures, it is interpersonal relationships that matter in post-Soviet Russian politics. This point was boldly expressed in an article written by an American diplomat and published in a Russian newspaper in the fall of 1995.[2] Although the Russian Foreign Ministry protested the public release of such a critical article by a diplomatic official, this merely drove home Moscow's sensitivity to charges that Russian politics is a matter of power-sharing among rival clans. The article also suggested that the population is largely excluded from the political process, and characterized the public as apathetic and disillusioned.

The question of Russians' apathy is open to debate. Russian society does participate in nongovernmental and quasi-governmental associations in neighborhoods and workplaces. Even dance societies, cultural groups, and civic clubs play their part in Russian politics. By the mid-1990s, nascent economic interest groups in particular were developing across the country. In February 1996, for example, several mayors formed the Association of Coal Mining Towns to promote their shared economic interests. The same month Russian scientists banded together to protest budget cuts to the Russian Academy of Sciences. The presence and activity of these organizations alone does not necessarily constitute an institutionalization of pluralism. But clearly Russian citizens desire to make their distinct interests heard.

A Party System?

The post-Soviet Russian government scrambled to adopt regulations, registration procedures, and electoral laws to structure the emerging multiparty system. A fluctuating number of factions and blocs developed within the Congress of People's Deputies. One year after the collapse of the Soviet Union, about two dozen parties were formally registered in the Russian Federation. A much larger number of political organizations—by some counts more than a thousand— did not formally register, but in one way or another had surfaced as countrywide political groups. (The disparity between the number of formal parties and in-

---

2. Thomas Graham, "The New Russian Regime," *Nezavisimaya gazeta*, November 23, 1995.

formal groups illustrates the "gatekeeping" power retained by the government in the form of registration procedures.) By the end of 1992 there were more political organizations than there were seats in the Russian legislature.

The December 1993 parliamentary elections forced some discipline upon this chaotic and amorphous congeries of party groups. By the time of the deadline in September, 140 national groups had registered. Only 35 of these managed to submit the requisite number of signatures to participate in the elections. Consolidation and invalidation reduced voters' choices still further, with 13 "electoral associations" ultimately appearing on the ballot. Of these, only eight managed to obtain the 5 percent of the vote required to gain Duma seats allocated through proportional representation (PR). (See Table 5–1.)

Russia's party system was finally beginning to coalesce. As the first Russia-wide elections to be held since the demise of the Soviet Union, the 1993 parliamentary elections infused the victorious parties with a certain legitimacy and credibility that theretofore had been unknown in Russia. The

Table 5–1   1993 Duma Election Results, by Party

Source: Richard Sakwa, "The Russian Elections of December 1993," *Europe-Asia Studies* 47:2 (1995): 213. Published by Carfax Publishing Company, reprinted with permission.

Party	PR Seats	District Seats	Total Seats
Russia's Choice	40	30	70
Liberal Democratic Party	59	5	64
Communist Party of the Russian Federation	32	16	48
Agrarian	21	12	33
Yabloko	20	3	23
Women of Russia	21	2	23
Russian Unity and Accord	18	1	19
Democratic Party of Russia	14	1	15
Russian Movement for Democratic Reform	0	4	4
Dignity and Charity	0	2	2
Civic Union	0	1	1
New Names	0	1	1
Cedar	0	0	0
Independent (no party affiliation)	n/a	141	141*

* Most "independent" deputies subsequently joined party fractions.

performance of these parties in the newly constituted parliament helped establish a legislative record by which they could be distinguished. And the procedural requirements imposed by the new Constitution nudged the parties to take up the arcane democratic arts of compromise and coalition building.

Not that everyone was pleased with the election results. Almost a quarter of the popular vote went to Vladimir Zhirinovsky's ultranationalist Liberal Democratic Party. Another 12 percent went to the Communists. Some of the more radical voices in Yegor Gaidar's Russia's Democratic Choice bloc called upon Yeltsin to dissolve the Duma—just as he had done with the last parliament only months earlier. But cooler heads prevailed. Democracy affords voters the right to decide for themselves which parties can best represent their interests. Mistakes can be corrected with the next election. What is most important about Russia's founding election is not so much the distribution of political power that resulted, but the establishment of the principle of popular sovereignty.

Soon after the 1993 parliamentary elections, the new Duma members further consolidated into party fractions. Similar to *Fraktionen* in Germany, Russia's fractions are the official, registered political groups within the legislature. Only groups with at least 35 members could register as fractions after the Duma elections. (Fractions registered before the elections were not subject to this requirement.) It is important for blocs, parties, and other political groupings to formally register as a means of effectively wielding political power within the parliament. Not only do fractions impose institutional structure upon their members, but in addition committee chairmanships are allocated to fractions on the basis of their size. Further, a Duma Council, whose powers include the setting of the legislative calendar, is composed of fraction and committee representatives. Legislators apparently have understood the importance of these institutions; although 141 "independent" candidates were elected to the Duma without a specific party affiliation, fewer than a dozen deputies were not members of a fraction or party by the time the new Duma had consolidated. (See Table 5–2.)

Despite clashes over policy, most of the fraction leaders judged Duma Speaker Ivan Rybkin (of the Agrarian Party) to have exercised his office with professionalism and fairness. The 1993–95 Duma served out its term without being dissolved or suspended, which was something of an accomplishment given recent Russian politics.

New registration procedures were in place for the December 1995 parliamentary elections, and 8,000 candidates and 43 parties registered by the deadline. The Central Electoral Commission's official list included both large, established parties and more idiosyncratic, ad hoc organizations. Illustrative of the latter was the group labeled as the "Electoral bloc including the leaders of parties for the defense of children (Peace, Good and Happiness); 'Russian women'; for orthodoxy (Faith, Hope and Love); the Popular Christian-

Table 5–2   Fractions in the Duma after December 1993 Election

Source: Michael McFaul, "Russian Politics: The Calm Before the Storm?"
Current History 93:585 (October 1994): 317.

Fraction (Leader)	Number of Deputies
LDP (V. Zhirinovsky)	57
Russia's Choice (Y. Gaidar)	71
New Regional Politics (V. Medvedev)	64
Agrarian Party (M. Lapshin)	55
CPRF (G. Zyuganov)	45
Yabloko (G. Yavlinsky)	27
Party for Russian Unity and Accord (S. Shakrai)	33
Women of Russia (Y. Lakhova)	23
Democratic Party of Russia (N. Travkin)	15

monarchist party; for the unity of Slavic peoples; for agricultural workers' 'land-mother'; for the defense of invalids; for those who have suffered from the authorities and who have been cheated." Although this single bloc secured over 145,000 votes, it garnered only 0.21 percent of the vote. And the Beer Lovers' Party, which even in the land of vodka managed to secure more than 400,000 votes, was allocated no seats. About 64 percent of the eligible voters participated in the elections, with only about 1.5 percent choosing the "against all" option on their ballots.

Despite the political and geographical fragmentation evident in post-Soviet Russia's first years, therefore, electoral politics seemed to be solidifying around a handful of viable parties. Indeed, over half the deputies elected in 1995 had served in the first Duma, and all but four of the 43 parties vying for "party list" seats failed to secure the 5 percent of the vote required to be awarded seats. (See Table 5–3.) Yabloko's Grigory Yavlinsky welcomed these developments as the conclusion of Russia's "infantile stage of multipartyism."

This time it was the Communist Party of the Russian Federation (CPRF) that received the largest number of votes cast. And in the words of the British magazine *The Economist*, "Nobody could sensibly accuse Russians, of all people, of voting for Communists in ignorance of the possible consequences."[3] Or could they? The meaning of labels such as communism, reformism, and conservatism had been contorted and twisted during the campaign, throughout the perestroika era, and indeed throughout the Soviet era. The Russian

---

3. "The Devil They Don't Know," *The Economist*, December 23, 1995: 59

Table 5–3   1995 Duma Election Results, by Party

Source: Open Media Resource Institute

Party	PR Seats	District Seats	Total Seats
CPRF	99	58	157
Our Home Is Russia	50	5	55
Liberal Democratic Party of Russia	50	1	51
Yabloko	31	14	45
Agrarian Party of Russia	0	20	20
Power to the People	0	9	9
Russia's Democratic Choice	0	9	9
Congress of Russian Communities	0	5	5
Forward, Russia	0	3	3
Ivan Rybkin Bloc	0	3	3
Women of Russia	0	3	3
Gurov–Vladimir Lysenko–Pamfilova	0	2	2
Communists–Working Russia–For the Soviet Union	0	1	1
Govorukhin Bloc	0	1	1
Trade Unions and Industrialists of Russia–Labor Union	0	1	1
Other Unions and Blocs	0	8	8
Independent (no party affiliation)	0	78	78

Duma was now dominated by fewer than a half-dozen parties, and the number of fractions shrank to seven (CPRF, LDP, NDR, Yabloko, the Agrarians, Popular Power, and Russian Regions). But what could be said about the ideologies they represented?

The Ideological Spectrum

Evaluating the general political philosophies of Russia's political parties presents frustrating conceptual difficulties. The West's Cold War–era practice of defining "Communism" as the left endpoint of an ideological spectrum offers little assistance in post-Soviet Russia. If "conservative" and "orthodox" are characteristics of the right side of the ideological spectrum, where should one place the revolutionary Communists of contemporary Russia who long for a return to the old (Soviet) order? Should "reformists" be placed on the left (with progressives) or on the right (with laissez-faire capitalists)? Other issues on which Russia's emergent parties can be distinguished do not lend themselves to the traditional left-right spectrum. Nationalism and imperialism are two critical issues coloring Russian politics in the mid-1990s, but they are not easily placed on the familiar left-right continuum. The task becomes even more difficult with the unusual combinations of values that are amalgamated within some party platforms.

This is not simply a methodological problem. It illustrates the amorphous nature of contemporary Russian politics. In the first months of the 1996–99 Duma, coalitions were built between "reformers" and Communists against nationalists. Such alliances resulted more from political expediency than from any harmony of fundamental values. The subordination of ideology to short-term tactical gains becomes especially clear when one recalls that the Communists and nationalists were frequently allied against the democrats in the 1993–95 Duma. In other words, the coalition building in modern Russian politics resembles the forging of alliances in nineteenth-century Europe's balance-of-power system. In both systems, ideology matters less than political survival.

A significant portion of Russia's political landscape consists of a congeries of parties in the amorphous center known as the "swamp." This center is largely defined by what it is not—and it is not "extremist" in the way that the parties identified by colors (communist Reds, ultranationalist Browns, environmentalist Greens) seem to be. Within the swamp, and to some extent even at the extremes, Russian politics is characterized not so much as a competition of ideologies as a clash of personalities. Nonetheless, three loosely defined groups (not parties) have emerged from the morass of post-Soviet Russian politics to have particular influence in defining the political debate. These three groups are the new Communists, the reformists, and the conservative/nationalists. It bears emphasizing that these categories are fluid and amorphous, and not mutually exclusive. Still, they help to better define Russia's political landscape in the mid-1990s.

The New Communists

The resurrection of communist parties in the former Soviet Union and Eastern Europe in the 1990s has forced a revision of the triumphalist thesis about the "end of history" brought on by the Cold War's demise. The victory of the Communist Aleksandr Kwasniewski over Solidarity leader Lech Walesa in Poland's 1995 presidential election was especially sobering. So was the near-victory in 1996 of Communist Gennady Zyuganov in post-Soviet Russia's first presidential election.

The CPSU's days were numbered when Article 6 was stricken from the Soviet Constitution in March 1990. Pressure for its repeal had been building rapidly throughout the Soviet Union, although even the advocates of repeal did not anticipate the systemic collapse that soon would result. Dissident historian Roy Medvedev predicted, "Even after the removal of [the CPSU's] guaranteed monopoly under Article 6 of the constitution, it will remain the ruling party for a long time to come."[4] But in defiance of this prediction, the Soviet Union's—and Russia's—political landscape was unrecognizably altered within a few months.

The subsequent proliferation of political groups gave voice to long-suppressed interests, but Russia's immediate political future was less dependent upon these political groups than on the simple fact that the CPSU was being officially abandoned and publicly vilified. Yeltsin resigned from the Party in July 1990. (Gorbachev resigned only after the failed coup of August 1991.) In the wake of the coup, Yeltsin, now president of the RSFSR, suspended Communist Party operations throughout Russia. In November 1991 he banned the Party outright.

Die-hard members of the defunct CPSU continued to hold occasional meetings in gloomy cafeterias and abandoned union halls—a somewhat pathetic spectacle when contrasted with the ostentatious pomp of Party meetings in the pre-Gorbachev era. On July 5, 1992, these partisans even staged a "Twenty-Ninth Congress of the CPSU." Another Congress was held in March 1993, where the "Union of Communist Parties—CPSU" was created to coordinate the activities of the various Communist-oriented parties across the former Soviet Union. But these efforts to prop up the corpse of the CPSU were merely a sideshow to the more meaningful efforts to create a viable successor party. A disparate collection of ad hoc groups competed for the mantel—and the property—of the defunct CPSU. Sovietwide Communist movements included the Nina Andreeva's Communist Party of Bolsheviks (the name of the Soviet Communist party from 1934 to 1952), and the Workers' Union of Communists (established in December 1991 by Aleksei Prigarin). But with the Soviet Union breaking apart while these groups issued defiant pronouncements about the glorious Soviet future, their efforts to preserve a unionwide Party ultimately were in vain.

Meanwhile, within the RSFSR itself efforts were made to create a new Russian Communist Party. For most of the Soviet period the RSFSR did not have a Communist party of its own. The Russian Communist Party that had developed in the crucible of revolution at the opening of the twentieth century had been abolished with the formal creation of the Soviet Union in December 1922. Lenin opposed a separate Russian party as a potential vehicle for Great Russian chauvinism. Presumably the all-union CPSU would be adequate for representing legitimate Russian interests. This does not explain, however, why Lenin saw fit to allow separate Communist parties in the other Soviet repub-

---

4. *The Guardian*, April 20, 1990.

lics. But it does provide today's CPRF with a basis for distancing itself from the sins of the Soviet period.

Thus, with the Soviet edifice crumbling, Party elites in Russia were motivated by the desire to establish a Communist base separate from the moribund CPSU. In June 1990 Ivan Polozkov and others (including Gennady Zyuganov) established a Russian Communist party, which, incidentally, claimed to represent "genuine" Communists in contradistinction to the "revisionist" agenda of the CPSU under Gorbachev. Other early efforts to establish a Russian Communist organization included Anatoly Kryuchkov's Russian Party of Communists, Viktor Anpilov's Working Russia, and Aleksandr Rutskoi's People's Party for a Free Russia. Numerous smaller groups, often with geographically limited appeal, developed as well. But virtually all that these groups had in common was a distaste for Yeltsin and a nostalgic desire for power. The seemingly monolithic Party of Lenin had been transformed into a fractious collection of political opportunists and ideological pretenders. Roy Medvedev, undeterred by his failed prediction about the CPSU's staying power, sought in 1991 to unite the "progressive forces" of the failed Party into a "new Russian party of left-wing, socialist-oriented forces." Although he did manage to establish the Socialist Workers' Party, he succeeded only in further fracturing the Communists' potential base of support. In 1992 Gennady Zyuganov helped establish the National Salvation Front to unite the left and right opponents of Yeltsin. Yeltsin summarily banned it.

For the first couple of years, therefore, post-Soviet Russia constituted an unfriendly environment for Communist organizations. Yeltsin's decrees facilitated the seizure of their property and the banning of their activities. Much of the public, infused with a desire for post-Soviet salvation and absolution, simply saddled the Communists with all the sins of the Soviet regime and the shortcomings of the Russian state. And the Communists themselves, recently cast out from their positions of privilege, fought over the scraps of the tattered ideology which might still provide meaning for their past, if not solace for their political demise. The fracturing of the once-mighty Party stood in stark contrast to even the recent past. As a political player, Communism was generally dismissed as a spent force.

The CPRF: Communism Resurgent

Before long, however, this assessment would have to be revised. In the winter of 1992–93 the Russian Constitutional Court scaled back Yeltsin's decrees blocking Russian Communists and the National Salvation Front. Basking in the partial vindication of the Court's ruling and savoring the growing public dissatisfaction with Yeltsin's reform programs, the Communists' prospects began to improve. The public was already showing signs of selective amnesia, recalling the order and certainty that characterized the country in the supposedly happier days of Soviet rule and overlooking the price at which that order was purchased. Over a dozen new Russian Communist groups quickly sprang up to capitalize on these conditions. But it was the Communist Party of the Russian Federation (CPRF), established in mid-February 1993, which most effectively claimed the legacy of the old CPSU. Gennady Zyuganov, the former mathematics teacher who earlier had established the National Salvation Front, was elected the CPRF's chairman. Zyuganov was no Johnny-come-lately; he had joined the CPSU in 1966 and was appointed to the Central Committee's propaganda department in 1983. Nevertheless, under his direction the Russian Communists reinvented themselves as a party that could gain significant public support in genuinely democratic elections. We have already observed the CPRF's success in the 1993 and 1995 parliamentary elections.

With about a half-million members, the CPRF is by far the largest party in the Russian Federation. It also is among the best organized, drawing upon an organizational structure that never entirely dissolved with the demise of the CPSU. In place of the Politburo, the CPRF has established a Central Executive Committee to direct the regional and local bodies and to preserve the party's ideology. The party is especially strong in the industrial cities, among older Russians, and among Russia's "new poor." Veterans and *apparatchiki* from the Soviet period also are well represented. Critics say that the CPRF represents the misfits and the feckless—the detritus of the Soviet system who could not find a home in the other post-Soviet parties across the political spectrum.

The CPRF is no radical, neo-Bolshevik organization. Rather, it is neoconservative in the sense that it decries the changes that the once-great Russian/Soviet state has recently undergone. The party under Zyuganov postures as a kinder, gentler Communist party, committed to reversing the "failed" and "ill-considered" policies of Yeltsin's government. Although it unrepentantly displays the Soviet-era hammer and sickle, it disowns the bureaucratization and corruption of its predecessor and publicly embraces multiparty democracy. Zyuganov has assured Western business leaders (and, more importantly to him, potential investors) of his party's commitment to markets and private property. To the more traditional Leninist faithful in Russia, he rationalizes this acceptance of (regulated) capitalism with reference to the Soviet Union's New Economic Policy (NEP), which had allowed limited private enterprise. Lenin himself introduced the NEP in 1921, although it was dismantled by Stalin soon after Lenin's death in 1924.

Despite Zyuganov's reassurances, much of the CPRF's doctrine worried the stewards of Russia's tenuous political and economic reforms. The party's 1995 election manifesto called for the "voluntary" re-establishment of the Soviet Union, cradle-to-grave social guarantees, renationalization of industry, collectivization of land, and a political distancing from the West. Indeed, there is evidence of tension within the party between (apparent) moderates such as

Zyuganov and harder-line ideologues such as Anatoly Lukyanov, the former chairman of the Soviet parliament. Of the latter category, Aleksandr Shabanov, the party's main ideologist, has argued that Western individualism does not suit Russia, and suggested that the country must return to promoting "community," even at the expense of personal freedoms. Some of the worst crimes perpetuated against humanity were justified on such logic. Nevertheless, the CPRF is generally careful to distance itself from Stalin and his excesses, claiming instead a Leninist heritage updated for the 1990s.

The RCWP

The same cannot be said for the other major post-Soviet Russian Communist party, the Russian Communist Workers' Party (RCWP). Led by Viktor Tyulkin, the RCWP dismissed the CPRF as an insincere pretender to the esteemed mantel of Communism. Yeltsin prohibited the RCWP from participation in the 1993 elections because of its role in the October 1993 "events." The party re-emerged in 1994. Recognizing its weak position as the 1995 parliamentary elections approached, the party sought an alliance with Zyuganov's CPRF. The RCWP was rebuffed and ran independently. The RCWP came up one-half percent short of the 5 percent threshold for party-list representation and took only one district seat. Without a power base in the legislature but still endorsed by more than 3 million voters, the RCWP later was courted by Zyuganov in his 1996 presidential campaign. This time, however, the RCWP rebuffed Zyuganov, whose already-suspect commitment to communism was further diluted by the exigencies of his presidential campaign. Viktor Anpilov, a high-profile leader of the Working Russia faction within the RCWP, nevertheless chose to endorse Zyuganov and was stripped of his position within the RCWP for his "betrayal" of the cause of "real" Communism. Later, Anpilov's faction was split into smaller factions.

At the same time, however, the radical Communist groups have shown some solidarity in the face of the CPRF's moderation. In October 1996 the RCWP and four other Communist groups formed the Union of Communists and Socialists of Russia. The group's staying power remained to be seen. In any event, its total membership paled in comparison with the CPRF.

The Agrarian Party

Closely related to the Communists is the Agrarian Party, founded in early 1993 by Mikhail Lapshin. The party embraced in particular the first element of the old Bolshevik slogan of "land, bread, and peace." The Agrarians' own slogan is "Land for those who work it." The idea of land reform traditionally has resonated with the Russian population, which remains overwhelmingly rural. The Agrarians championed the interests of collective farmers and state cooperatives, rather than private agricultural interests. Although the Agrarian Party also fell short of the 5 percent threshold in the 1995 elections, it secured 20 district seats in the Duma. Shortly after the elections the Agrarians announced that they, too, would support Zyuganov's presidential campaign. As a more moderate group, the Agrarians did not join the radical Union of Communists and Socialists of Russia.

Reformist Parties

The hardest category to define is that of the reformists. Most post-Soviet Russian politicians claim to support some conception of reform. But the category is generally understood to comprise those parties committed to market economics and democratic pluralism. Two of the four parties that surmounted the 5 percent threshold in the 1995 Duma elections could be considered reformist by this definition.

Our Home Is Russia

The Chernomyrdin government was behind one of these reform parties, Our Home Is Russia (usually identified by its Russian acronym, NDR). Although Yeltsin technically declined formal association with the party, he clearly supported it. NDR thus represented the incumbent government and the presidency. Although it stands for the status quo and has taken a centrist position on various economic and political issues, NDR was committed to the democratic and market reforms initiated by Yeltsin. It secured slightly more than 10 percent of the popular vote and a total of 55 seats in the 1995 Duma elections.

In the years after those elections a schism began to develop between NDR's Duma faction and the Chernomyrdin-led party in government. The Duma group, led by Sergli Belyaev, showed increasing independence. It even opposed the Chernomyrdin government's draft of the 1997 budget. This schism perhaps illustrates the different institutional perspectives of the various branches of government.

Yabloko

More vigorous in its commitment to democracy and market economics is the Yabloko party. The party was founded and led by Grigory Yavlinsky, an American-educated, free-market economist, whose name provided the first syllable of the party's moniker. (Co-founders Yuri Boldyrev and Vladimir Lukin contributed the other two syllables.) In 1990 Yavlinsky helped write the renowned Five Hundred Day Plan to create a market economy in Gorbachev's USSR; the plan was never implemented, however. He later helped the city of

Nizhny Novgorod to become a laboratory for ambitious economic reform programs. In 1993 Yabloko secured 33 seats in the Duma. In 1995 it garnered slightly less than 7 percent of the popular vote—the least of the four parties gaining proportional representation. Personal and doctrinal disputes between Yavlinsky and Boldyrev threatened to fracture the party after the 1995 elections.

Russia's Choice

Yegor Gaidar's Russia's Choice had been the primary reform bloc in 1993, representing the incumbent, pro-Yeltsin forces after the October events. In 1995 the organization was reconceived as a party bearing the name Russia's Democratic Choice (RDC). But with Chernomyrdin replacing Gaidar as prime minister, RDC lost its institutional advantage. Gaidar refused to ally his group with NDR, and Yavlinsky refused Gaidar's request for an alliance. Somewhat isolated and anachronistic, RDC failed to clear the 5 percent threshold in the 1995 Duma elections. It also secured nine district seats. Several other reformist parties did secure district seats, but even a generous definition of the term places reformist strength in the 1996–99 Duma at about a quarter of the seats.

Although the reformists share a general commitment to Western-style democracy and capitalism, political unity has eluded them. An unwillingness to compromise has caused part of the fractiousness among the reformists. Yavlinsky refused an alliance with Gaidar in both 1993 and 1995, and then turned down requests for cooperation from other reformist Duma fractions. Criticism of Yavlinsky mounted as the 1996–99 Duma leadership was being established. He was accused of cutting a deal with the CPRF to facilitate the election of their candidate for speaker, Gennady Seleznev. In the floor vote, Yabloko deputies supported the longshot candidacy of Vladimir Lukin, thus splitting the reformist vote from the otherwise electable choice of the anti-Communist bloc, Ivan Rybkin. Although a member of the Agrarian Party, Rybkin had earned a reputation for professionalism and fairness in his position as speaker of the 1994–95 Duma. Later, Yabloko deputies were calling for Yeltsin's resignation while NDR generally defended the president.

Divisions among the reformists continued in the fall of 1996 as Gaidar's RDC sought a "liberal" alliance with the Peasants' Party and others. Gaidar made a point of excluding Yabloko from consideration as he regarded it a "social democratic" party, not a "liberal" one. Meanwhile, local branches of Yabloko and the CPRF supported a common candidate in the September 1996 gubernatorial election in the Leningrad oblast. Their joint candidate was running against an NDR candidate. Clearly, the divisions within the reformist camp ran deep.

The divisions within the reformist ranks may reveal a primary flaw with their political approach: Their commitment to liberty and pluralism may be manifesting itself as an unwillingness to compromise individual beliefs. But in addition to possible shortcomings on the part of reformist leaders, the general cause of reform is so vague as to allow quite varied interpretations and prescriptions. The timing, order, and extent of the reform programs are a matter of vociferous debate. As a result, the various fractions of the 1996–99 Duma that might be classified as reformist found their collective strength weakened in the face of a more disciplined opposition.

Conservative/Nationalist Parties

The conservatives and nationalists generally promote a stronger state and a restoration of Russian greatness. For this they are occasionally associated with the Communists, but conservatives and nationalists usually do not share the Communists' ideological beliefs. Neither are the conservative/nationalist parties necessarily averse to some of the reformists' economic objectives, although conservatives and nationalists usually reject the liberal pluralism often associated with reform. Mostly conservative/nationalist parties are committed to the nation of Russia over the individuals that constitute it.

The Liberal Democratic Party

Best known within the conservative/nationalist group is the Liberal Democratic Party (LDP). The appealing name was established when Vladimir Bogachev and Lev Ubozhko founded the rather innocuous Liberal Democratic Party of Russia in the summer of 1989. The party, committed to market capitalism and the rule of law, became the first party to be registered in the Soviet Union. But in a parallel of Austria's Freedom Party under the ultranationalist Jörg Haider, Russia's LDP soon came under the extremist sway of Vladimir Zhirinovsky, who re-established the party as the Liberal Democratic Party of the USSR in March 1990. Zhirinovsky ran for the presidency against Yeltsin (and others) in 1991 and came in third with more than 6 million votes. He was associated with the conservative/nationalist organizations Nashi ("Ours") and Pamyat ("Memory") before rising to prominence within the LDP. As a leader of the LDP, Zhirinovsky supported the August 1991 coup against Gorbachev.

The LDP was reregistered as a Russian political party in 1992. In 1993 Zhirinovsky led the party to a surprising victory in parliamentary elections, garnering the largest number of proportional representation seats in the Duma. As the reformist forces reeled, Zhirinovsky deadpanned: "Today, the whole world knows about me." The LDP had most effectively employed Western-style campaign tactics, which would become de rigueur in the next parliamentary elections two years later. In 1995 the LDP received somewhat less support, with 11 percent of the PR vote, but this was the second best showing of all the parties running. Under Zhirinovsky, the LDP established itself as a well-known and potentially powerful force in Russian politics.

Zhirinovsky's political rhetoric is an odd amalgam of ethnic chauvinism, sexism, and anti-Westernism. He has flirted with anti-Semitism (notwithstanding his own father's being Jewish) and calls for the domination of the former Soviet Union by Russia (although he was born in Kazakhstan). Zhirinovsky's brand of nationalism is therefore not so much Great Russian chauvinism as it is Russian imperialism. Indeed, his preferred vision for Russia is essentially the Soviet Union—a vision shared with many Communists. But unlike Zyuganov's CPRF, Zhirinovsky's LDP supported Yeltsin's military invasion of Chechnya. That the LDP was virtually the president's sole major supporter in the Duma on this issue was something of an embarrassment to the Yeltsin leadership.

It is impossible to imagine the LDP without Zhirinovsky. The party gained notoriety in the West for Zhirinovsky's outrageous statements about taking back Alaska from the United States, initiating a third world war, re-establishing the Soviet Union, and jointly deporting Jews (a "small but troublesome minority") in cooperation with would-be American President Pat Buchanan (whose 1996 candidacy Zhirinovsky endorsed). He describes the party's official ideology with obfuscation: "center-right moderate conservative party, standing on a patriotic platform."[5] But at its core his message is one of great power expansionism. In his autobiography, *The Last Thrust South*, Zhirinovsky calls for the expansion of the Russian empire southward, not merely to the old Soviet boundaries (the Transcaucasus and Central Asia), but to include Turkey, Afghanistan, and Iran as well. Promoting a return to international spheres of influence, he recommends that the United States make similar imperial forays into Latin America.

The fortunes of Zhirinovsky and the LDP were declining in 1996, particularly after his poor showing (less than 6 percent to Yeltsin's more than 35 percent) in the first round of presidential elections in June. Further, in October 1996, a Moscow court ordered Zhirinovsky to pay 10 million rubles (about $1,800) for making slanderous statements. Zhirinovsky might possibly feel a need to rein in his rhetoric. The LDP nevertheless retained about 50 seats in the Duma, gained its first seat in the Federation Council in late 1996, and was poised to exploit growing nationalist sentiment among the population.

The Congress of Russian Communities

Other parties have competed for the nationalist vote, although none has come near the LDP's level of success. Yuri Skokov's Congress of Russian

---

5. Richard Sakwa, "The Russian Elections of 1993," *Europe-Asia Studies* 47:2 (1995): 205.

Communities (KRO) seemed to be heading for a parliamentary victory in mid-1995, particularly after recruiting the popular former General Aleksandr Lebed to head the ticket.

Lebed was credited with disobeying the 1991 coup leaders' orders to storm the Russian parliament building. American and Russian pundits at the time portrayed Lebed as a Russian Colin Powell. Quite unlike Powell, however, Lebed earned his nationalist credentials heading a military operation in defense of ethnic Russians in the Dniester region of Moldova. His outspoken criticism of Defense Minster Pavel Grachev and his unwillingness to comply with troop reduction orders caused him to be removed from that position in the summer of 1995. But this only bolstered Lebed's projected image as a Russian patriot fighting a corrupt, feckless political leadership. At the same time he has vociferously opposed the invasion of Chechnya (see Chapter 9) and has advocated the re-integration of Belarus and Ukraine with Russia. Although he claims to support the principles of democracy, he believes Russia is not yet ready for it. Instead, he has openly expressed admiration for Augusto Pinochet's dictatorial methods in developing Chile's economy and society in the 1970s.

The business of protecting Russians in the Near Abroad is popular with Russian nationalists, as is the call for firm, even undemocratic leadership. But in an illustration of the fragility of post-Soviet Russia's political parties, the KRO suffered from the public squabbles between Lebed and Skokov. On the day of the 1995 elections, the party, once expected to win a feature slot in the 1996–99 Duma, failed to surmount the 5 percent threshold. Even Gennady Zyuganov, who in the campaign had expressed interest in an alliance with the KRO, now backed away from the association. Nevertheless, the KRO did secure five district seats, one of which was held by Lebed. Skokov was removed from the party leadership and replaced with a more radical nationalist, Dmitry Rogozin.

Lebed went on to run (with a third-place showing) as a candidate for president in 1996. In an effort to shore up his support among nationalists for the second round of voting, Yeltsin made Lebed the head of the National Security Council. A few months later, however, Lebed was removed in the wake of accusations that he was plotting a coup. Although no longer associated with the KRO, Lebed's political odyssey spurred speculation about the nationalists' agenda.

Russia's nationalists and their ultraconservative allies have provided some of the most colorful, provocative, and controversial statements since the country's independence. It is easy to write off much of this—particularly Zhirinovsky's antics—as the eccentric, clownish excesses of political expression in the uncharted frontier of Russian democracy. As political actors the LDP, KRO, and their ilk may not be especially harmful to Russian democracy. But the nationalist sentiment that propelled the LDP to two substantial victories is a force to be reckoned with. Whereas the Communists tap into dissatisfaction with the economic pains of market transitions, the nationalists play upon Russians' ethnonational pride and great power pretensions. Many Russians still smart from their empire's humiliating demise under Gorbachev and resent Yeltsin's alleged obsequiousness toward the West. They chafe at the conditions placed on their country by the International Monetary Fund and the Council of Europe. They fret over the widespread Westernization of Russian music, literature, film, and language. They revile the foreign carpetbaggers who buy up rights to Russia's vast natural resources and raise land prices with their business and housing developments.

Accurate or not, these perceptions resonate with a significant segment of Russia's population. Although the policy prescriptions of the LDP and other nationalist parties are unlikely to alleviate the core complaints, their populist message obviously has succeeded in drawing popular support away from the reformist parties.

Other Parties

Many parties, fractions, and political groups in contemporary Russian politics are not easily placed in the three categories defined above. Most of these are relatively small and without much influence. One, however, has tremendous potential power and has managed some impressive legislative victories. This electoral bloc, Women of Russia, combined three women's groups in October 1993—only two months before the first Duma elections. It managed to match the 9 percent of the PR vote achieved by Yabloko and the Agrarians, securing a combined total (party list and district races) of 23 seats.

The party has defined itself as a left-leaning centrist party, committed to "equal rights, equalization of opportunity, and partnership." With well over half of the Russian electorate composing the bloc's self-defined constituency, Women of Russia represents a potentially powerful force. A 1995 article in *Pravda* warned that "women must be satisfied or [they] will turn to politics." Apparently they already had. Several months later, with the tactical advantage of appearing first among 43 on the ballots, Women of Russia was expected to win a large share, perhaps even a plurality, of PR votes in the December 1995 Duma elections. The unpredictability of Russian politics made itself felt here, however. The party fell short of the 5 percent PR threshold and secured only three district seats.

Russia's embryonic party system was continuing to stabilize and even mature in the mid-1990s. Although nowhere near a successful institutionalization of "party government"—perhaps a good thing, given the Soviet Union's gross malformation of that concept—Russia's political landscape was becoming dominated by political groups and electoral blocs that were rapidly making the business of Russian elections a meaningful process.

Russia's Developing Electoral System

Like the making of sausages and laws, the process of Russian democracy is not for the squeamish. Russian elections fall significantly short of the democratic ideal in a variety of ways. For example, candidates and parties commonly purchase lists of signatures necessary for registration from "signature farmers," who pay potential voters for their signatures. Various charges of electoral irregularities have been lodged against the government as well, such as the alleged pressuring of state employees to sign candidate registration lists during working hours. Similar pressures have been reported within the military ranks. Election officials have been accused of ballot stuffing and otherwise manipulating electoral results. The outcome of the 1993 parliamentary election was widely understood to have been tainted by outright falsification.

By the time of the 1995 parliamentary elections, electoral campaigns had become more sophisticated. So had the skirting of electoral laws. Many parties contesting the elections placed high-profile names on their party lists to attract voters to the party. This turned out to be something of a bait-and-switch tactic, as the celebrities would subsequently decline to take the seats allocated to them by the election, leaving them to be filled by lesser party figures. Some groups sought to secure greater free media time for their candidates by splitting into several parties and then consolidating their electoral strength by pulling out the "shadow" parties at the last minute. Still other parties forewent such Byzantine procedures and simply sold spaces on their party lists to raise funds. The Russian "green" party, Cedar, made particular use of this tactic, selling slots to business leaders whose environmental credentials were suspect. The party's only prominent environmental activist, Sergei Zaligin, resigned in protest. Several months after the Duma elections, a Duma deputy from the LDP revealed that about half the members of his fraction had purchased their places on the LDP's party list for an average of $1 million each.

Russia's Central Electoral Commission (TsIK) is charged with ensuring the propriety and legality of elections. Yeltsin created the TsIK shortly after he dissolved the Supreme Soviet in September 1993. He appointed Nikolai Ryabov, a loyal ally, to the post of chairman. Ryabov oversaw the groundbreaking of Russia's new electoral process, presiding over two Duma elections in two years as well as post-Soviet Russia's first presidential elections. (In November 1996 Ryabov became Russia's ambassador to Czechoslovakia, and was replaced as TsIK chairman by Aleksandr Ivanchenko.) Besides establishing regulations and procedures for such electoral concerns as party registration, the TsIK has also sought to limit the influence of money in political campaigns. It established clear limits on the amount of money Russian parties could receive and spend, but because adequate investigation and enforcement were hard to come by these limits were routinely violated in the 1995 parliamentary campaign. In addition, some parties were bribed with large cash payments to drop out of the race and endorse the former opponents. The TsIK has also established regulations concerning the use of media and the length of campaigns—again, with mixed success.

An understanding (subsequently corrected by the Constitutional Court) that legislators are immune from criminal prosecution enticed various big- and small-time crooks, many under indictment, to seek sanctuary in the form of legislative office. Some of these were attracted to Cedar and other parties that sold their party-list slots. Others were ideologically attracted to (and initially welcomed by) such parties as Zhirinovsky's LDP.

Despite all these affronts to the democratic ideal, Russia's electoral results have been largely honored by the parties and accepted by the masses. Further, over 400 international observers from the Council of Europe, the European Union, and the Organization for Security and Cooperation in Europe judged the 1995 parliamentary elections to meet basic standards of democracy. Five hundred OSCE observers passed similar judgment upon the 1996 presidential elections. What has been remarkable is the speed with which Russian society has accepted the institution of democratic elections.

Legislative Elections

The Russian parliament, the Federal Assembly, is divided into two chambers. The Federation Council is the upper house and is composed of regional governmental leaders. The lower house, the State Duma, is popularly elected.

State Duma

The State Duma is made up of 450 deputies. Half of these are elected by direct election in single-member districts. The remainder are awarded seats from party lists, apportioned through proportional representation.

Deputies to the Duma serve four-year terms and are not subject to term limits. (The first Duma deputies, elected in 1993, served a special two-year term.) Russian citizens at least 21 years of age and otherwise qualified to vote (Russia's minimum voting age is 18) are eligible to run for a Duma seat. Candidates must collect signatures from 1 percent of a district's voters to run for a district seat, unless directly nominated by a party. Candidates running for seats allocated by proportional representation merely need to be placed on a party list. (That party must itself submit signatures to be registered.) The Constitution requires that no candidate run unopposed. Deputies of the Duma may not simultaneously hold office in other branches of government, although members of the other branches may be candidates for Duma seats. Only parties receiving at least 5 percent of the national vote may take their proportional allocation of seats.

Federation Council

Like the U.S. Senate, the Russian Federation's upper house is based upon the representation of the federation's subnational territories. Each of the country's 89 regions sends to the Federation Council two representatives: one from the regional executive and one from the regional legislature. The first election to the Federation Council in 1993 was exceptional, however, as Yeltsin had dissolved the regional legislatures in the wake of the October 1993 events. The chamber's 178 seats were therefore filled by a direct vote of each region's population. Almost 500 candidates vied for 178 seats.

The new (1994–95) Russian legislature was charged with the task of adopting new laws that would provide for the filling of the next Federation Council. The Constitution simply states that "the procedure for forming the Federation Council . . . shall be established by federal law." The Constitution does not prescribe a length for the Federation Council's term of office.

In the fall of 1995, only weeks before the term of the Federation Council was due to expire (on December 12), the president and the legislature battled over a suitable electoral law. The debate partly turned on the question of whether the Federation Council would be a full-time body (which the sitting members of the Federation Council desired). Instead, the law that finally was passed provided for a part-time Federation Council, whose membership would comprise the head of each regional executive (that is, the governor) and the head of each regional legislature. In other, words, these regional leaders would have to split their time between their regional and federal positions.

In addition, the political battle over the electoral law centered on how these regional governors and legislative leaders were to obtain their regional offices. Regional governors had largely been appointed by Yeltsin, a practice that would make the Federation Council largely hand-picked by the president. It was eventually determined that all regional executive and legislative leaders must be popularly elected by December 1996. It remained unclear whether the composition of the Federal Assembly is to change each time a regional leader changes. Further, confusion arose on the matter of choosing regional legislative leaders from bicameral parliaments. Several regions had not settled the issue of which chamber the legislative leader would be drawn from.

Presidential Elections

The president of the Russian Federation may serve two four-year terms. The presidency is open to all Russian citizens at least 35 years of age who have resided in the country for at least 10 years. The president is elected by a direct vote of the citizenry through a two-round process. An initial election selects the two top candidates, who then compete in a runoff election. Voters are afforded the option of choosing "none of the above" in Russian elections. (An informal organization, dubbed Nyet, was established by human rights activists in the spring of 1996 to encourage voters to make that choice.) The winner of the two-person race must receive more votes than this "protest" vote. Failing this, new elections must be called within three months. It is unclear whether the losing candidates from the first round could run in the new elections.

Arrangements for presidential elections are made by the Federation Council. Russian elections follow a stricter schedule than do American elections, with the candidates' "media campaigns" limited to the month prior to election day. Free television time is also allocated to candidates on the basis of a lottery. Strict limits are placed upon campaign finance.

The 1996 Campaign

Post-Soviet Russia's first presidential campaign was held in June 1996—five years after Yeltsin became president of the RSFSR. Seventy-eight presidential candidates had registered by the March 3 deadline. (These candidates were nominated by 94 official organizations. Of the 94 organizations, 15 supported Yeltsin, two supported Aleksandr Lebed, and two supported Valery Zorkin.) All candidates were required to submit their previous two years' tax returns and a million signatures supporting their nomination, with no more than 70,000 from any one region. Only 11 candidates met all of the requirements to participate in the elections.

The candidacies that attracted the most attention were those of Yeltsin (as the incumbent), Zhirinovsky (as the most controversial), and Zyuganov (with the greatest support of potential voters in the spring of 1996). In addition, Grigory Yavlinsky, Aleksandr Lebed, and renowned eye surgeon Svyatoslav Fedorov attempted to unite their followers behind one of them as an alternative to Yeltsin and Zyuganov. This potential "Third Force," as it was dubbed, never materialized.

The most tragic character in the presidential elections was Mikhail Gorbachev. He announced his candidacy on March 21, claiming that the need for his return was obvious. Still hailed abroad as a heroic figure, Gorbachev was truly a prophet without honor in his own country. Opposed by conservatives and Communists (for destroying the Soviet Union) and the reformists (for never renouncing socialism), Gorbachev has endured various humiliations during his retirement from the Soviet presidency. For example, shortly after Gorbachev found himself to be a citizen of Yeltsin's Russia, Yeltsin stripped him of his government-issue limousine and office space. At other times this former leader of the Soviet empire was forced to wait at the Moscow airport while his bags were searched.

During the presidential campaign, Gorbachev's popularity ratings never rose above 1 or 2 percent. Neither the founding of the Civic Forum movement in

April 1996 to support Gorbachev's candidacy nor his own efforts to secure the support of the Third Force could make Gorbachev anything more than a pathetic relic from the once-heady days of perestroika.

1996 Election Results

The 1996 presidential elections were simultaneously a referendum on Yeltsin's leadership (including the war in Chechnya), a test of the democrats' ability to unite behind a single candidate, and a gauge of the communists' resurgent strength. Yeltsin was shameless in his election-season populism, promising the payment of mounting wage arrears, across-the-board salary increases, a solution to the Chechen imbroglio, top-level cabinet reshuffling, and even free automobiles to potential voters. He did, however, firmly retain his verbal commitment to political and economic reform, casting Zyuganov's platform as a return to the stagnation and oppression of Brezhnevism. For his part, Zyuganov portrayed Yeltsin's leadership as inept, allowing the decline of Russian prestige and the increase in crime and inequality.

Initial surveys showed Zyuganov's popularity ratings far ahead of his competitors', with Yeltsin placing a poor fourth or fifth. But as election day neared, leaders of various democratic, centrist, and other non-Communist groups gradually united behind Yeltsin. Chernomyrdin's NDR of course endorsed Yeltsin's candidacy early on. Soon Yegor Gaidar and Anatoly Chubais also threw their support to Yeltsin, splitting with some other members of Russia's Democratic Choice. Boris Gromov of the My Fatherland party also supported Yeltsin. Patriarch Aleksii II of the Russian Orthodox Church called on voters to ensure that the Communists not be returned to power—a veiled call to vote for Yeltsin. Leaders in the Near Abroad showed a preference for Yeltsin, with the CIS presidents declaring unanimous support for his reelection. Even Chechen rebel leader Dzhokar Dudaev's widow, an ethnic Russian, declared her support for Yeltsin. So did the leadership of the nationalist Pamyat movement.

Zyuganov was supported by various Communist and nationalist groups, many of which drew together under a broad coalition named the Popular Patriotic Union of Russia. Among these was the CPRF and the Agrarian party. (The Union of Communist Parties–CPSU withheld support). And toward the end of the campaign, presidential candidate Aman Tuleev withdrew himself from the race and pledged support for Zyuganov. But Zyuganov's support did not appear to be as broad as Yeltsin's. In the end, most polls indicated that Russian voters were less concerned about ideology than about their personal living conditions. Many indicated that their support for Yeltsin hinged on their assessment of whether he could ensure salaries and pensions would be paid on time and whether he could restore their lost savings. Foreign-policy issues hardly figured into their voting. Perhaps surprisingly, neither did the issue of ethnic Russians' rights in the Near Abroad prove to be of any significance in the presidential race.

On June 16, 1996, Russians cast the plurality of their votes (35 percent) for Yeltsin, with Zyuganov coming in second with 32 percent. The two men thus were set to compete in a runoff election. Aleksandr Lebed placed third with almost 15 percent of the vote, potentially placing him in a "kingmaker" position. (See Table 5–4.)

In the two weeks prior to the runoff election, Yeltsin took a number of additional actions to shore up his support. Most importantly, he appointed Aleksandr Lebed the secretary of the Russian Security Council and the presidential national security adviser. In turn, Lebed endorsed Yeltsin in the runoff. Yeltsin also fired his Defense Minister, Pavel Grachev (whose relationship with Lebed had been one of open disdain); the head of the Presidential Security Service, Aleksandr Korzhakov; First Deputy Prime Minister Oleg Soskovets; and the director of the National Security Service, Mikhail Barsukov. All four men supported the military invasion of Chechnya, opposed the holding of presidential elections, and generally were regarded as hard-liners. Their dismissal clearly was intended to bolster Yeltsin's reformist credentials.

With Lebed's endorsement, Yeltsin sought the support of the other members of the Third Force. Fedorov endorsed Yeltsin outright, but Yavlinsky

Table 5–4   Results of the 1996 Presidential Election, First Round

Source: *Rossiiskaya gazeta*, June 22, 1996.

Candidate	National Vote (%)
Boris Yeltsin	35.3
Gennady Zyuganov	32.0
Aleksandr Lebed	14.5
Grigory Yavlinsky	7.3
Vladimir Zhirinovsky	5.7
Svyatoslav Fedorov	0.9
Mikhail Gorbachev	0.5
Martin Shakkum	0.4
Yuri Vlasov	0.2
Vladimir Bryntsalov	0.2
"Against all candidates"	1.5

stopped short of a formal endorsement, instead urging voters not to vote for Zyuganov.

Russian elections are held on holidays—traditionally on Sundays. But Yeltsin successfully pushed for the runoff election to be held on a Wednesday (July 3), hoping that his likely supporters would be less inclined to be out of town. The third of July was nevertheless declared an official holiday, and many did use the day for vacations. Russia's mass media also seemed to work to Yeltsin's advantage, with most news programs and newspapers repeating Yeltsin campaign themes while giving little exposure to Zyuganov's speeches and statements.

In the final days of the runoff campaign Yeltsin's health became a major issue. He abruptly canceled campaign appearances and did not show up before the media on July 3 to vote as scheduled in Moscow. Yeltsin had had a history of heart problems, and his time in power had been marked by periodic mysterious absences. Many speculated that alcohol may play a role in some of his apparent health problems. Nevertheless, Yeltsin won the second round handily, with 53.7 percent of the vote to Zyuganov's 40.4 percent. It was evident that voters were less concerned with Yeltsin's long-term ability to govern than with the prospect of a Communist as president. Almost 5 percent of the voters chose "against all candidates." Total voter turnout was over 67 percent. Although Zyuganov complained about media bias and other irregularities, he accepted his defeat. Foreign observers from the OSCE, the Council of Europe, and the European Parliament deemed the runoff election "free, unbiased, and fair."

The Regions

The governors (executives) of Russia's 21 autonomous regions have been directly chosen in free elections since 1991. In the 68 nonautonomous regions, however, the decision of voters was confirmed (and occasionally rejected) by Yeltsin's decree. In a 1994 decree, Yeltsin also granted himself the power to appoint and dismiss governors and to set the dates for regional gubernatorial elections. A 1996 ruling by the Constitutional Court upheld these powers in cases where regions had no applicable electoral laws.

Yeltsin dissolved the nonautonomous regional soviets (legislatures) after dissolving the federal legislature in October 1993. The regional soviets' powers were transferred to the regional governors. Regional legislatures were reorganized, and new elections were held alongside the federal parliamentary elections on December 12, 1993.

For the 1995 elections, the involvement of the federal president in confirming regional elections was terminated. Still, as discussed above, not all of these leaders were up for reelection in 1995. Only a dozen regions held elections for governor on the same day as the Russian parliamentary elections, December 17, 1995. Most of the winners had originally been appointed by Yeltsin.

Regional executives' terms were set to expire in December 1996. Regional legislative elections were set to be held at the same time. On March 2, 1996, Yeltsin issued a decree allowing regional legislative bodies to set the date for regional elections on their own. All regions require a second round if no one candidate wins 50 percent plus one vote in the first round. (The one exception is Primorsk krai, whose regional electoral law requires that the winner garner more votes than all rivals put together.)

As regional electoral campaigns got underway in the late summer and fall of 1996, Communist and anti-Communist umbrella organizations began to form in an attempt to increase their strength in the regions. The pro-reform All-Russian Movement of Public Support for the President, which had been created to unite democrats and centrists behind Yeltsin's presidential reelection bid, was subsequently redirected to the regional campaigns. Over a score of political organizations, including the NDR and Russia's Democratic Choice, joined the renamed All-Russian Coordinating Council. (Yabloko opted only for observer status.) Meanwhile, the "red-brown" coalition of Communists and nationalists that had backed Zyuganov's run for president reestablished itself as a force to increase Communist, Socialist, and nationalist representation in the regions. The Popular Patriotic Union of Russia elected Zyuganov as its leader.

Between September 1, 1996 and January 4, 1997, over 50 regional elections and runoff elections were held. Although some elections were invalidated or required a later runoff, the election season produced about 26 pro-Yeltsin governors, 16 opposition governors, and several independents.

As the power of regional officials to affect living conditions and local development continued to increase in the mid-1990s, it was becoming clear that regional elections would matter at least as much as the national elections for Russia's future.

Prospects

Within its first five years of existence, the Russian Federation adopted a new Constitution and held two parliamentary elections and one presidential election under its auspices. Numerous regional and local elections also were held. Although there were occasional accusations of irregularities (particularly with regard to the referendum approving the Constitution itself), Russia has made tremendous progress toward the democratic ideal of regular, fair elections and real choices among defined political parties.

Suggested Readings

Dallin, Alexander. *Political Parties in Russia*. Berkeley: International and Area Studies, University of California at Berkeley, 1993.

Kartsev, Vladimir. *!Zhirinovsky!* New York: Columbia University Press, 1995.

Kiernan, Brendan. *The End of Soviet Politics: Elections, Legislatures, and the Demise of the Communist Party*. Boulder, Colo.: Westview Press, 1993.

Lentini, Peter, ed. *Elections and Political Order in Russia: The Implications of the 1993 Elections to the Federal Assembly*. Budapest: Central European University Press, 1995.

McFaul, Michael, and Sergei Markov. *The Troubled Birth of Russian Democracy: Parties, Personalities, and Programs*. Stanford, Calif.: Hoover Institution Press, 1993.

Rees, E. A., ed. *The Soviet Communist Party in Disarray: The XXVIII Congress of the Communist Party of the Soviet Union*. Houndmills (UK): Macmillan Press, 1992.

White, Stephen, et al. *How Russia Votes*. Chatham, N.J.: Chatham House, 1996.

6

Political Culture and Democratic Values

If hell, as Thomas Hobbes once said, is truth seen too late, the road to hell must now be paved twice over with the thousands of books claiming to discover the "truth" about Russia—while the tortures of the damned are reserved for those, diplomats especially, who committed the fates of millions in the confident belief that they could predict correctly the way in which the Soviet rulers would respond.

— Daniel Bell[1]

Perceptions of Russia

The awesome immensity and harshness of the Russian landmass, the terrible sweep of the country's history, and the disconcerting inscrutability of its people have been a source of endless speculation and commentary. Each country is unique, of course, but Russia's temporal and geographical vastness and unrelenting political oppression have earned it a category of its own. Russia's uniqueness has inspired and intrigued writers through the ages. Alexander Blok called it "the Sphinx." Shakespeare wrote of the unusual length

---

1. Daniel Bell, "Ten Theories in Search of Reality: The Prediction of Soviet Behavior in the Social Sciences," *World Politics* 10:3 (April 1958): 327. © 1958, The Johns Hopkins University Press.

of Russian nights, and Dostoyevsky of the length of its days. Maxim Gorky reviled the tsarist double-headed eagle as an "actively pernicious bird," and Abraham Lincoln admired Russia's lack of pretension, "where despotism can be taken pure, and without the base alloy of hypocrisy." Boris Pasternak called the Soviet Union "an asylum without God, soulless, senseless." Lincoln Steffens called it "the future."

For most of the post–World War II period, comparative political science followed in this tradition, treating Russia, and particularly the Soviet Union, as a special type of country that did not fit easily within the methodological requirements of social scientific analysis. The most common approach was to label the Soviet Union a "totalitarian" state—one that sought to control virtually all aspects of society through a powerful, ideologically defined party, which wielded such weapons as propaganda, surveillance, mass media control, and economic centralization.[2] But although the totalitarian model captured the essence of Stalin's Soviet Union (and Hitler's Germany), it was of little help in understanding the possibilities for change within the totalitarian system.

It was primarily a small confrerie of academics, engaged in the arcane craft of "Sovietology," who sought to understand the Soviet and Russian people with especial analytic depth. And even then, Sovietology tended to focus on the incomparable uniqueness of its subject. In the West a relatively small number of left-leaning intellectuals (such as Steffens) saw Soviet Communism as "the future." But as the Stalinist Terror and the Brezhnevite stagnation revealed the true nature of Sovietism, its utopian appeal faded.

Periodically the Soviet Union would come under the rule of a new leader—from Stalin to Khrushchev, to Brezhnev, to Andropov—and some would anticipate fundamental changes from the new leadership. To be sure, each Soviet leader initiated a raft of economic and political reforms, some of which substantially altered the particulars of the country's domestic policy. But the essence of Sovietism, one-Party rule, was never threatened. Alternatively, a "convergence theory" was popularized, anticipating the gradual drift of the capitalist West and the communist East toward a common middle ground—a "third way." But this too was revealed to be a chimera. Still others expected that the Soviet people would eventually rise up and overthrow their oppressors, as the East Germans, Hungarians, and Czechoslovakians had tried to do in the 1950s and 1960s. Yet expectations for a "Second Russian Revolution" faded with each passing year.

Increasingly the Soviets, and especially the Russians, were presumed by Western analysts to be incapable of escaping their political repression. Russia's

---

2. For a classic statement of totalitarianism, see Carl J. Friedrich and Zbigniew Brzezinski, *Totalitarian Dictatorship and Autocracy* (New York: Praeger, 1962).

thousand-year tradition of authoritarian rule, under Kievan princes, Romanov tsars, and Soviet Communists, was assumed to have predisposed the Russian people to passivity, to accepting paternalistic (though not especially benevolent) rule. Russia's stillborn efforts at republicanism, in the last weeks of the short-lived Kerensky government in 1917, only reinforced the notion that Russians were "undemocratizable." And so during the Cold War, while Western academics and politicians sought to understand how the war-torn countries of Europe and the underdeveloped nations of the Southern Hemisphere might be securely wedded to democracy and capitalist modernization, "Soviet Russia" was eventually abandoned as beyond salvation. (It is interesting to note that a relatively small number of Western Sovietologists devoted their careers to trying to "prove" that the Soviet Union had, in fact, developed into a functioning civil society. Their claims were fatally undermined in the final years of Gorbachev's rule.)

The Transition to Democracy

While the Soviet Union's seven years under Gorbachev largely validated the thesis of Sovietism's irredeemability (it could not be reformed, only destroyed), it undermined the conception of Russians as a passive people. But given the preconceptions developed during the Soviet period, it is not surprising that most Western governments and universities, as well as Gorbachev himself, did not ever really understand the enormous power of the newly liberated citizenry until after the entire Soviet edifice had collapsed. The Soviet Union was not conquered by the West in a culmination of the Cold War; it was torn apart by its own people, infused with a sense of self-determination and liberated by a regime that had lost the ability or the stomach to continue oppressing them.

Immediately after gaining independence, Russia's post-Soviet leadership took pains to distance itself from the old regime. The banishment of the Communist Party, Yeltsin's public commitment to democracy and capitalism, and the country's close cooperation—even friendship—with its erstwhile adversaries in the West all forced a rapid and thorough reevaluation of Russia's essence. It was as though the crude and heavy blanket of Soviet Communism had been pulled back to reveal a relatively sane society and leadership. Perhaps Russia could be a "normal" country after all. Perhaps U.S. President George Bush's "New World Order" had indeed materialized. Perhaps we were all of the First World now.

But were analysts of Russia simply substituting one oversimplification of Russia for another? Soviet totalitarianism had collapsed, but Russian democracy had not yet fully materialized. In its first five years after independence Russia disappointed the new optimists. Yeltsin's unconstitutional dissolution of the parliament in 1993 raised questions about the principle of "rule of law" in Russia. The forced resignations of a pro-Western foreign minister and pro-market economic advisers in 1995 undermined the government's commitment to reform. The Duma's symbolic efforts to restore the Soviet Union in 1996 suggested imperialist ambitions. More importantly, the Russian people began to demonstrate a recidivistic attraction to the ghosts of the past: through substantial electoral support for Communists and nationalists, through violent hostility toward successful entrepreneurs. It was as though the hard lessons learned through 75 years of Sovietism (and centuries of tsarism) were forgotten with the passage of a few months. Perhaps the Russian people really were "beyond democracy."[3]

The case of Russia raises interesting questions not just about the Russians but about democracy itself. Is it simply a matter of setting into place the proper institutions, laws, and leaders? Or does it require a particular mindset on the part of the people? Can it be imposed from without, or does it need to arise from within? The record in other countries is mixed, and so it is in Russia. Certainly the Bolsheviks had been able to suddenly, even brutally, impose upon the Russians a new political system. But was Sovietism a foreign (or "universal") system, discovered by Marx and imported by Lenin? Or was it simply another variant of the unique, crypto-authoritarian Russian culture? Historians and political scientists have devoted years to debating these questions, and it is unlikely that they will be resolved in the near future. But they are crucial questions to consider as we examine the prospects for Russian democracy.

Democracy

Divining the prospects for democracy in Russia first requires a closer look at democracy. In recent years the boundaries of the term have become hazy. The Cold War, for all its faults (even without triggering a thermonuclear conflagration, the Cold War imposed its costs), at least had the advantage of conceptual clarity. From the American perspective, democracy resided alongside capitalism and virtuousness as inseparable elements of a trinitarian ideal that characterized the countries of the West. The "Second World" countries similarly were endued with an unholy triad of characteristics, quite the opposite of the West's. It was all quite simple. But after the perestroika-inspired revolutions of 1989, the old shortcut of identifying democracies by their presumably associated characteristics (Do they belong to NATO? Does most of the

---

3. On this theme see Robert V. Daniels, "The Revenge of Russian Political Culture," *Dissent* 41:1 (Winter 1994): 32–34.

population own a car and telephone? Is the currency convertible?) has become less reliable. It became necessary to define more precisely democracy itself.

This is a difficult task. Just about every country in the world, from Switzerland to Iraq, claims to be a democracy. If the label is to mean anything, surely it cannot be stretched to cover such a range of countries. Not that many people take seriously Saddam's claims to be the legitimate president of a democratic state. Few consider his "election" in 1995—a choreographed performance of government-appointed election officials coercing the public to indicate support for the man referred to in the state-run media as the "beloved leader"—to be in any way related to democracy. But this is an easy case. With some effort, we might be able to identify all the countries that are nominally based on the rule of law, and that allow the people freely to choose the individuals or parties that make and implement the laws. This is a definition for procedural democracy. And as we saw in Chapter 3, it exists in Russia today.

Hence the contradiction in the pessimist's claim that Russia's parliamentary elections in December 1995 strengthened the antidemocratic hue of the Russian government. The degree to which a country is democratic (and it is well to consider democracy a continuous variable) is not measured by the proportion of self-professed "democrats" in the legislature. More to the point of procedural democracy is how the legislators are selected and whether they have adequate power to carry out their mandate. So the fact that Russians freely chose "Communists" or "nationalists" or even "monarchists" is less important in measuring Russia's possession of procedural democracy than the fact that they made their choice freely. Procedural democracy affords voters the ability to make unwise choices—an opportunity occasionally seized with gusto even by Americans.

Russia falls back a few notches on the continuum of procedural democracy for its maldistribution of formal powers. As will be observed in Chapter 7, the Russian Duma is weak, even compared with the French National Assembly, as extensive power is vested in the executive. Nevertheless, constitutional checks on the Russian president do exist. Although the constitution and electoral laws would benefit from some tinkering, the people are afforded enough of a voice to move post-Soviet Russia onto the list of procedural democracies.

But as political scientists and normative thinkers, we ought to ask whether procedural democracy is enough. (Indeed, some consider "pure" procedural democracy, without the proper political culture, to be dangerously susceptible to tyranny.)[4] Leaving aside the question of whether democracy, capitalism,

---

4. Karl R. Popper has made this argument. Similarly, Alexis de Tocqueville feared that "democratic despotism" would emerge from slavish and simple adherance to the doctrine of popular sovereignty. Finally, consider Aristotle's criticisms of democracy as a form of mob rule.

and virtuousness really do always appear together as conceptualized in the liberal trinitarian ideal, does the presence of procedural democracy ensure the existence of "Western" liberal democracy? This question suggests that there is more to democracy than procedures. There is something more organic, more elemental, on which it is based. And that ingredient springs from the society rather than from the government.

Russia's democratic institutions are still being established. But even if clear and consistent electoral laws were in place; even if the convoluted electoral system could produce a parliament precisely reflecting the people's will; even if that parliament had clearly defined, adequate powers to act on the people's expressed preferences—if, in other words, a perfect constitution could be imposed upon Russia—Russian democracy still would require one vital element: a supportive political culture.

Political Culture and Civic Culture

A country's political culture is the set of basic values, beliefs, attitudes, and assumptions the people hold about their political system and political life in general. It derives from any number of sources, just as nonpolitical culture does. History and geography play major roles in the shaping of political culture and thus militate against any sudden change in its composition. But political culture does evolve with economic, political, societal, and other forms of development.

The notion that a particular set of societal values and beliefs supports democracy was advanced in the 1960s by Gabriel Almond and Sidney Verba; they termed it a "civic culture."[5] A civic culture includes "participant" characteristics: a widespread belief among citizens that they have the ability and obligation to participate in the political system, that the overall population constitutes a cohesive society, that political institutions and decisions matter. But a civic culture also includes "subject" and "parochial" orientations, which restrain the citizens' level of political activism. The governmental system as a whole is understood to be legitimate and efficacious. Citizens have a basic trust in their society, and maintain a respect for tradition. Overall, the civic culture blends tradition and modernity, acquiescence and participation. It is a delicate balance that, according to Almond and Verba, is urged by a society's modernization—"the democratic opportunity"—but also requires "other investments of energy, resources, and imagination."

---

5. See Gabriel A. Almond and Sidney Verba, *The Civic Culture* (Princeton, N.J.: Princeton University Press, 1963).

In recent decades political scientists have derided the concept of civic culture as a product of Western, or perhaps American, ethnocentrism.[6] Certainly Almond and Verba's precise formulation, as well as the methods they applied, were not impervious to improvement. But in their desire to display their universalist credentials, some Western analysts have strayed from the crucial idea that democracy is based upon values, and not simply institutions. The people in a democracy must accept and embrace those values; they must feel they have a stake in the system; they must have reason to trust their fellow citizens. Creating democracy has as much in common with Peter Pan ("Say quick that you believe!") as with a Field of Dreams ("Build it and they will come").

Russia's Political Culture

This puts the thesis about Russia's congenital absolutism in perspective. If there is any significance to the concept of political culture, then Russians may find it difficult, perhaps even impossible, to make an expeditious transition to democracy. As a society, Russians have learned to be skeptical about their ability to genuinely influence government policy. This skepticism should come as no surprise. Russia's experience with Soviet rule taught them not to place blind faith in the bare institutions of democratic governance. Constitutions, legislatures, elections, the bureaucracy, the media, the schools, the courts—all were subordinate to the Party, and thus could not be relied upon to protect, let alone serve, the interests of the people. Soviet ideology claimed that the Communist Party of the Soviet Union was inherently endued with the people's interests, although the Party had an omniscient, "enlightened" understanding of those interests as befits a vanguard party.

Of course, a healthy skepticism about political elites might serve the citizens of a democracy well. But the experience with Soviet rule and an understanding of tsarist history might place Russian attitudes beyond skepticism to the realm of cynicism and potentially even nihilism.

Defining Russia's political culture in the wake of its experience with Soviet Communism is no easy task. The jarring changes to Russia's developmental course at the end of the millennium speak toward not so much an "evolutionary" transition to democracy (or anything else), but rather a "revolutionary" transformation away from the ossified, brittle Soviet system. If Russia is undergoing a systemic change, no single, stable political culture can be identified. Indeed, democratic and antidemocratic attitudes may both be present at

---

6. For several critiques of political culture, see Gabriel A. Almond and Sidney Verba, eds., *The Civic Culture Revisited: An Analytic Study* (Boston: Little, Brown, 1980).

the same time, even in the same individual. But there may be evidence of attitudinal shifts that provide answers to questions about the development of a new political culture. To what extent did Leninist ideology take root? How deeply runs the cynicism bred by the Soviet years? Are elements of a civic culture emerging at all?

Attitudes about Economics

An important study by Miller, Reisinger, and Hesli[7] based upon the University of Iowa Post-Soviet Citizen Surveys (PSCS) sheds welcome light on the topic. It paints a picture of an ideologically disjointed population. On economic attitudes, for example, about a third of Russia's citizens in 1992 believed in the Sovietesque notion that personal incomes should be regulated to ensure that "no one earns more than others." In 1995, that figure had risen to over half (53 percent). Presumably the growing income differentials within the society offended the majority of Russians (and presumably this 53 percent did not consider their own incomes to be substantially above the median). This is consistent with several other studies that have found the majority of Russians believing their own standards of living to have dropped since independence. It also corresponds with surveys that have found a substantial majority of Russians believing (against the laws of mathematics) that their incomes rank in the lowest quartile of the population.

More importantly, the PSCS data suggest the continued importance of the value of equality that had been central to the Soviet Union's official ideology. We have already observed (in Chapter 4) that the Soviet leadership's egalitarian shibboleths did not necessarily translate into practical equality, especially between the party apparatchiki and the workers. But the gross disparities that did exist were discreetly hidden from view in remote dachas, on the shelves of restricted stores, and behind the doors of special Party resorts.

Post-Soviet Russia's wealth is ostentatious. Trendy young "biznesmeny" and raffish Mafiosi sport pounds of gold chains, bracelets, and watches. Entrepreneurs open exclusive restaurants catering to Western hard currency—rubles not accepted. Wealthy families build grandiose homes the size of Soviet-era apartment blocs. Most galling for the common Russian, this wealth is largely denominated in Western goods: Italian suits, German cars, Japanese cellular phones. Russians are not especially known to accept easily the superior wealth of others. A venerable Russian joke illustrates how Russian envy is frequently mischannelled. A Russian peasant is granted one wish by God, with

---

7. Arthur H. Miller, William M. Reisinger, and Vicki L. Hesli, "Understanding Political Change in Post-Soviet Societies: A Further Commentary on Finifter and Mickiewicz," *American Political Science Review* 90:1 (March 1996): 153–166.

the caveat that his neighbor will receive double whatever is granted. The peasant agonizes over his decision. Finally he calls toward heaven, "O Lord, strike out one of my eyes so that my neighbor may go blind!"

Although average personal wealth in Russia is increasing by some measures, the disparity of wealth in the country is increasing as well. Notwithstanding periodic claims to the contrary during the Soviet period, Russia's fledgling middle class is not sizable. Instead, one sees in Russian society the manifestations of two extreme values toward equality: the ostentatious flaunters of wealth who presumably value opportunism, and the resentful poor who yearn for a just "leveling" of society. The Post-Soviet Citizen Survey found 61 percent of Russians in 1995 believing the state should be responsible for their standard of living and 22 percent placing that responsibility upon the individual. Only 17 percent took a middle position.

The PSCS data reveal a slightly more laissez-faire trend concerning attitudes toward private property. The 1992 survey found 46 percent of Russians holding negative views about privatization. That figure fell 10 points to 36 percent in 1995. When only Russians with some higher education are considered, the 1995 figure drops to only 19 percent. Comparing Russian attitudes toward equality and privatization suggests that Russians appreciate the presumed benefits of privatization (better services and greater selection of goods, perhaps) while resenting the harsh environment and garish excesses of "wild capitalism." Although these attitudes seemed to be moving in opposite directions between 1992 and 1995, they are not necessarily irrational. Russians collectively are not strongly committed to their understanding of capitalism. Shortly before the June 1996 presidential election, a survey by the All-Russian Center for Public Opinion Studies (VTsIOM) found that only about a third of the population supports a market economy, while over 40 percent favored an economy based on state planning.[8]

Attitudes about the Old Party

Russians' attitudes toward Communists are especially discordant. In 1992, Miller et al. found 47 percent of the Russian population believing that Communists have "too much influence in politics." In 1995 that figure had dropped to about 16 percent. In 1995 also, 42 percent believed the "democratic reformers" had too much influence. What could account for this reversal? Some see it as another example of Russians' inevitable attraction to authoritarian rule. Others interpret it as a simple nostalgia for simpler, more certain times. Still others (including Miller et al.) explain the attitudinal shift

---

8. *Open Media Research Institute Daily Digest* 74 (April 15, 1996): 1.

at least in part upon changes in the Communists themselves. As observed in Chapter 5, this explanation has some credibility.

During his tenure as president, Boris Yeltsin has done his best to reduce the lingering support for Communism and Communist parties. Although his decrees making certain Communist parties illegal were scaled back by the Constitutional Court, Yeltsin has worked to constrain those parties' ability to publish newspapers and hold demonstrations. In an especially symbolic move, Yeltsin declared on the 79th anniversary of the Russian Revolution that November 7th would, henceforth, officially be called Harmony and Reconciliation Day. He also charged a new government commission with developing ideas to commemorate the victims, rather than the victors, of the 1917 Revolution.

It nevertheless should be recalled that Russia has undergone no formal "de-Communization" efforts the way that, say, postwar Germany underwent de-Nazification. Without such a concerted effort, Russia's attitudes about Communists and Communism will remain mixed for some time, left to drift while a definitive evaluation of the relative beneficence and malevolence of the Soviet system is lacking. Thus, the VTsIOM survey found 41 percent of Russians believing that the pre-1990 Soviet political system was best suited to their country, 27 percent believing Western-style democracy was preferable, and only 9 percent supporting their current system as the best option. Such attitudes do not lend themselves to political stability.

Attitudes about Political Efficacy

In terms of perceived political efficacy, Russia's political culture comes up short. Russians' assessment of the political choices available to them is especially illuminating. A 1995 poll conducted by the International Foundation for Electoral Systems found that a large segment (41 percent) of the Russian voters sees no great difference between the various party platforms. Such attitudes naturally produce pessimism about the worth of voting. This pessimism may be partly justified. As observed earlier, Russia's political parties do not have strong ideological identities and are distinguished primarily by their names and the personalities of their best-known members.

Similarly, the PSCS found that 56 percent of the voters regard the federal government as incapable of improving their lives. The confusion, infighting, and provocative rhetoric from Russia's politicians has not endeared the citizens to the new democratic procedures. Sophomoric and insulting behavior by the LDP's Duma fraction is a case in point. Shortly after the 1995 elections the LDP deputies accused the liberal governor of Nizhny Novgorod, Boris Nemtsov, of trying to arrange the assassination of Vladimir Zhirinovsky. The alleged assassin supposedly aborted his vile task "after he listened to a speech by Zhirinovsky." The fraction has also provoked fistfights on the Duma floor, and Zhirinovsky's antics are well known. A September 1996 article in the Russian daily *Moscovsky Komsomolets* described a tawdry list of misbehavior in the Duma's offices and meeting rooms, including sex, drinking, public defecation, and theft. The reformists attributed these incidents to staff hired by the Communist deputies. The Communists in turn have blamed the LPD. The LPD calls the reports "gross slander and outright lies."

Whatever the precise facts surrounding the parliamentary antics, the Russian people generally are not convinced that they see effective, positive change as a possible product of their system. Certainly the national elections in Russia still are characterized by a sense of confusion and novelty. In addition to the more traditional candidates, film producers, actors, musicians, and a circus magician ran for Duma seats in 1995.

The respectability of the democratic system has also been tarnished by the preference of bullets to ballots in a number of campaigns. The run-up to the 1995 parliamentary elections suggested that some political battles were becoming a matter of life and death. On December 5, a bomb exploded in the Parliament office of Nikolai Lysenko, leader of the extremist National Party of Russia. (Lysenko was arrested several months later for allegedly staging the explosion himself, but the overall point holds.) Three days later, a candidate from Our Home Is Russia, Mikhail Lezhnev, was slain. Four days after that, Aleksandr Kashcheev, campaigning for a Duma seat in Stravropol, was shot at while driving. These incidents came on top of earlier assaults on, and assassinations of, various other Russian politicians and government officials. Although the 1996 presidential election was not marred by this level of violence, a bomb explosion at a Moscow metro station five days before the polls opened was thought to be a terrorist act aimed at disrupting the elections.

Perhaps all this helps to explain why barely half the electorate voted in the 1993 parliamentary elections. Two years later voter turnout had risen to 65 percent, but many voters had to be lured to the polls with dangled incentives. In Khabarovsk, voters were entered in a lottery for a trip to Israel. In Chechnya they received free meat. (Suddenly seized by a sense of propriety, election officials in St. Petersburg prohibited the provision of beer at the polls—not because of its effects on voters' judgment, but because of the advantage it might afford to the Beer Lovers' Party.) Yet although voter turnout is low by Soviet standards (with some regions posting turnouts above 100 percent!), they compare favorably with American rates. And whereas 17 percent of the voters in 1993 chose the protest choice of "against all candidates," less than 3 percent made use of this option in 1995. The 1996 presidential election showed a further increase in voter turnout and a further decrease in the use of the "against all candidates" option. Russians may not be enamored with their political system, but voter behavior in post-Soviet Russia suggests a significant willingness to participate in elections which for years had been mere empty forms.

The Emergence of a New *Weltanschauung*

Russia has not yet developed a civic culture, but it has demonstrated that it is not wholly saddled with the "subject" political culture sometimes ascribed to tsarist Russia and the Soviet Union. Instead, the emergence of post-Soviet Russia's political culture hinges in large part upon the coalescing of society around a set of shared values. Some of the more important debates are described below.

Communitarianism or Individualism?

One of the major differences between Marxist-Leninist ideology and Western liberalism concerns the focus of state policy, and indeed the very repository of life's value. Although the debate between communitarianism and individualism quickly enters the realm of the existential, in practical terms it turns on the relative importance of the community and the individual. As interpreted by the Soviet regime, Marxism-Leninism placed the good of the former above the good of the latter. In practice, the "community" was frequently conflated with the "state," leading to the mistreatment, humiliation, impoverishment, and even torture and execution of individuals for the sake of meeting five-year plans and preserving the regime's hold on power.

In countless subtle ways the Soviet system sought to impress upon individuals their subordination to the community at large: requiring the performance of pro bono community work, housing citizens in communal apartments, consolidating peasants on collective farms. In the first months after the 1917 revolution, some regional soviets even mandated that young, unmarried women were "communal property" and required that they register at the local "Commissariat of Free Love." Although such outrageous measures as this were eventually reined in, the basic message that individuals' interests and rights were less important than those of the community was reinforced through official policies, the educational system, the arts, and myriad other channels.

Liberal conceptions of democracy and capitalism are based upon a more individualist philosophy. Liberal individualism holds that promoting the interests of individuals is the sine qua non of governmental institutions. Individuals are understood to possess rights that the state cannot violate. To a strict individualist, communities are mere reifications—abstract collectives that in reality are nothing more than the aggregate of the individuals who compose them. Of course, just as the Soviets twisted the principles of communitarianism into a justification for their oppressive policies, individualism also can be taken to injurious extremes. At the logical endpoint, individualism disintegrates into anarchy. For most political practitioners, the debate between communitarianism and individualism is less a competition between two opposite value systems, but rather a search for a compromise between two endpoints. Most accept that the individual cannot be separated from the community, and that the community cannot exist without individuals.

By virtue of their experience under Soviet rule, Russians understand the dangers of subordinating individuals to the community. On the other hand, the "wild capitalism" that characterizes much of the post-Soviet economy demonstrates to Russians the dangers of neglecting community interests. With the lifting of Party-imposed community principles, Russian cities have endured an upsurge of graffiti, litter, and other abuse of public spaces. Light-bulbs are stolen from stairwells in apartment buildings and even from military installations. In contemporary Russia, the slang term *kidat* (literally, "throwing" [away]) has increasingly been applied to interpersonal relations where people renege on contractual and social obligations—failing to pay back loans, breaking contracts, and otherwise repudiating agreements.

With such selfish and inconsiderate behavior resulting from the lifting of enforced communalism, Russians' newfound freedom can be frightening. An anonymous Russian woman articulates the dilemma in her country: "Freedom is an abstraction. For most people, freedom means safety. Here, though, physically it's still fairly dangerous."[9] Perhaps as an illustration of this thinking, another 1996 poll VTsIOM found 79 percent of Russians preferring order to democracy. One cannot help but hear the ghostly echo of Lenin's words: Liberty is "so precious that it must be rationed."

The task for Russians is to find a balance that suits their society. Naturally, the development of a societal consensus on the relative value of individuals and community is inextricably linked to the development of a political culture, and thus the development of a political system.

Western or Slavic?

Russian society has historically been torn between conceiving of itself as essentially European (and part of a "Western" civilization) or uniquely Slavic. As observed in Chapter 2, the debate between "Westernizers" and "Slavophiles" has been going on for centuries. It was particularly salient during the reigns of Peter I and Catherine II, both of whom sought to import Western values, arts, and culture to Russia. The collapse of the Cold War's institutionalized dualism has raised the debate anew.

Many in Russia, particularly younger people, now seek to move their nation into a position within the Western world. The desire to be "Western" is

9. Barbara Zingman, "Not-So-Bleak Russian Future," *The Louisville Courier-Journal*, December 20, 1995: 15A.

illustrated in Russian teenagers' penchant for American jazz and Snickers candy bars. (Former General Aleksandr Lebed has derisively called these youths "the Pepsi Generation.") Western fashions, slang, and values are being adopted by increasing numbers of Russians. Western (and particularly American) television has become enormously popular. Even Russia's version of *Sesame Street* (*Ulitsa Sezam*) has been introduced to Russian television, dispensing lessons about democracy and freedom to Russia's future voters. And Pepsi signed a contract with Russia's Energiya Corporation to film Russian cosmonauts drinking a can of Pepsi in space.

On the other hand, Russians have not abandoned their Slavic, or even their Soviet, heritage. In fact, the farther east of Moscow one moves, the more likely one is to encounter hostility to "Westernism." Miller et al. found in 1995 that two-thirds of Russians consider themselves to be "Soviets." Boris Yeltsin was forced to remove his foreign minister, Andrei Kozyrev, because of popular perceptions that he was too "pro-Western." The rise of nationalist parties, discussed in Chapter 5, underscores the importance of this issue to many Russians. The Westernizer-Slavophile debate has obvious implications for Russian alliance-building and foreign policy. (See Chapter 12.) But it also bears upon the formation of Russia's political culture and its polity. Many latter-day Westernizers desire that Western-style political and economic institutions be adopted for their country. And Slavophiles insist just as fervently that the adoption of such institutions will mean the mongrelization, or worse, of the Russian people.

Prospects

Russia's political culture is a product of over one thousand years of experiences, as well as the country's geography and climate. The weight and influence of Russia's political culture therefore is not easily overcome.

But political culture does change. New experiences, foreign influences, and demographic changes collectively shape the political culture slowly but continually. In the words of one political analyst, "Political culture builds up and changes like a series of geological deposits."[10] For Russia's political culture, the final decade of the twentieth century has been one of tremendous tectonic activity.

---

10. Robert V. Daniels, "Russian Political Culture and the Post-Revolutionary Impasse," *The Russian Review* 78:3 (1984): 618.

Suggested Readings

Brown, Archie, ed. *Political Culture and Communist Studies*. Armonk, N.Y.: M. E. Sharpe, 1985.

Mead, Margaret. *Soviet Attitudes Toward Authority*. New York: William Morrow, 1955.

Petro, Nicolai N. *The Rebirth of Russian Democracy: An Interpretation of Political Culture*. Cambridge: Harvard University Press, 1995.

Shalin, Dmitri, ed. *Russian Culture at the Crossroads: Paradoxes of Post-communist Consciousness*. Boulder, Colo.: Westview Press, 1996.

Solzhenitsyn, Aleksandr Isaevich. *The Russian Question: At the End of the Twentieth Century*. N.Y.: Farrar, Straus and Giroux, 1995.

Tucker, Robert C. "Culture, Political Culture, and Communist Society," *Political Science Quarterly* 88 (June 1973): 173–190.

Tucker, Robert C. "Sovietology and Russian History," *Post-Soviet Affairs* 8 (July–September 1992): 175–196.

Wyman, Matthew. "Russian Political Culture: Evidence from Public Opinion Surveys," *The Journal of Communist Studies and Transition Politics* 10: 1 (1994).

Part III

State Structures and Relationships

7
Constitutional Structure

The emergence of an independent Russia from the wreckage of the Soviet Union hastened the process of redefining Russia as a political entity. Although questions of Russia's national identity and geopolitical role might be debated without resolution for years to come, the establishment of Russia as a sovereign state required the immediate creation or co-option of governmental structures. The first order of business for the post-Soviet Russian leaders, therefore, was to secure both de jure and de facto power. The Russian Soviet Federative Socialist Republic (RSFSR) warranted its own governmental apparatus throughout the Soviet period by virtue of its status as one of the 15 Soviet Socialist Republics that composed the USSR. But for the Russian leaders who sought to secure Russia's de facto political independence, the existing governmental structure was inadequate on two counts. First, it was clearly subordinate to the all-union government (that is, Soviet Moscow). And second, the RSFSR's government suffered from the same centralized structure and Party monopoly that by the late 1980s was perceived as illegitimate or, perhaps worse, ineffectual, by the increasingly restive population.

To correct both these inadequacies, President Boris Yeltsin and his lieutenants redefined Russia's basis as a political entity: declaring first its autonomy
and then its full independence from Soviet Moscow, and banning all political
parties from state organizations and enterprises. (As noted earlier, they also
banned the Communist Party of the Soviet Union outright.) Yeltsin bolstered
Russia's political independence in symbolic ways as well, such as by adopting
the pre-Revolution Russian flag and renaming the country the Russian Federation (*Rossiiskaya Federatsiya*). None of this is to say, of course, that Russia
was recreated tabula rasa, with its peoples and culture cleansed of all traces of
Soviet contamination. The disintegration of the USSR did not and could not
return the peoples that had lived within it to a Hobbesian state of nature.
Instead, the new Russian Federation (as well as the other successors to the
USSR) co-opted many of the institutions, laws, and physical and economic
infrastructure that had been part of the Soviet state. What made the Russian
Federation unique—what most clearly distinguished it from the Soviet state—
was the source of its political legitimacy and the basis of its political authority.
These came to be explicitly expressed in the new Russian Constitution.

Constitutional History

It bears emphasizing that the mere expression of laws, rights, and principles
in an adopted constitution does not ensure their observance by the government. To be observed and honored, a constitution must reflect the values and
interests of the people who derive authority from it, if not also those who live
under it. The Soviet Constitution did not, and the Soviet system represented
a textbook case of divergence between expressed principle and actual practice.

The Soviet Union

Since its founding, the Soviet government claimed its authority from a written
constitution. The first post-Revolution Russian constitution was adopted in
1918, then replaced in 1924 with a new document that took into account the
new "union" of the country's various "republics." In 1936 that constitution
was replaced with the so-called Stalin Constitution, and in 1977 yet another—
the Brezhnev Constitution—was adopted. This last was arguably the most
liberal, in that it softened or eliminated provisions that smacked of Stalinism
and added various individual and human rights guarantees. Brezhnev claimed
that the new constitution reflected the USSR's achievement of "real existing
socialism." This putative achievement permitted the official abandonment of
the "dictatorship of the proletariat" and ushered in a "state of all the people."
While the Soviet authorities seldom allowed expressed constitutional principles to stand in the way of strategic objectives, the constitutions did perhaps

impose tactical obstacles that constrained—or at least required official justification for—the most grievous abuses of power. Although never subject to the disciplines of judicial review or checks and balances found in the United States, the development and implementation of policy in the Soviet Union could only flout the constitution so far. To the extent that the Soviet leadership desired to foster the belief that it drew its legitimacy from the constitution, it limited its abuses of power. For example, the regime felt it necessary to respect at least the form of the legislative process and periodic elections. It is in this way primarily that the Soviet Union's constitution "mattered."

Like the United States, each of the semisovereign territorial units of the union—the "republics"—possessed its own constitution. These constitutions contained provisions relating to the distinct features of the republics and were meant to underscore their autonomy. Article 76 of the 1977 Soviet Constitution required that all union republics adopt constitutions consistent with the new all-union document. In the following year Russia, with the 14 other republics, obliged. This would be the constitution inherited by Russia's post-Communist leaders.

The RSFSR and Russia

The 1978 Constitution of the RSFSR was, of course, a product of Russia's Communist leadership and was consistent with the stated principles of the greater Soviet regime. In style and substance, the Russian Constitution resembled its Soviet counterpart. As such, the Russian Constitution was tainted and thus considered unsalvageable by the shepherds of Russian independence in the Yeltsin era. Only days after Russia's declaration of sovereignty on June 12, 1990, therefore, a commission was established to draft a new document. The Constitutional Commission, chaired by Boris Yeltsin, produced two drafts in as many years. Both were debated in the Russian Congress of People's Deputies, where numerous amendments and counterproposals were vetted. The most protracted debates centered on the distribution of governmental powers, both "horizontally" (among the primary branches of government) and "vertically" (between the central government in Moscow and the various regional and local bodies). These issues proved intractable, and no new constitution was adopted.

At the time of the Soviet Union's formal dissolution in December 1991, the Russian government still was operating under the 1978 Soviet-era constitution. Unable to agree on a completely new replacement constitution, the Russian parliament resorted to amending the old constitution—precisely the reverse mission and outcome of the American Constitutional Convention two centuries earlier.

The factions within the Russian legislature had their own reasons for offering their particular amendments: their constituencies had particular grievances; they desired to promote an ideological agenda; they sought to bring the constitution into conformance with existing practices. Most important, the constitution served as a battleground for fighting out the allocation of power between the presidency and the parliament. As a result of all these disparate amendments, the constitution came to comprise a rather motley congeries of sweeping principles and narrow provisions, of class interests and individual rights, of Soviet Millenarianism and Western pragmatism, of centralized presidential power and decentralized parliamentary prerogative. The constitution of course suffered from these contrasts—indeed, the amended document was self-contradictory. Yet despite its formal powers, the Constitutional Court lacked the recognized authority and stature to resolve these problems effectively. The legislature and the executive alike were left to choose among the provisions which suited their agendas at the time.

The issues on which the Constitutional Commission's draft constitutions had foundered continued to plague the new Russian government. The debate about federalism became only more vociferous with time. Of increasing concern were the parallels between Russia's acquisition of independence from the multinational USSR and demands for autonomy by the national groups within the Russian Federation. At least temporarily, the regions were mollified in the spring of 1992 by the new Federation Treaty, which spelled out the vertical distribution of powers. (The Federation Treaty and associated issues are discussed in Chapter 9.)

Efforts to amicably settle questions about the horizontal allocation of power, however, were less successful. Ideological differences and political competition had come to divide the parliament and the president, and both branches claimed to have a superior claim of democratic legitimacy. The Russian Congress of People's Deputies had been popularly elected in March 1990, and although the election stemmed from the Zeitgeist of democracy and anti-Sovietism, the country could hardly be considered a functioning democracy at the time. Soviet apparatchiks and Communist Party functionaries employed their institutional advantages over unknown and poorly organized "reform" candidates. (In a sense, the very notion of "reform" in Russia is so broad as to be almost meaningless, as practically all Russian politics conducted with the intent of creating a post-Soviet state were by definition "reformist." See Chapter 5.) The result was a Russian parliament populated with many of the same faces, and whose commitment to democratic reform, though in many ways genuine, disagreed mightily with that of Yeltsin.

Constitutional Crisis

The interbranch conflict and constitutional crisis eventually became unbearable for Yeltsin. By temporarily stabilizing the issue of regional autonomy, the adoption of the Federation Treaty in April 1992 shifted the focus of Yeltsin's opposition from the peripheral region to the Russian White House. Now, the parliament was obstructing Yeltsin's plan to stabilize the country as a viable state with an operating free-market economy—goals Yeltsin presumed were shared by most of his countrymen. No doubt Yeltsin's populist instincts, which had served him so well in the aftermath of the 1991 coup, told him that an out-of-touch parliament could not survive a truly democratic election. Yet legislative elections were not scheduled to be held until 1994. (Yeltsin's own term as president was set to expire in 1995.)

In March 1993, with political sniping between the two branches worsening, a turning point arrived. The parliament convened an emergency session and imposed constitutional amendments that effectively reduced the presidency to a ceremonial office. Furious, Yeltsin responded with a televised statement that he had issued a decree creating a "special governmental regime" to confront the intolerable constitutional crisis. He also announced that a nationwide "vote of confidence" in the parliament would be held the following month. But despite widespread confusion and mutual accusations, in subsequent days Yeltsin spoke no further about his "special regime." The parliament eventually agreed to a modified popular referendum to be held on April 25. The referendum entailed two sets of questions: a vote of confidence in Yeltsin and in his social and economic programs, and a poll of whether presidential and parliamentary elections should be held earlier than their scheduled dates. The Constitutional Court ruled that the rescheduling of elections could be accomplished only by an affirmative vote by a majority of the potential electorate (not simply a majority of the votes cast), thus imposing a larger electoral burden upon the second set of questions. The voters affirmed their support for Yeltsin and his programs by decisive if not overwhelming majorities, but the vote for rescheduling elections failed to meet the Court's criteria. (See Table 7–1.)

Meanwhile, Yeltsin resurrected the effort to replace Russia's constitution. In June 1993 a Constitutional Assembly (distinct from the earlier Constitutional Commission) was convened in Moscow to reconcile the Constitutional Commission's 1992 draft constitution with a new draft by the Kremlin. (All told, six drafts were on the table at the time.) The federalism issue was reopened, and the question of the central government's structure—parliamentary or presidential—continued to bedevil the effort . Nevertheless, by the middle of July a new draft constitution was approved. The procedure for adopting and ratifying it, however, remained unclear. Many segments of the country were not inclined to recognize the authority of the Constitutional Assembly—a phenomenon with some resonance in American history.

At the same time the constitutional crisis continued to worsen. Yeltsin and the parliament traded political fire, until finally, on September 21, 1993, Yeltsin again appeared on television to announce his signing of a new decree— his 1,400th as president. The decree suspended the existing parliament and set

Table 7–1   Results of April 25, 1993 Referendum

Source: "A Battle Not the War," *The Economist*, May 1, 1993: 49.

	% "yes" (of votes cast)	% "yes" (of potential electorate)
1. Do you have confidence in the President of the Russian Federation, Boris Yeltsin?	57.4	37.7
2. Do you approve of the socio-economic policies carried out by the President of the Russian Federation and the Government of the Russian Federation since 1992?	53.7	34.0
3. Do you consider it necessary to hold early elections for the President of the Russian Federation?	49.1	30.9
4. Do you consider it necessary to hold early elections for the Congress of People's Deputies of the Russian Federation?	70.6	44.8

elections for a new legislative body, the State Duma, to be held in December. The Duma, whose name was borrowed from the pre-Revolutionary legislative body, would serve as the lower house of a bicameral National Assembly. In the days following this decree the Kremlin promulgated election rules, announced that the presidency would also be up for early election (in June 1994), and specified the structure of the temporary government that would be in place until the constitution was approved.

Yeltsin's actions were deemed a presidential coup, even by sympathetic supporters. The legality of the decree certainly was open to question. But the parliamentary leadership did not afford itself the option of taking the high road. Instead, Duma speaker Ruslan Khasbulatov interpreted Yeltsin's decree as cause for a coup of his own. Within hours, the parliament had decreed that Yeltsin had forfeited the presidency, and it swore in Vice President Aleksandr Rutskoi as acting president. Two years earlier Yeltsin had chosen Rutskoi as his running mate to shore up his popularity with the military and conservatives. No doubt Yeltsin now recalled that it had been Gorbachev's hand-picked vice president, Gennady Yanayev, who had turned on President Mikhail Gorbachev in the 1991 coup attempt. In a further parallel to the 1991 coup attempt, the parliament also acted to replace Yeltsin's defense and security ministers with its own selections.

For two weeks a standoff ensued between the White House and the Kremlin, each claiming to represent the real government. But after Rutskoi initiated an attack to seize the Moscow mayor's office and a television station on October 3, Yeltsin ordered Russian troops to storm the parliament and arrest its leaders. In the confusion he also suspended the Constitutional Court and established a state of emergency in Moscow. With his main governmental rivals now suspended, in prison, or dead (more than 100 people died in the October "events," as they came to be known), Yeltsin made a final push to establish a new constitutional order. A new draft constitution, presumably tailor-made to suit Yeltsin's vision for his country and his rule, was put before the country with the intention that it would be subject to a plebiscite at the same time as the already-scheduled parliamentary elections—on December 12, 1993.

Yeltsin's constitution was approved with 58 percent of the votes cast. With an official 55 percent turnout rate, the vote met both of the thresholds deemed necessary for approving the constitution (a simple majority of "yes" votes, with at least half of the electorate voting).[1] The election was generally acknowledged to have been conducted and tallied fairly, but many voiced concerns about this particular method for adopting a constitution. Voters had barely a month after publication of the draft to consider the new constitution before voting. Yeltsin had discouraged public campaigns against the draft constitution. And, of course, the coups and countercoups of the fall hardly were conducive to reasoned discourse about the structure of a new Russian government. Nevertheless, the new constitution was understood to be more legitimate and suitable than the old one, and it managed to alleviate the constitutional crisis that had been fermenting since Russia declared its independence from the Soviet Union in 1990.

The Yeltsin Constitution

> We, the multi-national people of the Russian Federation, united by a common destiny on our land, asserting human rights and liberties, civil peace and accord, preserving the historic unity of the state, proceeding from the commonly recognized principles of equality and self-determination of the peoples honoring the memory of our ancestors, who have passed on to us love of and respect for our homeland and faith in good and justice, reviving the sovereign statehood of Russia and asserting its immutable democratic foundations, striving to secure the well-being and prosperity of Russia and proceeding from a sense of responsibility for our homeland before the present and future generations, and being aware of ourselves

---

1. The official figures were later disputed. Subsequent reports indicated that the actual voter turnout amounted to 46 percent of the potential electorate. The constitution was nevertheless approved. See ITAR-TASS report, May 5, 1994.

as part of the world community, hereby approve the CONSTITUTION OF THE RUSSIAN FEDERATION.[2]

The preamble to the Russian Constitution reveals some of the antino-mies that characterize Russia, or at least that illustrate competing visions for Russia: self-determination of multinational peoples and historic unity of the sovereign state; honoring the memory of ancestors and securing well-being for future generations; sensing responsibility for the homeland and belong-ing to a larger world community. By its preamble, the Constitution at once promises to preserve Russia as a historical entity and to transform it into a democratic, peaceful state that recognizes human rights.

The Yeltsin Constitution nevertheless expresses an identity and a goal for post-Soviet Russia. As the Soviet constitutions of 1936 and 1977 were known as the Stalin and Brezhnev Constitutions, respectively, it is fitting to label Russia's 1993 constitution with Yeltsin's name. Not only was he the best-known politician associated with its drafting, but clearly the draft also re-flected most of Yeltsin's wishes. Like the 1958 French Constitution, which presumably was drafted for President Charles DeGaulle, the Yeltsin Consti-tution was created with the needs and desires of Yeltsin in mind. Indeed, the French and Russian constitutions themselves are similar, particularly by their creation of a powerful presidency with control over the cabinet and various prerogatives concerning foreign policy.

Unlike the United States Constitution, the constitution of the Russian Fed-eration is detailed and specific, comprising 137 separate articles. A mix of old (Soviet) principles and specifically anti-Soviet ones, the Yeltsin Constitution specifies a separation of state power into three branches (Article 10), ensures "ideological pluralism" by proscribing any state-sponsored ideology (Article 13), and maintains a separation of church and state (Article 14). Forty-eight articles grouped as "Human and Civil Rights and Freedoms" provide a liberal and expansive, even majestic, expression of human rights. The listing of affronts to human rights which are proscribed by this chapter serves as a catalog of the various abuses practiced by the Soviet state: diminution of human dignity, pro-longed detention without judicial action, invasion of privacy, forced renuncia-tion of opinions, censorship, and many others.

Nevertheless, a loophole in Article 55 allows human rights and civil rights to be restricted "to the extent necessary for upholding the foundations of the constitutional system, morality, or the health, rights and lawful interests of other persons or for ensuring the defense of the country and state security." Article

---

2. Belyakov, Vladimir and Raymond, Walter J. (eds.), "Preamble," *Constitution of the Russian Federation: With Commentaries and Interpretations* (Lawrenceville, VA: Brunswick Publish-ing Co., 1994).

56 provides for states of emergency, in which case rights and freedoms may temporarily be restricted. Nevertheless, the chapter of the constitution that comprises the Human and Civil Rights and Freedoms is specially protected from the regular constitutional amendment process, and certain rights are protected from restriction in all events.

The Institutions of Government

The Presidency

The Yeltsin Constitution designates the president as the head of state. Like the president of France, however, the Russian president possesses powers far beyond the ceremonial role that "head of state" implies. In this sense, Russia has an "executive presidency." The Russian president appoints the prime minister (with the Duma's consent), appoints governmental ministers (after vetting by the prime minister), and nominates justices (for approval by the Federation Council). He may call referenda and grant pardons.

The constitution also grants to the president the power to issue decrees and directives, which are legally binding throughout the country so long as they do not contradict the constitution or federal laws. Although this power is potentially enormous, it is limited by the willingness of the federal and local bureaucracies to implement the decrees. Yeltsin has felt some frustration in this regard, and in June 1996 he resorted to the peculiar device of decreeing that all decrees must be faithfully executed. When this failed to appreciably bolster the effectiveness of his decrees, Yeltsin, in November 1996, issued yet another decree, this time requiring concrete measures be taken to implement decrees within one month of their issuance. Agency heads were also required to submit reports on progress in implementing specific decrees. There was little reason to expect these measures would succeed where others had failed.

Although his power over the bureaucracy is severely limited, the president wields considerable power over the federal parliament and cabinet. If his choice for prime minister is rejected three times by the Duma, he has the power to dissolve the Duma and call new elections. If the Duma passes a vote of no confidence in the government, the president may either dissolve the Duma or dismiss the government. However, the Duma may not be dissolved when it has initiated impeachment charges against the president. The president may introduce martial law and declare a state of emergency, but while either of these is in effect the president may not dissolve the Duma. A new (or, one supposes, renewed) government must be appointed only when a new president takes office.

The president also wields formal power over the regions of the federation. The constitution permits him to use "reconciliatory procedures" to settle differences between the federal and regional authorities. He also may suspend acts of the regional executives if he finds that they contradict the federal constitution or federal law, until "the appropriate court" decides the question. As noted above, he may declare states of emergency and martial law in particular regions.

No provision exists in the Yeltsin Constitution for a vice president. Perhaps the memory of Rutskoi's and Yanayev's betrayals were still too fresh. In the event of a president's incapacitation, presidential powers pass to the prime minister. (This was done for 23 hours on November 5–6, 1996, while Yeltsin underwent cardiac bypass surgery.) If a president dies or is permanently incapacitated, new presidential elections must be held within three months. The acting president may not dissolve the Duma, call a referendum, or propose constitutional amendments.

The president takes the lead in conducting Russia's relations with other countries. The president is commander-in-chief of the armed forces and is generally responsible for conducting the country's foreign policy. He appoints ambassadors and other diplomats. The constitution affords him the power to approve the country's military doctrine and to chair the Security Council, although numerous informal and formal structures are involved in the drafting of military and foreign policy (see Chapter 12). The president conducts international negotiations and signs international treaties (which require ratification by the parliament) and recognizes foreign diplomats.

In the making and directing of policy the president is assisted by the "power ministries" of defense, foreign affairs, interior, and security. Unlike the other ministers, which report to the prime minister, the power ministers report directly to the president. In addition, the president is advised by a network of formal and informal consultative groups. The Presidential Council, with 28 members in 1996, advises the president on a broad range of issues, but as an institution it is seen as somewhat ceremonial. Even more ceremonial was the presidential Social Chamber (later recast as the Political Consultative Council) through which Yeltsin heard advice from representatives of a broad range of political parties. In the fall of 1996 Yeltsin created the Consultative Council, which ostensibly was designed to resolve issues between the executive and legislative branches. Its membership included the president, the prime minister, the chairman of the Federation Council, and the speaker of the Duma. Some speculated that the body was designed to co-opt the legislative leadership.

As Yeltsin's presidency progressed, some charged that he was ignoring his expert advisers and increasingly turning to a shadowy clique of cronies. Chief among these was Aleksandr Korzhakov, head of the presidential security service, whose role in Yeltsin's policy toward Chechnya was speculated to be crucial. (In the spring of 1996 Yeltsin elevated Korzhakov to the level of federal minister, but weeks later Yeltsin fired Korzhakov altogether in the aftermath of a vague coup allegations.)

In the winter of 1996, several members of the Presidential Council, including Yegor Gaidar and human rights advocate Sergei Kovalev, resigned to protest Yeltsin's unrelenting military campaign in Chechnya. The resignations were triggered by a report on the status of human rights in Russia released by the Presidential Human Rights Commission, another body whose moral authority and political expertise Yeltsin was allegedly ignoring. Kovalev had been on this commission as well and led the wave of resignations.

Overall, the distinction between the president and the government is vague, given the president's influence over the makeup and actions of the cabinet and prime minister. Yet when it suited him to do so, Yeltsin blamed social and economic problems upon the actions of "incompetent ministers."

The Government

Although the president's decision-making powers are considerable, the constitution formally places executive power in the government. "Government" is defined in the European sense, meaning the prime minister (formally called the chairman of the government), deputy prime ministers, and federal ministers. Collectively, the federal ministers compose the cabinet. In its capacity as the executive branch, the government is charged with carrying out the laws and policies of the Russian Federation. The government also submits a federal budget to the Duma and oversees the implementation of the final budget.

The prime minister is nominated by the president and confirmed by the Duma. If the Duma rejects a nominee, the president must make a new nomination (the same candidate may be renominated) within one week. If the Duma rejects three consecutive nominations, the president makes a fourth nomination and dissolves the Duma. One might expect this provision to militate against the Duma's hasty rejection of nominees. After the Duma is dissolved, new parliamentary elections are called.

Once confirmed, the new prime minister proposes a list of nominees for deputy prime ministers and a cabinet. The president may accept or reject those nominees. Government ministers may not simultaneously hold legislative seats. After Yeltsin's reelection in July 1996 the Russian cabinet included 24 ministries (see Table 7–2). In addition to the heads of ministries, three first deputy prime ministers help oversee policy. Further, a number of deputy prime ministers (seven as of August 1996) coordinate government policy among several ministries within larger administrative "departments" (see Table 7–2).

The Duma's powers over the government are complex and heavily checked by the president. A simple majority of deputies in the Duma may pass a vote

Table 7–2   Cabinet of Ministers of the Russian Federation (as of August 1996)
Source: ITAR-TASS, August 15 and 22, 1996.

••

Prime Minister: Viktor Chernomyrdin

First Deputy Prime Ministers
• Industry, Construction, Transport, Communications, Natural Resources: Aleksei Babidhev
• Social Policy: Viktor Ilyushin
• Economics: Vladmir Potanin

Deputy Prime Ministers
• Head of Government Administration: Vladimir Babichev
• Minister of Foreign Trade: Oleg Davydov
• Minister of Finance: Aleksei Bolsnakov
• Agriculture and Environmental Protection: Aleksdandr Zaveryukha
• Media: Vitaly Ignatenko
• CIS, National, and Regional Policy: Valery Serov
• Science and Education: Vladimir Fortov
• Without Portfolio: Oleg Lobov

Ministers
• Agriculture: Viktor Khyltsun
• Civil Defense and Emergencies: Sergei Shoigu
• Commonwealth of Independent States: Aman Tuleev
• Communications: Vladimir Bulgak
• Construction: Yefim Basin
• Culture: Yevgenii Sidorov
• Defense: Igor Rodionov
• Defense Industry: Zinovy Pak
• Economy: Yevgeny Yasin
• Foreign Affairs: Yevgeny Primakov
• Fuel and Energy: Petr Rodionov
• Health: Tatyana Dmitrieva
• Industry: Yurii Bespalov
• Internal Affairs: Anatoly Kulikov
• Justice: Valentin Kovalev
• Labor and Social Development: Gennady Melikyan
• Nationalities and Federal Relations: Vyacheslav Mikhailov
• Natural Resources: Viktor Orlov
• Nuclear Energy: Viktor Mikhailov
• Railway Communication: Anatoly Zaitsev
• Social and Professional Education: Vladmir Kinelev
• Transport: Nikolai Tsakh
• Chairman of the State Privatization Committee: Alfred Kokh
• Director of Federal Security Service: Nikolai Kovalev

of no confidence in the government. The president may either accept the Duma's vote, in which case he announces the government's dissolution, or he may reject the vote of no confidence. If the Duma's vote is rejected, the Duma may pass a second vote of no confidence within three months of the first. In this case, the president must either announce the government's resignation or dissolve the Duma. Once again, self-interested deputies might be hesitant to push the president to the wall. This was illustrated in 1994, when the Duma passed a vote of no confidence in the government. After its first vote of no confidence was rejected by President Boris Yeltsin, the Duma was unable to muster a majority to pass a second, more destabilizing vote of no confidence.

The Legislature

Like most democratic governments (and some nondemocratic ones), Russia's legislature takes the form of a bicameral parliament. This Federal Assembly, as it is known, is charged with the usual representation and lawmaking tasks, as well as providing certain checks on the other branches of government. It is, however, significantly less powerful than the Congress of People's Deputies which it replaced.

Federation Council   The Federation Council serves as the upper house, and in several ways it resembles the U.S. Senate. Like the Senate, the Federation Council is constituted on the basis of equal geographical representation. Each of Russia's 89 regions sends two representatives to the Federation Council, for a total of 178 members. And, like the Senate, the Federation Council ratifies treaties (along with the Duma) and possesses the power to impeach the president. The Federation Council possesses powers relating to the Russian Federation's justice system, including approving and dismissing the prosecutor-general, and approving or rejecting the president's nominees for justices on Russia's three high courts. In addition, the Federation Council approves internal border revisions, approves presidential decrees of martial law, and "decides the possibility" of deploying the military abroad.

Members of the Federation Council elect a chairman and a deputy chairman, who preside over its sessions. (Yegor Stroev, a former Politburo member now associated with the Our Home Is Russia party, was elected chairman in 1996.) Legislative work is conducted in various policy committees. Sessions are to be open to the public, except as stipulated by the Federation Council's code of procedure.

As observed in Chapter 5, half of the Federation Council is to be composed of regional governors (although the number was slightly higher in the 1994–95 Federation Council due to direct election). As executives, these governors have tended to be more loyal to the federal executive (that is, the president) than the members of the lower house. In its first year, the post-

1995 Federation Council did indeed prove to be more inclined to support Yeltsin's policies. The proportion of Communists in the upper house was less than that of the lower house, and only 28 of the 178 deputies were considered "oppositionists."[3]

State Duma   As is true for many parliamentary systems, Russia's lower house, the State Duma, is the more powerful of the two chambers. Because its 450 deputies are directly elected as representatives to the federal parliament, the Duma enjoys a stronger mandate than the Federation Council. The Duma is the more important and more powerful chamber in the making of legislation, as it initiates all legislation and can override a rejection of a bill by the Federation Council. The constitution also provides for the censure of the government by the Duma. The term of office for Duma deputies is four years. The Duma elects a speaker to preside over the body. (The Duma elected in December 1995 chose Gennady Seleznev, a member of the CPRF, as its speaker.)

The constitution reserves for the Duma various powers: approving the president's nominee for prime minister, deciding votes of confidence, appointing and removing the chairman of the Central Bank, appointing and removing the officer for human rights, initiating articles of impeachment against the president, and issuing declarations of amnesty. The Duma used this last power shortly after it convened in 1994, granting amnesty to the leaders of the 1991 attempted coup against Gorbachev and the 1993 "October events" against Yeltsin.

Russia's separation of powers doctrine forbids deputies in the Duma from holding official positions in the executive or judicial branches. The practical significance of this provision became clear in 1995, when a number of governmental ministers (including Foreign Minister Andrei Kozyrev) won seats in the Duma and were forced to choose between their two offices. The constitution does not address the question of whether members of the Federation Council may simultaneously serve in other branches.

Lawmaking

The making of federal laws involves checks and balances between the two houses of parliament and the president. All bills are introduced in the Duma, although legislative proposals may be initiated by members of either house, as well as by the president, the government, the three central courts, and the regional legislatures. The Duma deliberates upon bills in committee (there were 28 standing committees in 1996), after which they are submitted to the

---

3. According to *Obshchaya gazeta*, January 11–17, 1996.

entire body for approval or rejection. Within five days after a bill is adopted by the full Duma (usually by a majority vote), it is passed on to the Federation Council for consideration. The Federation Council need not consider a bill at all, unless it concerns the federal budgetary and financial matters, international treaties, Russian borders, or matters of war and peace. The Federation Council has 14 days to approve the legislation (again by majority vote) or to reject it. If it does not act within the 14 days, the legislation is considered approved. If the Federation Council rejects a bill, it is returned to the Duma for repeat consideration. A two-thirds vote of approval by the Duma overrides rejection by the Federation Council.

Once a bill has passed out of the Federal Assembly, either with bicameral acceptance or with a two-thirds vote of the Duma, the legislation is forwarded to the president. If he signs it within 14 days, it becomes law and is made public. If the president rejects the bill, it is returned for repeat consideration by the two legislative chambers. A two-thirds vote of approval by both chambers overrides the president's veto. In 1996 the Constitutional Court upheld an additional method for the president to block legislation: he may return to the Federal Assembly a law which he finds to be legally flawed or improperly passed. In effect, the president can exercise judicial review.

The adoption of federal constitutional laws requires a three-quarters majority of the Federation Council and a two-thirds majority of the Duma before going to the president for approval.

The Judiciary

Awareness of Russian, and especially Soviet, history causes Russians to be skeptical about what passes for justice in their country. During the Soviet period the courts were an instrument of the Communist Party of the Soviet Union. Stalin used show trials to destroy his political enemies, and cruel punishments often were meted out against "enemies of the state." Even after Stalin's death, the Soviet judiciary system was politically controlled, with virtually all judges above the local level belonging to the CPSU. In addition, the KGB's Fifth Chief Directorate, established in 1969, maintained a vast network of informants and infiltrators to seek out and eliminate political dissent. Its information, of whatever degree of veracity, often found its way into trials of Soviet citizens. The judiciary's ties to the Party and the KGB made it a feared institution indeed.

The Russian Constitution therefore takes pains to ensure that the courts are strong enough to protect the people's rights, but accountable enough to prevent abuse. Toward the goal of defending the constitution, the Russian Federation has adopted the principle of judicial review. That is, the courts may assess the constitutionality of established laws, striking down those which are in conflict with constitutional principles. In addition, the courts are deemed to be independent of the other branches. Article 121 states that "judges shall be irremovable," although federal law may make provisions for the suspension of a judge's powers.

Specific constitutional provisions prohibit Soviet-era practices which made a mockery of the term "Soviet justice." Under Chapter 2 of the Yeltsin Constitution, all accused persons have a right to an attorney and to have their case heard by a judge or a court; in capital cases a jury trial is guaranteed. Court proceedings are required to be open. All persons are equal before the law, and persons may not be tried in absentia. The constitution affirms the Western principle that persons are considered innocent until proven guilty in accordance with federal law. To prevent a return to KGB-era domestic surveillance, the constitution prohibits the "gathering, storage, use and dissemination of information concerning the private life of an individual without the individual's consent" (Article 24).

State prosecution in the Russian Federation is conducted through the federal prosecutor's office, under which all regional and local prosecutors are centralized. The prosecutor's office is headed by the prosecutor-general of the Russian Federation, who is nominated by the president and confirmed by the Federation Council. Lower-level prosecutors are appointed by the prosecutor-general.

The Russian Federation uses three high courts. Justices on all three are nominated by the president and confirmed by the Federation Council. The Constitutional Court has 19 justices, all of whom serve 12-year terms and who must retire at age 70. The Constitutional Court conducts judicial review at the federal level. It decides the constitutionality of federal laws and presidential decrees (but not of actions), of regional constitutions, and various treaties. It settles disputes of competence between federal bodies and between the central and regional governments. The Constitutional Court's rulings have not always been heeded by the other branches of government; Yeltsin's suspension of the court during the 1993 October events is a case in point. But since the adoption of the Yeltsin Constitution, the executive and legislative bodies have displayed a professional respect for the court's authority.

The Supreme Court of the Russian Federation is the highest court of appeal for civil, administrative, and criminal law. In matters of impeachment, the Supreme Court must verify the Duma's findings of presidential criminality, and the Constitutional Court must verify that the proper impeachment procedures are followed. The Supreme Court has established a degree of credibility and independence, overruling such actions as the Central Election Commission's disqualification of Yabloko from the 1995 Duma elections.

The Supreme Arbitration Court of the Russian Federation is the highest such court of appeal for cases concerning economic matters. The Russian judiciary system includes a network of courts of arbitration, which settle economic disputes.

Amendments

About half of the articles of the Russian Constitution may be amended by the parliament with a two-thirds majority in the Duma and a three-fourths majority in the Federation Council. These amendments require ratification by two-thirds of the regions of the Russian Federation. The other constitutional articles—those found in the three chapters concerning basic principles of the constitutional system, human and civil rights, and procedures for amending the constitution—are protected from legislative amendment. Those articles can only be amended by a Constitutional Assembly, convened by a three-fifths vote of both legislative chambers. Any new draft constitution produced by a Constitutional Assembly requires either adoption by a two-thirds vote of the Assembly or a majority vote of the Russian electorate.

Despite some disputes about the legitimacy of its adoption, the Russian Constitution has largely been accepted by the political elites and the general population. Protracted academic debates and political arguments over the constitution's particular provisions continue to fill the pages of journals and newspapers. Yet the 1993–95 Duma managed to work with the president and the regions in general conformity with the constitution's stated principles.

Still, political forces in Russia continue to seek major constitutional amendments. Shortly after re-establishing dominance in the Duma in the wake of the 1995 elections, the Communists (led by Gennady Seleznev in the Duma) began attempting to amend the constitution to increase parliamentary oversight of the government and the president. Some within the party sought to eliminate the presidency. Others hinted that they might try to replace the constitution altogether. The Communist Party of the Russian Federation's parliamentary platform, adopted in August 1995, had called for abolishing the presidency (after a transitional period). In February 1996, Gennady Zyuganov "clarified" that the CPRF wanted to "redistribute" balance between legislative and executive; not abolish the presidency. Yeltsin defended the institution of a strong presidency in a television interview in March 1996, suggesting the Russians need "a strong hand" over them and rejecting parliamentary democracy as a structure in which "no one is responsible." Some speculated that Zyuganov planned to support the shift toward Duma power as a payoff to parliamentary supporters during his 1996 presidential campaign. Zyuganov's defeat in that campaign reduced the likelihood that the balance of constitutional power soon would be shifted. Yet at the same time more moderate forces, including Grigory Yavlinsky, continued to push for a reduction in presidential powers.

Prospects

One of the most important symbols of Russia's break with its Soviet and Communist past is its constitution. Although the Yeltsin Constitution created a new set of governmental and political structures to carry Russia into its post-Soviet future, the constitution could not guarantee a particular course for Russia's development. The road leading from the mere creation of structures to their institutionalization is long, arduous, and poorly marked. It could be decades before Russia's political system has been fully institutionalized.

Suggested Readings

Belyakov, Vladimir V. and Walter J. Raymond, eds. *Constitution of the Russian Federation: With Commentaries and Interpretations.* Lawrenceville, Va., and Moscow: Brunswick and Novosti, 1994.

Smith, Bruce L. R. and Gennady M. Danilenko, eds. *Law and Democracy in the New Russia.* Washington, D. C.: The Brookings Institution, 1993.

Tolz, Vera. "Drafting the New Russian Constitution," *RFE/RL Research Report* 2:29 (July 16, 1993): 1–12.

Unger, Aryeh L. *Constitutional Development in the USSR: A Guide to the Soviet Constitutions.* New York: PICA Press, 1981.

Yeltsin, Boris. *The Struggle for Russia.* New York: Random House, 1994.

Yakovlev, Alexandre. *The Bear that Wouldn't Dance: Failed Attempts to Reform the Constitution of the Former Soviet Union.* Winnipeg: Legal Research Institute, University of Manitoba, 1992.

Part IV

Issues and Policies

8
—

Social and Economic Policy

As the primary successor state to the Soviet Union, the Russian Federation inherited much from the old order. To some of this the Kremlin has jealously clung: its nuclear deterrent, its seat on the United Nations Security Council, its status as one of the primary victors of the Second World War. But at the same time the Yeltsin leadership has struggled to extricate Russia from many of the Communist-era social and economic structures that arguably contributed to the failure of the Soviet state. It is no exaggeration to say that Boris Yeltsin is trying to move his country from the Second World to the First World, although steering this course without drifting into the Third World will take unprecedented skill, courage, and luck.

From Second to First World?

The classification of countries into three worlds was adopted by Western analysts, who perceived that the international political order that congealed after the Second World War comprised three large blocs of countries, grouped by political and economic characteristics. That the three groups came to be known as "worlds" underscores the depth of the fundamental differences that were presumed to divide them. The distinction between the first and second worlds was most starkly defined: democracies with free-market economies, politically aligned with the United States, were considered members of the First World; Marxist-Leninist states with centrally planned economies were assumed to be under the tutelage of the Soviet Union and were assigned to the Second World. There was little conceptual place for hybrids; that is, it was difficult to conceive of a state with a centrally planned economy closely aligned with the Soviet Union that was democratic.

Western analysts essentially understood there to be a natural coincidence of capitalism, democracy, and alignment with Washington. The converse—that central planning, Marxist-Leninist ideology, and alignment with Moscow necessarily went together—was only partially discounted with the Sino-Soviet split in the 1960s. What was most important, conceptually, about the First World/Second World divide was that it fit neatly with the bipolar character of the Cold War. It also was reinforced by a geographical tidiness, in that most of the First World countries (with some exceptions, such as Japan) were located to the west of the iron curtain, and most of the countries of the Second World were to its east.

The bipolar conception of the world was complicated by the existence of numerous countries whose social, political, and economic characteristics did not readily suggest placement in either the Western or Eastern blocs. Mostly these countries were considered "undeveloped" or "underdeveloped," suggesting that with their eventual "development" would necessarily come membership in one of the two camps. Alternative development scenarios were not given serious consideration. Although these countries were pursued as potential allies, or at least as friendly votes in the UN General Assembly, they were left out of the First and Second Worlds and relegated to the Third World—a sort of geopolitical purgatory before ascending to "modern" status.

Thus, politically the Third World was not directly associated with the bipolar order. Indeed, many of these countries themselves sought to institutionalize their nonalignment through such organizations as the Group of 77. But it was the Third World's level of socio-political (under-)development that became most salient to Western political scientists. Increasingly their research turned to the question of how a Third World country could achieve a type and level of political and economic development that warranted membership in the First World. Modernization theory, popularized by Walt Rostow and others, presumed a natural, linear movement of these countries as the forces of industrialization and urbanization created social forces that would demand democracy.[1] Other theories, including those based on Marxist thought, offered alternative predictions and prescriptions.

---

1. See, for example, W. W. Rostow, *The Stages of Economic Growth* (New York: Cambridge University Press, 1960).

In a practical sense the Cold War order provided for the testing of development theories. Without a doubt the tangible differences in living conditions between West and East—between the First World and the Second—helped foster popular dissatisfaction with the regimes of the Soviet bloc. The differences were most starkly illustrated in Germany. For almost exactly four decades Germany was a single nation split between two states: one firmly grounded in the First World, and the other in the Second. Although Communist East Germany was widely considered one of the most prosperous, successful countries in the Soviet bloc, its government still was forced to rely on walls, soldiers, and the backing of the Soviet Union to stem the flow of its citizens to the free and more prosperous West German state.

When the anti-Communist revolutions finally erupted throughout the Soviet bloc in 1989–91, popular dissatisfaction with living conditions provided fuel for the counterrevolutionary fire. The importance of living standards was further in evidence as the post-Communist polities took their first steps toward creating new societies, embracing the consumer culture of the West and especially of the United States with shameless abandon. Yet although the enticements of First World prosperity helped steal the hearts of the Second World's denizens away from the more idealistic appeals of Marxist-Leninist ideology, the Second World's collapse did not result from unfulfilled consumer desires alone.

On a structural level, the countries of the Second World progressively became weakened by the command economy's inability to meet the demands placed upon it by the state and the military, as well as by the consumer. And the societal alienation that characterized most Second World societies, particularly Brezhnev's Soviet Union, further weakened the bond between citizen and state. To the extent that each of these contributed to the revolutions of 1989–91, the new governments of Eastern Europe and the former Soviet Union were faced with the immediate need to correct the institutional cause, and not merely the individual manifestations, of social and economic reverse development.

Social Policies

Under Yeltsin the Russian state has undertaken the monumental effort of rebuilding Russian society. Little by way of instructive experience is offered by the Gorbachev years, which focused primarily on economic reform and which pursued societal reform only to the extent that it contributed to stabilizing the state. By contrast, the reformers who found themselves at the levers of post-Soviet Russian power sought more fully to "normalize" society. This was a tall order indeed.

Housing, Health Care, and Education

Until its final years, Tsarist Russia was largely rural and agrarian, leaving housing and health care essentially to the individuals' responsibility and ignoring the need for formal education except for the most privileged classes. The Bolsheviks exploited the physical and intellectual impoverishment that resulted from this neglect. For all its faults, the Soviet regime did manage to provide adequate levels of social services to a population that historically had been denied them. The enormous, indistinguishable apartment buildings were hastily erected by the new regime in the major cities may have lacked charm and working elevators, but they met the needs of a rapidly urbanizing population. Health care may not have been state of the art, but it helped increase life expectancy by more than 30 years between 1917 and 1966. Education may have been tainted by Party propaganda and Marxist-Leninist revisionism, but it raised the country's literacy rate from below half to virtually 100 percent.

By and large today's Russian population still expects these basic services to be maintained. Part of the burden falls upon the business sector, which still provides to employees many of the social services previously guaranteed by the Soviet state. A large number of enterprises own their own stocks of employee housing, run child-care facilities, administer retirement accounts, provide unemployment compensation, and so forth. Since many firms and enterprises are now privately owned, their provision of social benefits is akin to the provision of fringe benefits such as insurance and sick leave by Western private firms. But in Russia the state still bears the brunt of popular expectations for social guarantees.

The 1993 Russian Constitution ascribes to the state a paternalistic role that is somewhat reminiscent of the Soviet constitutions. Article 7 defines the Russian Federation as a "social state" whose policies "shall aim to create conditions ensuring adequate living standards and the free development of every individual." The social guarantees established in this article include a minimum wage, protection of work and health, and "state support for the family, motherhood, fatherhood, childhood, invalids, and aged people." In its first five years, the new Russian government has been only partly successful in fulfilling these obligations.

The constitution assigns governmental responsibility for health, education, and social security to the federal government (Articles 39, 41, and 43). State-run hospitals continue to provide free care, but many medicines have become unaffordable. Ultimately, the market has taken on the task of allocating higher-quality social services.

Health Policy   One of Russia's greatest health care challenges lies in the battle against alcohol abuse. Russians' consumption of alcohol is legendary, and the toll this has taken on personal health, economic productivity, and family stability is well documented. Fighting alcohol abuse was one of the first major elements of Mikhail Gorbachev's program to save the Soviet Union. That effort was simultaneously derided as too simplistic (for assuming the country's enormous problems were caused primarily by drunkenness) and too ambitious (for assuming alcoholism could be stemmed by governmental decree). On both scores the critics seem to have been vindicated. Gorbachev soon learned that saving his country would require much more than sobering up the population, and he turned by degrees to allowing public criticism of governmental policy, to fundamental economic restructuring, and ultimately (and perhaps fatally) to democratization. Meanwhile, Soviets who found their access to vodka restricted turned to the black market for noxious, often fatal *samogan* (moonshine).

Perhaps without the hubris of his predecessor, Yeltsin has picked up the cause of alcoholism. This provides enormous joke potential for Russians, who widely perceive their president to have a weakness for the bottle. (In a 1996 campaign brochure, Yeltsin acknowledged that denying his drinking would be useless; Russians would say, "What kind of Russian man are you if you can't drink?") Although Moscow has continued to launch periodic anti-alcohol campaigns, Yeltsin's government was initially hesitant to severely restrict sales of alcohol for fear of public reaction. In 1994 Yeltsin did issue a decree banning alcohol and cigarette advertising, but it has not been vigorously enforced. The parliament passed a law to take effect in 1996 that bans such advertising from television, but there was little reason to expect this law to be any more successful than Yeltsin's decree.

In early 1996 the government adopted measures that increased governmental control over alcohol. Unlike Gorbachev's decrees, which sought to increase productivity by restricting the availability of alcohol, the new laws used a market approach by imposing taxes and duties on alcohol sales. Not coincidentally, these funds could be a boon to the strapped Russian treasury.

Yeltsin's Council on Social Policy has ranked drug abuse as a problem at least as serious as alcoholism in Russia. Drug use was decriminalized in 1991, although sale and possession remained illegal. Police seizures of drugs and arrests have increased a hundredfold since the Gorbachev era, and still authorities are overwhelmed by the problem. (Some law enforcement authorities themselves have been accused of drug sales and related corruption.) Private and quasi-governmental organizations have appeared in Russia to combat drugs and their abuse, including Narcotics Anonymous and the International Association Against Drugs and Drug Trafficking.

Housing The 1993 Constitution assigns responsibility for housing to the regional governments (Articles 130 and 132). The federal government nonetheless plays a role in augmenting the country's housing stock and in expanding home ownership opportunities. Homelessness is a growing problem in Russian cities (see Chapter 4). Moscow and St. Petersburg are the main centers, of course, with estimates running into the tens of thousands of persons. Although not extraordinarily high in comparison with major American cities, these figures are extremely high by Soviet standards.

In the Brezhnev period virtually all urban housing was owned by the state, and about half of this was under the direct administration of enterprises for their employees. Gradual and cautious privatization of housing began under Yuri Andropov, expanded under Mikhail Gorbachev, and reached a plateau under Boris Yeltsin in 1994, with about 30 percent of the overall housing stock privately owned. But further privatization was stalled by the new parliament and increasing public unwillingness to subject such a basic necessity to the uncertainties of the market. Yeltsin issued presidential decrees in December 1993 and June 1994 that authorized mortgage lending and other housing ownership instruments. In February 1996 he issued another decree, which expanded mortgage lending. In March 1996, Yeltsin issued yet another decree calling on the government to create a federal program to subsidize housing construction. The program was announced under the title of "My Home," with echoes of the government party "Our Home Is Russia." Yet notwithstanding Yeltsin's decrees, there was no immediate indication of how the government might fund these programs.

Foreign aid has helped Russia's efforts to create new housing. For example, the German government has helped fund housing for Russian soldiers returning home from their posts in East Germany. America has earmarked some foreign aid exclusively for Russian housing. And the World Bank has authorized a $400 million loan to construct housing in five Russian cities and has provided a $300 million loan to privatize housing controlled by firms. Partly as a result of foreign assistance, housing construction in Russia increased 9 percent in terms of housing units and 25 percent in terms of floor space between 1994 and 1995.

Education   Formal education serves a crucial role in any society. In the Soviet Union it created a literate, potentially productive citizenry out of the intellectually impoverished masses. In the Soviet Union education also served as a tool of control, with the state's official doctrine and ideology thoroughly woven into the curriculum. This was not simply a matter of grafting propaganda onto a course in history or economics; instead, the social sciences and humanities and even the natural sciences were reinterpreted and recast through the lens of Soviet ideology.

Rebuilding a state-run educational system in post-Soviet Russia therefore requires that the ideological bias be removed from curricula, textbooks, and teachers. It requires that the educational system regain a sense of legitimacy. And to the extent that the leadership wishes to create a liberal, civil society, it requires that the educational system not simply become the handmaiden to a new, post- (or even anti-) Soviet ideological elite.

The Yeltsin Constitution guarantees free and compulsory public education through the ninth grade (Article 43). Although technically a federal responsibility, the administration and even funding of education falls largely upon local authorities. Inadequate local resources and insufficient federal funds have left many school systems with decaying buildings, outdated textbooks, overworked teachers, and virtually nonexistent technical equipment. The condition of Russia's public schools has spurred a "marketization" of education. Numerous private schools are springing up to serve elementary and secondary grades. Admission to a university requires the completion of one's secondary education, which is neither compulsory nor free. Preparatory schools have become especially popular with the country's newly rich families, with more than 100 private preparatory schools registered in Moscow alone in 1994.

The status of Russia's universities has suffered in the post-Soviet environment. Despite its ideological bias, Soviet higher education enjoyed international recognition for its rigor and technical focus. In these ways the Soviet Union's system of higher education served the economic system and the sciences well. But in Yeltsin's Russia, the search for short-term economic savings has conspired with efforts to de-ideologize education to restructure the university system. Many universities are slated to be privatized by the State Property Committee, although it is unclear how and when this would happen. In the meantime, scarce resources and underpaid teachers are taking their toll, just as they are with primary education. Students in Russian universities encounter widespread corruption and frustration. In 1996 a diploma could be secured at many universities for a bribe of $5,000 to $10,000, a situation that has rapidly debased the value of a Russian diploma. More importantly, the universities are less able to provide the educated workforce necessary for a technologically advanced economy. And they are less successful in producing citizen elites who can serve as leavening in the nascent civil society.

The pedagogical latitude for professors and teachers in higher education is broader, as are some educational opportunities for students. But alternatives are also enticing. Professors are leaving for occupations that pay better than the typical $30–$50 per month that education does. Students are choosing to study abroad (and not infrequently to stay abroad). Thousands of the brightest young urban elites leave the country each year to study in the United States and Western Europe. There is no guarantee that they will be able to resist the material and other enticements of the societies in which they study. Partially offsetting this hemorrhage of educated, promising elites is a trickle of Soviet-era émigrés who are returning to Russia. They see economic opportunities in the country's emerging market, and they maintain some visceral attachment to the land of their childhood. Many Russians place faith in these returning citizens, with their Western-nurtured idealism, values, education, and training, to assist Russia's moves toward democracy and market economics.

Women's Issues

As Russia has become more of a democracy and allowed greater voice to disaffected groups, the status of women has emerged as a political issue. Women in Russia, as have their counterparts in many societies, historically have been marginalized from politics and government and relegated to second-class roles in business and work. The ideology touted by the revolutionary Bolsheviks made a strong commitment to gender equality. After seizing power, the Bolsheviks continued to show an awareness of women's issues in their policies and proclamations. By the 1930s the Soviet government declared the "women's question" to be resolved. To be sure, in some ways the living conditions of Russian women improved in comparison to the end of the Tsarist period. For example, women's participation in the workforce climbed to about 90 percent, with women taking jobs as doctors and educators, as well as the more traditionally female occupations. Women were also represented at various levels of the government and the Party. The Soviets and their defenders seldom ignored an opportunity to hold up these statistics against those of Western societies.

Despite the advances of Russian women under the Soviets, it is clear that the Party acted too hastily in declaring the women's question closed. All through the Soviet period, women were seriously underrepresented in the higher levels of business, government, and the Party. They also suffered under what was called the double burden whereby their opportunity (obligation, really) to join in the workforce carried with it the expectation that they remain responsible for running their households. Finally, it is worth recalling that discussions of equality in the Soviet Union are by their nature relative, and thus ignore the absolute quality of life. Whatever the degree of equity between men and women, that equity merely allowed women to share in the unsatisfactory, often oppressive, occasionally unbearable, life that Soviet men experienced.

By many measures the disintegration of the Soviet Union and the collapse of the Communist Party improved the lives of all Russians, yet at the same time the rise in unemployment and the general development of "wild capitalism" have worked disproportionately against women. A 1996 survey found that the proportion of women in particular jobs is inversely proportional to the salary bracket. It also found widespread unemployment among urban women. Notwithstanding some success by the Women of Russia political party, women remain underrepresented in the parliament and the government. Less than 14 percent of Duma deputies elected in 1993 were women, and in the 1995 elections that figure dropped to barely 10 percent. By contrast, over 30 percent of the members of the USSR Supreme Soviet in 1984 were women. (In the United States House and Senate, the percentages were 11 and 6, respectively.)

Russian society remains patriarchal and discriminatory. In the newspapers typical help-wanted ads aimed at women call for "leggy blondes" and "women who know how to be sexy." Sexual harassment in the workplace is common but virtually unrecognized as such in Russia. Vladimir Zhirinovsky gave voice to the more patriarchal, even misogynist, aspects of Russian culture. He has repeatedly insisted that men are properly provided with the right to lead and make decisions in family and government. He has repeatedly ridiculed the political party Women of Russia as "Spinsters of Russia." And as his time in the national spotlight wore on, Zhirinovsky's speeches adopted an odd eroticism that seemed to play to his intended audience.

Reforming societal attitudes like sexism and chauvinism is an ambitious undertaking. Indeed, the experience with attempted societal reform under the Communists makes one wonder whether the government should be in the business of remaking culture, even when the prevailing culture demonstrates serious shortcomings. But instead of seeking to prescribe Russian attitudes, the government can legitimately proscribe unacceptable behavior through its laws. And this has been the path taken by Russia's advocates for women. Numerous laws, as well as constitutional provisions, prohibit discrimination against women and guarantee their equal participation in society. The country's labor code includes a chapter titled "Female Labor," which protects women from "arduous jobs and jobs with harmful working conditions." (Although perhaps well-intentioned, this provision might have the effect of hindering "equal participation in society.") Maternity leave and "child care leave" are also provided for. Russian law also is recognized to be relatively liberal on reproductive issues, including access to abortion. (Partly as a result of this the number of abortions have exceeded the number of live births by more than 2 to 1 in recent years.)

But many other laws concerning women are decidedly less liberal. Wife-beating (traditionally endemic in Russia and increasing in recent years) falls under the category of "hooliganism," and even then prosecution is possible only if serious injuries are inflicted and the beating was witnessed. The party Women of Russia introduced the country's first domestic violence legislation and workplace equity bill in the early 1990s, but these were stalled in the Duma. And in any event, the passage of laws does not guarantee their enforcement. Few oversight mechanisms are in place to ensure the observance of regulations and laws relating to the protection of women.

Calls for legislative reform of women's issues were increasing in the mid-1990s. In a 1996 speech given on International Women's Day (March 8), Yeltsin acknowledged the need to improve the lives of women in Russia. He hinted that new policies and legislative proposals would be forthcoming. In the same month, 53 women's associations called upon the Duma to improve women's legal status in Russia. They expressed greatest concern with economic inequality and job discrimination. And new women's organizations, including United Russia, continued to spring up around the country in 1996. But for the time being, the relative deprivation of women seemed to be overshadowed by calls to address the absolute deprivation of the society as a whole.

Economics

Article 8 of the Russian Constitution makes an unequivocal commitment to market economics: "A unified economic space, the free movement of commodities, services and finances, and support for competition and freedom of economic activity shall be guaranteed in the Russian Federation." Yet as with so much of the constitution, there is no clear indication how this guarantee is to be realized.

Economic reform serves as the second horn of Moscow's post-Soviet dilemma. Not only does adopting a market economy require some retraction of the state's social guarantees, it also raises the danger of all manner of economic turbulence, including inflation, unemployment, disrupted trade relationships, and financial destabilization. The problem of transforming a centrally directed economic system into a market-based economy was not a practical issue until the late 1980s, when halting reforms were undertaken in Eastern Europe, the Soviet Union, and other Second World countries. In no country has the transition been easy. Even in the former East Germany, which presumably was best equipped for the transition by virtue of its absorption by the prosperous Federal Republic of Germany, introducing market mechanisms has meant severe economic dislocations and enormous cost. Not only does Russia have no such patron, but it also has been subjected to the unhealthful logic of socialist economics longer than any other country in the world. Its transition is surely the most difficult.

The problem of establishing a market economy where once there had been a developed command economy differs from the task of economic development in less industrialized, less differentiated countries. The Soviet economy had not existed merely as a malformed "system" in need of correction; it was a fully integrated facet of the state itself. In other words, the distinction between state and economy that is so central to liberal capitalism was absent in the Soviet Union. When the state collapsed, therefore, the economy collapsed with it. The notion of an economic "transition" is hence misleading, for at the time of the Soviet Union's demise Russia possessed precious little in the way of an economic "system" to transition from. Rather, Russia faced the necessity of constructing a new economic system.

Initial Steps

In the first months after Russia's independence from the Soviet Union, the elite's commitment to achieving a market economy was not in question. Yeltsin, who had frequently berated Gorbachev for dragging his feet on economic and political reform, now set about the task of creating out of the physical and institutional wreckage of the Soviet economic apparatus a working market economy. The ground had been prepared a year before Russia's actual independence, as the Russian Soviet Federative Socialist Republic in December 1990 enacted the Law on Ownership, which accorded private property an equal status with state property. This law eliminated one of the central Marxist principles from the state's economic doctrine. But as Gorbachev had demonstrated so effectively in the 1980s, an economic system cannot be created by decrees alone.

To navigate the country's movement through the uncharted waters of marketization, Yeltsin assembled a crew of advisers with impeccable free-market credentials: Anatoly Chubais, Yegor Gaidar (who also served as the Russian Federation's first prime minister), and Boris Fedorov. These were like-minded, relatively young, men whose ideological sympathies lay more with the free market economist F. A. von Hayek than with the more interventionist ideas of John Maynard Keynes, let alone Karl Marx. The term "perestroika" was seemingly banished from the Kremlin as the new Russian leadership sought to distance itself from the half-hearted, unpopular reforms of the Gorbachev era.

Price Reform

Yeltsin's economic advisers, under the leadership of Chubais, took up price liberalization as its first task. They generally followed the program begun in 1988 in Poland, which by the early 1990s was recognized as remarkably successful. Adopting what some have called a form of "shock therapy," the Russian leadership in January 1992 liberalized virtually all prices (that is, subjected them to the forces of the market rather than the decrees of the state). Although skeptics predicted widespread strikes and even riots, the liberalization of prices proceeded rather smoothly. The government did retain control over some prices, including necessities like heating oil and bread. And the country encountered a predictable bout with inflation triggered by price liberalization. But the general freeing of prices from the impossibly complicated mathematical models and ideologically driven objectives of the bureaucrats at Goskomtsen (the Soviet price-setting agency) was an impressive feat that demonstrated the new leadership's commitment to reform.

Privatization

The Chubais team adopted as its next task the privatization of industry. Soviet industries had been owned by the state and regulated by their respective ministries in Moscow. The management of each enterprise operated within a complicated administrative hierarchy. Creating a market economy required that these state enterprises be freed from governmental ownership and political control. As noted above, the 1990 Ownership Act had permitted citizens of the RSFSR to own "productive assets," but it did not provide for the prerequisite privatization of those assets. With the collapse of the Soviet Union and its ministries, industries fell under the aegis of "nomenklatura capitalism," whereby the well-connected Soviet-era industry leaders traded influence and even "productive assets" for sundry bribes.

The Chubais team reasoned that only legitimate market forces could break the corruptive influence of nomenklatura capitalism. But how could state assets be transformed into private ones? The answer turned on matters of efficiency, justice, and politics. A voucher program used with some success in post-Communist Czechoslovakia served as a rough guide for the Russian program. Each Russian would be issued his or her "share" (by virtue of citizenship) of the state's assets in the form of a certificate. In the fall of 1992 the federal government gave each Russian citizen a voucher worth 10,000 rubles. The vouchers entitled their holders to invest in state enterprises that the government would put up for auction, but they could also be sold directly for cash. Mutual funds were also established. By the time the voucher program expired in June 1994, more than 2,600 state enterprises had been privatized. This accounted for about 70 percent of Russian industry and about six of every seven industrial jobs.

Smaller consumer-oriented businesses, such as retail shops and private services, were ignored by the voucher program. Still, almost all of these businesses are now privately owned. Indeed, most of Russia's small businesses appeared only after the demise of the Soviet state. As of 1996, the State Committee for the Support of Small Businesses estimated that the country had 877,000 small firms (with fewer than 200 workers each), accounting for about one-eighth of the country's gross domestic product.

To say that the voucher program was successful in privatizing industry is not to say that privatized enterprises are necessarily efficient. Creating productive factories from outdated, poorly organized, and even obsolete industries requires more than merely privatizing them. The reformers reasoned that firms owned by private investors would be subject to substantial pressures for reform. But many of the new owners were in fact the old Soviet-era administrators. Russians began to speak of "nomenklatura privatization" (or sometimes "piratization"), in which Soviet-era directors bought their enterprise with state approval, using insider knowledge and strategic positions. Other firms came under the control of "workers' cooperatives," which logically would not be especially accepting of the downsizing, layoffs, and pay cuts required by the new market environment.

Further, privatization does not even guarantee the presence of suitable market forces. Many of the Soviet Union's industries comprised of only a few enormous factories; about a third were absolute monopolies. Without domestic competition, these firms may be under little pressure to correct inefficiencies. Even foreign competition is blunted in some industries, as many firms continue to receive government "transfers" (subsidies) as a hedge against layoffs and worsening unemployment. The replacement of Prime Minister Gaidar with the more centrist Viktor Chernomyrdin, himself a former director of the Russian gas monopoly Gazprom, in 1992 helped to ensure the continuance of subsidies.

Privatization therefore could accomplish little without the collaboration of market forces. The results were predictable: Russia's inefficient auto industry, for example, continued to produce inferior vehicles. Firms that competed mostly against imports (such as those in television manufacturing) experienced substantial drops in production but did not undergo comparable levels of personnel layoffs. In fact, no firms at all were forced to close until late 1994, when Russia's Federal Bankruptcy Agency moved against several hundred bankrupt state enterprises. Although no firms were forced to close, the number of declared bankruptcies increased from 10 in 1993 to more than 1,000 in 1995.

After the conclusion of the voucher phase of privatization on June 30, 1994, Russia's State Property Committee, under the leadership of Chubais, continued to oversee the development of private assets. In January 1996 Yeltsin replaced Chubais with Aleksandr Kazakov. Although Yeltsin's forcing of Chubais's resignation was widely understood to be a concession to the resurgent conservative tide after the 1995 Duma elections, Kazakov had been a protégé of Chubais, and thus no strategic changes in privatization were forthcoming.

Kazakhov was replaced with Alfred Kokh after Yeltsin's reelection in the summer of 1996. Kokh, too, was considered a member of the Chubais team, and described himself as an economic "radical." The privatization program thus was expected to remain on track. Meanwhile, the government initiated a "cash" phase of privatization in the spring of 1995. In this phase, new shares are sold to raise investment funds and to bring in outside investors. Privatization sales were expected to raise 7.7 trillion rubles for the government in 1996. The final phase of privatization entailed mortgage auctions, also conducted by the State Property Committee.

Part II of the Russian Civil Code came into force March 1, 1996. Sometimes called the country's "economic constitution," this set of laws addresses obligations in purchases, sales, donations, leases, loans, credit, and contracts— but not land. Part III of the Civil Code, which was still being drafted in early 1996, covers industrial ownership, among other things.

Land

In addition to the privatization of industry, the new Russian leadership faced the issue of private land ownership. Stalin's collectivization of agriculture in the 1920s and 1930s spawned famines and otherwise damaged the Soviet Union's agricultural sector for decades. In some ways the country continues to suffer from the effects of collectivization. Endless reforms of the country's agricultural sector, including Khrushchev's ill-fated "virgin lands" program, could not surmount the inherent flaws of collectivization. Because of this experience, as well as historical injustices toward Russia's landless peasantry (such as the treatment of serfs in tsarist times), land reform remains an emotional issue in Russia. In 1993 it was taken up with some electoral success by the Agrarian Party.

The first significant moves toward the privatization of land began under Gorbachev, who in 1990 allowed the leasing of private plots. In Russia a 1991 Land Code provided for the breakup and privatization of kolkhozy and sovkhozy (collective and state farms). But numerous obstacles, including intragovernmental turmoil and local opposition, prevented more than modest progress. Conservative farm lobbies (a phenomenon for which the American reader might have an appreciation) in particular opposed the breakup of the collective farms. Responding to these groups, the Congress of People's Deputies in 1992 imposed a five-year ban on the resale of land. Other limitations on land sales were instituted, and as of 1995 all but about 10 percent of Russian agricultural land remained under the control of collective farms. Three-quarters of the privatized farms are grouped within the oblast (region) of Nizhny Novgorod, which grants its own credits to newly privatized farms.

Collective farms technically are owned by the workers, but in practice this has meant institutional control and bureaucratic administration, reminiscent of the Soviet period. After all, the Soviet state was also alleged to have been controlled by the "workers." The collective farms are considerably less efficient than truly private farms, a phenomenon illustrated in the 1970s when the government first allowed produce sales from small private plots. Since that time the equipment and soil quality at collective farms has declined further.

More recently, Yeltsin signed a 1996 decree "on the constitutional rights of the citizen to land," which further clarified ownership rights and governmental powers. In essence the decree provides for the sale, purchase, and mortgaging of private farmland, provided that the land remain under Russian ownership and in agricultural use. (Although more than 40 million Russians own farmland, until Yeltsin's decree ownership could be transferred only through inheritance.) The decree further required that collective farms be privatized by the end of 1996, this proved to be a wildly optimistic target. The Agrarian Party immediately called Yeltsin's decree unconstitutional and fought back with legislative proposals intended to prevent foreigners from owning land and to limit the resale of land. As of the spring of 1996, the Land Code under consideration by the Duma contradicted Yeltsin's decree (and possibly the Constitution as well) by its proscription of land sales. The Agrarian's Land Code became stalled in the Duma with little chance of passage after Yeltsin's reelection in July. Until the Land Code issue is resolved, much of Russia's Civil Code cannot be implemented.

Budget and Inflation

An especially difficult part of the reformers' task is to contain the inflation and other negative side effects that can result from price liberalization. If one accepts the logic of the Phillips Curve, which holds that a country's levels of unemployment and inflation vary inversely, the dilemma faced by the Russian leadership is especially clear. Russian conservatives, generally unburdened by the economists' logic, railed against the appearance of both inflation (for robbing the people of purchasing power) and unemployment (for robbing the people of a livelihood.) The reformers, by contrast, initially insisted upon budget austerity to keep inflation in check, even if that meant scaling back social guarantees and triggering widespread layoffs. In fact, many viewed short-term unemployment to be salubrious, as it would facilitate the movement of labor from inefficient industries into productive positions. About 6.6 million Russians were unemployed in the fall of 1996.

The freeing of prices in January 1992 triggered inflation rates as high as 38 percent per month (in February). Russia's bout with hyperinflation (up to an annualized rate of 2,000 percent) was halted by the end of the year, although inflation remained at unacceptably high levels. In 1994 the Russian Central Bank demonetized all pre-1993 currency in an effort to stabilize the ruble. Monthly rates soon dropped into the single digits. Annual inflation amounted to 300 percent in 1994 and 131 percent in 1995. In August 1996 the monthly inflation rate fell virtually to zero.

In Russia, maintaining budget austerity meant not only reining in discretionary spending, but it also meant allowing segments of the workforce to go without pay. In September 1996, Russia's total wage debt had reached 40 trillion rubles (about $7.3 billion). Unpaid wages triggered strikes at almost 9,000 enterprises in 1995 and over 3,500 enterprises in the first 9 months of 1996. Although the strikers put forth a number of grievances, most of the strikes were prompted by unpaid wages. The situation of Russia's coal mining industry illustrates the dilemma. Mine operators were unable to pay their miners because their customers, primarily power stations, were unable to pay for deliveries. The power stations' inability to pay stemmed largely from the inability of their own customers, including government and military installations, to pay their utility bills. Federal law prevented the power stations from shutting off service to certain classes of customers, and the federal government delayed or suspended promised subsidies to the power stations.

The coal miners at the bottom of this hierarchy simply were not paid for much of the winter of 1995–96. A two-day strike in February 1996 forced the government into settling the miners' wage arrears and committing a total of $600 million to the coal industry for the 1996 fiscal year. It was unclear how this money would be obtained, given that the federal budget already was stretched beyond available resources. But Yeltsin faced an election, and he could not help but recall the debilitating strikes by coal miners in the Kuzbass region during the Gorbachev era.

The issue of wage arrears continued to hound the Russian government. At the same time as the coal miners' walkout, 250,000 schoolteachers also went on strike, demanding that their own back wages be paid. Long delays in the distribution of pension checks and the payment of other private and public benefits also provoked public clambering for governmental action. (Pension arrears reached 17 trillion rubles, or $3 billion, in the fall of 1996.) Continuing his shift from budget austerity to political responsiveness as the presidential election moved closer, Yeltsin blamed the Finance Ministry for the nonpayment of state employees and released a series of decrees promising money to soldiers, students, pensioners, and others. Most of these decrees were understood to be election-season posturing, and there was no indication whence the funds for these payments would come. Wage arrears remained an issue for the rest of the year, with doctors, miners, scientists, air traffic controllers, military workers, and others staging strikes. Although prohibited by law from striking, workers at two of Russia's nine nuclear power stations went on strike to protest nonpayment of wages in October. That month the Duma passed a bill imposing financial penalties for late payment of wages and pensions. It was unclear how effective this would be.

Other demands on the federal budget in the mid-1990s further eroded any hope of budget austerity. Such dubious enterprises as the military operation in Chechnya, though off-budget, threatened the government's solvency. Another contentious issue concerned the creation of a tax system. The Communist leadership had eliminated the various income and other taxes in the 1930s. Governmental operations and programs were funded by impounding funds directly from payrolls. Because the state and the employer were one, this was an expeditious process. The leaders of post-Soviet Russia were faced with the task of creating a tax system that took into account the expansion of the private sector. It has not been an easy process. In November 1996 Federation Council Chairman Yegor Stroev complained that only 16 percent of Russian companies were paying their taxes regularly and in full.

Banking

In 1991 the Soviet Union had only seven banks. Since that time several thousand banks have been established, but they remain an uncertain prospect for Russian savers. The Russian banking industry is still in its infancy, and tales of fraud and inexplicably frozen accounts abound. Some estimates place the number of legitimate banks at only about 50. The government has taken steps toward regulating these banks—by imposing reserve requirements, for example—but enforcement remains weak. Bankers and other lenders are clearly nervous about the solvency of the system, and this has allowed rumors and minor economic fluctuations to escalate into major banking crises. This was illustrated on August 24, 1995, when Russia's 2,500 banks suddenly halted their lending to one another on the basis of local news reports about the unsoundness of Russian banks, and because of an announcement by the Central Bank about extending the "ruble corridor" against the dollar, thus allowing greater fluctuation. Depositors who rushed to withdraw their funds found their banks closed. The Central Bank defused the crisis the next day by pumping millions of rubles into the banking system, but the instability of the system was made clear to everyone.

For these and other reasons, many Russians generally distrust banks and prefer to keep their savings in the form of cash—literally hiding their money in the mattress. Frequently they convert their rubles into dollars as a hedge against inflation. In July 1993 the government created a near panic by suddenly canceling old ruble currency and insisting on the use of new bills, which nevertheless were the same denominations. In the fall of 1995 the total of money privately held as cash was estimated to be worth about $20 billion. This "ruble overhang" helped to create a liquidity crisis. The government attempted to entice these funds back into the economy by offering "household-friendly" savings bonds in the fall of 1995.

The availability of investment funds constitutes another important issue. A well-publicized scheme that bilked thousands of investors in Sergei Mavrody's "MMM" investment fund has served as a cautionary tale against other would-be investors. The Russian government has established a respectable track record in fulfilling its repayment obligations with earlier bond issues, which distinguishes it significantly from its Soviet predecessors. The government has also helped to establish a regulated mutual fund market under the Russian Securities and Exchange Commission in 1994. Even after losing his post as first deputy prime minister in early 1996, Anatoly Chubais remained the chairman of that commission. He continued to work toward the establishment of a mutual fund market and a new stock exchange. In mid-1996, the government was developing protections for bank depositors and investors, including a federal depositor insurance fund to compensate depositors at closed banks.

Viktor Gerashchenko headed Russia's Central Bank from 1992 until 1995, when he was replaced by Tatiana Paramonova. Gerashchenko displayed a weakness for providing cheap credit to state enterprises, resulting in inflation. In November 1995 the post was raised to the equivalent of a federal minister. As of April 1996 the Central Bank chairmanship was held by Sergei Dubinin. Yevgeny Yasin, who has been the country's economics minister since 1994, is highly respected and has been involved with most of Russia's economic reform since the Gorbachev era.

Foreign Influences

Russia's economic restructuring has not been the purview solely of domestic politics; representatives of the international economy have contributed expertise and guidelines as well. Indeed, to the extent that Russia seeks access to foreign capital and markets, it must meet the minimum requirements of the investors and institutions that provide them. The International Monetary Fund (IMF) is especially important in that regard. Once considered the international headquarters of America's economic domination, the IMF now is courted by Russia for its loans. As it does with other borrowers, the IMF imposes certain conditions upon the Russian government. These conditions have generally concerned the reduction of government transfers, the continuation of budget austerity, and the reduction of tariffs. On the basis of Moscow's assurances in these areas, the IMF approved a record $10 billion, three-year "Extended Facility" loan to Russia in 1996.

The success of Moscow's application for membership in the World Trade Organization (formerly the General Agreement on Tariffs and Trade) requires further trade liberalization. And Moscow's desire to join the Organization for Economic Cooperation and Development (to which it applied in 1996) could be met only with even more drastic changes; it is unlikely that Russia soon will be invited to join. In addition, individual countries have conditioned Russian access to their markets upon a demonstrated commitment to human rights and democracy. Foreign markets have been crucial and lucrative for Russia. Production of Russian consumer goods dropped by half between 1991 and 1995, suggesting a potential rise in imports. Yet in 1996 Russia ran a foreign trade surplus worth $40 billion. (The majority of Russia's trade growth is with the other CIS states.) Russia has also sold treasury bills to international investors to cover its budget deficits. In 1995 receipts from these sales amounted to 1.4 percent of Russia's GDP. Russia also launched its first Eurobond issue in November 1996.

On the one hand, budgetary, fiscal, and other conditions imposed by the IMF and the United States provided the Russian government with the incentive and even justification for maintaining economic discipline. On the other hand, however, the economic conditions imposed by the West gave Yeltsin's foes an issue for opposing economic reform and international cooperation. The Communists and Agrarians in particular painted the West's loan conditions as a violation of Russia's sovereignty. Communist Aman Tuleev used the issue in his 1996 presidential campaign, claiming that the Yeltsin administration had made a secret agreement with the World Bank to close down most Russian coal mines in return for a $500 million loan. Similarly, CPRF presidential candidate Gennady Zyuganov described IMF officials as "agents ruling Russia like Hitler's gauleiters."

The Backlash

Russians exhibit a general appreciation for market principles. A survey in 1992 found that about half the urban population accepted that individuals are responsible for the welfare of their families, and two-thirds believed that entrepreneurs can run enterprises more efficiently than the state. Russians accepted an element of risk in day-to-day living. But accepting principles in the abstract is different from accepting the reality of their results. So when privatization and price liberalization brought unemployment and inflation, Russians began to revise their attitudes about the market. In the years after Russian independence, the general population grew increasingly resentful of particular aspects of economic restructuring.

This resentment has been manifested in a variety of ways, from private complaints and letters to the editor, to the increased support for the government's political opposition. As the 1996 presidential elections drew near, the government's commitment to tough economic measures slackened. The conservative opposition, sensing a potent campaign issue, put economic restructuring on trial. For example, in early 1996 the resurgent Communist Party used its strength in the newly elected Duma to launch inquiries into the government's privatization program. Even Yuri Skuratov, Russia's prosecutor-general, announced that his office would investigate allegations of illegality in the privatization program. Investigations were launched into certain cases in which the winning auction bids for natural-resource enterprises were cast by the banks conducting the auctions. Other tribunals ferreted out allegations of insider tips and arrangements.

Rather than address these attacks head-on, Yeltsin gradually distanced himself from the reformers, either firing or coercing the resignations of economic advisers Chubais, Gaidar, and Fyodorov. The future of Russia's economic restructuring came to hang between the Scylla of Yeltsin's tactical retrenchment and the Charybdis of Yeltsin's replacement by a neo-Communist president. Yeltsin's reelection in July 1996 provided some hope that his fresh electoral mandate would permit a recommitment to economic reform.

Suggested Readings

Åslund, Anders. *How Russia Became a Market Economy*. Washington, D.C.: The Brookings Institution Press, 1995.

Frydman, Roman, et al. *The Privatization Process in Russia, Ukraine and the Baltic States*. New York: Central European University Press, 1993.

Goldman, Marshall I. *Lost Opportunity: Why Economic Reforms in Russia Have Not Worked*. New York: W. W. Norton, 1994.

Isham, Heywood, ed. *Remaking Russia*. Armonk, N.Y.: M. E. Sharpe, 1995.

Jones, Anthony, ed. *Education and Society in the New Russia*. Armonk, NY: M. E. Sharpe, 1994.

Nelson, Lynn D., and Irina Y. Kuzes. *Radical Reform in Yeltsin's Russia: Political, Economic, and Social Dimensions*. Armonk, N.Y.: M. E. Sharpe, 1995.

Slater, Wendy. "Female Representation in Russian Politics," *RFE/RL Research Report* 3:22 (June 3, 1994): 27–33.

White, Stephen. *Russia Goes Dry: Alcohol, State and Society*. Cambridge (UK): Cambridge University Press, 1996.

9

Ethnicity and Federalism

The centripetal forces that helped dissolve the Soviet bloc and the Soviet Union itself continue to play themselves out in the former Soviet republics. The spectre of ethnonational unrest that lurked behind the bloodstained curtain of socialist fraternity now even more persistently haunts the Soviet Union's successor states. No issue cuts more directly to the very essence of Russia as a state and a nation; as a state, the Russian Federation requires political cohesion. As a people, Russians require a national identity. Both exigencies are complicated by the presence of ethnonational minorities with a desire for self-determination. How the government approaches these issues will determine the face of Russia at the opening of the new millennium.

The Prisonhouse of Nations

The tsars assembled their empire with sporadic annexations of contiguous lands—a process constitutionally distinct from the other European powers' acquisition of overseas colonies. And unlike other multinational European empires, namely the Austro-Hungarian, the Russian empire maintained authoritarian control over its disparate peoples: Lithuanians, Crimean Tatars, Ural Cossacks, and numerous others. Even semantic distinctions were telling; the tsar possessed authority over "all the Russias," rather than over the multinational peoples of the empire. Yet despite St. Petersburg's periodic attempts at Russification, the Russian state even in the nineteenth century was limited in its power to co-opt the national identity of its non-Russian subjects.

The Bolsheviks approached the Russian empire's multinational character with a new ideological perspective when they wrested control from the monarchy in 1917. Marxist doctrine saw national groups as a manifestation of bourgeois manipulation. Indeed, in Marxist writings the term "nationalism" was almost invariably preceded by the adjective "bourgeois." Marxism used class consciousness as an antidote to the false consciousness of national identity. And with the final triumph of the proletarian dictatorship that the Bolsheviks had putatively wrought, even class differences would disappear and the Communist rapture would commence.

Historians continue to debate how much of their Marxist rhetoric the Bolsheviks actually believed. Certainly Lenin thought the Russification policies of Aleksandr III and Nicholas II in the late nineteenth century were morally repugnant tools of imperial control. (This particular evaluation of Lenin's has evoked uncharacteristically few objections in the West.) And after seizing power, the Bolsheviks cut loose the Ukraine, Belorussia, the Baltic states, and other countries that had been forcibly joined to the Russian empire centuries earlier. But once the new regime's power stabilized, the Party maintained an ambiguous, even schizophrenic policy toward its disparate nationalities, summed up in the phrase "national in form, socialist in content."

As observed in Chapter 2, Moscow in the 1920s terminated the short-lived independence of the recently liberated states. But each of the 15 "titular nationalities" of the Soviet Union were accorded formal autonomy within their respective union republics. In addition, several union republics (notably the Russian Soviet Federative Socialist Republic) themselves contained "autonomous" areas that served as homelands for distinct national groups. Illustrative both of this institution's potent symbolism and political meaninglessness was the Jewish Autonomous Republic of Birobidzhan. Although it nominally provided a refuge for Jews, the republic was located in the barest reaches of Siberia, strictly controlled as part of a sensitive military zone along the Chinese border and overwhelmingly populated by non-Jews. Further, although Yiddish was deemed an "official language" of the republic, the authorities in Moscow banned Yiddish-language books as part of the 1949 decree prohibiting the teaching of Yiddish. Stalin's "anti-cosmopolitan" campaign during this time sent many Yiddish actors and writers to the Gulag. Analogous conditions were imposed on the RSFSR's other ethnic republics.

At the same time, the state worked methodically toward the objective of diluting ethnonational identities. Under the aegis of Marxian class identity, the regime sought to create a "new Soviet man"—a nonnational (or perhaps transnational) "Soviet" identity. The USSR's citizens were to become the vanguard of a new type of society, unburdened by the disunity of national, class, and religious cleavages. In many respects, however, the regime's understanding of "Soviet" bore a canny resemblance of Russianism.

Neither the attempts to placate national groups through limited self-government nor the attempts to assimilate them into a greater Soviet identity were ultimately successful. But the sheer strength of the Soviet regime did generally contain the "nationalities problem" for most of the twentieth century. This might be seen as part of a larger phenomenon, whereby totalitarian and often Communist regimes managed to assuage, but not eliminate, national animosities in Yugoslavia, in Czechoslovakia, and elsewhere.

We have already observed (in Chapter 3) how nationalism contributed to the ultimate demise of the USSR. The disaggregation of the union was facilitated by the very administrative segmentation that had been intended to defuse separatist tendencies. The nationalists effectively cut along the dotted lines that were their administrative borders. All the more troubling, therefore, that the map of the post-Soviet Russian Federation is criss-crossed with a spiderweb of dotted lines. Of course, in itself the presence of administrative divisions is not necessarily fatal; many of the 89 territorial divisions contain overwhelmingly Russian populations and serve as mere administrative districts. Still, a score of autonomous republics contain substantial non-Russian populations, and a few—including Chechnya—claim independence from Moscow. With almost one in five Russian citizens claiming non-Russian ethnic background, post-Soviet Russia must contend with the complicated ethnonational legacy of the tsars and the Soviets.

Federalism

As its name implies, the Russian Federation continues the use of federative structures that were officially characteristic of the Russian Soviet Federative Socialist Republic. The RSFSR was only partly a federal entity; theoretically, the Russian government in Moscow shared sovereign powers with the governments of 31 regions: 16 Autonomous Soviet Socialist Republics (ASSRs), five autonomous oblasts,[1] and 10 autonomous okrugs (districts). This theoretical autonomy was of course tempered by the universal control wielded by the Party. The 57 other regions, however, were not granted even that hollow

---

1. "Oblast" is usually translated as "region." However, throughout this book the English word "region" is used generically to apply to any of Russia's 89 administrative divisions. References to oblasts as a specific type of administrative division utilize the Russian word.

autonomy and were formally and fully subordinate to Moscow. Even on paper, therefore, the RSFSR was a hybrid of federal and unity systems.

After achieving independence from the Soviet Union, Russia underwent several changes to its quasi-federal governmental structures. For a time the idea of consolidating the various administrative regions of Russia into eight or 10 provinces was discussed, but it never moved beyond the conceptual stage. Meanwhile, on July 3, 1991, four of Russia's five autonomous oblasts were elevated to the status of "republic," from which the presumably redundant adjective "autonomous" had been dropped the previous December. (The Jewish Autonomous Oblast of Birobidzhan was not granted republican status.)

The sense of crisis and vulnerability that was compounded by the August 1991 coup attempt prompted the Russian Congress of Peoples Deputies to grant Boris Yeltsin new powers regarding the regions. "Presidential representatives," appointed by Yeltsin, were deployed to the regions as emissaries of Moscow. Elections in the nonautonomous regions were postponed for a year, with Yeltsin directly appointing regional governors in the interim. The (autonomous) republics, however, were permitted to elect their own leaders.

But Moscow's decrees were not accepted with equanimity in all the regions. Throughout the process of Russian independence, various okruga (districts), kraya (areas), and oblasti (regions) were also declaring some measure of their own autonomy. Then, on June 4, 1992, the Chechen-Ingush Republic was divided along its hyphen. When the smoke (temporarily) cleared at the end of 1992, Russia comprised 89 distinct administrative areas, of which 21 were republics (see Figure 9–1).

The relationship between the federal and republican governments—"center" and "periphery," in political scientists' vernacular—was once again reconstituted through the Federation Treaty, signed on March 31, 1992. Only two republics did not sign it. One of these, Chechnya-Ingushetia maintained that it was an independent country (or rather, two independent countries), and eventually (as Chechnya) became embroiled in a war with Moscow over the definition of independence. The other republic refusing to sign the Federation Treaty, Tatarstan, signed a bilateral treaty with Moscow in 1994 that effectively bound it to the Russian state. In this case one of Yeltsin's populist statements from the heady days of accelerating independence had come back to haunt him. In August 1990 he told an audience in Tatarstan to "take as much freedom as you can swallow." They did.

The Federation Treaty was incorporated as a new part of the heavily amended 1978 Constitution of the RSFSR. It was in some ways analogous to the aborted new Union Treaty between the Soviet republics and Moscow, which had been proposed by Gorbachev in 1991. The Union Treaty proclaimed that "each republic . . . is a sovereign state." This principle may well have been what precipitated the August 1991 coup. The 1992 Federation Treaty also outlined a shared sovereignty agreement between the center and

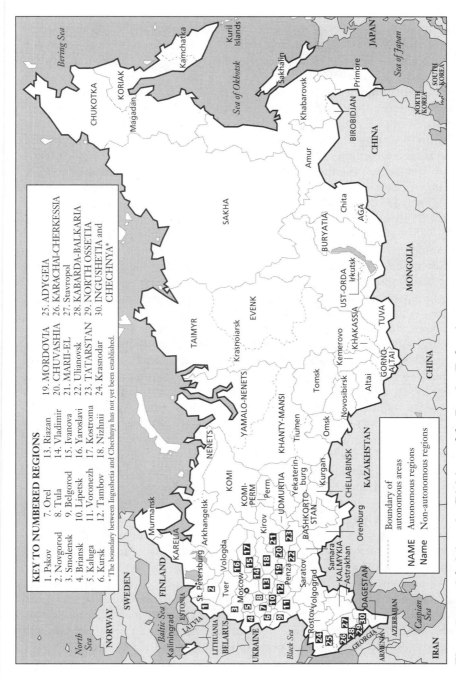

KEY TO NUMBERED REGIONS

1. Pskov	7. Orel	13. Riazan	19. MORDOVIA
2. Novgorod	8. Tula	14. Vladimir	20. CHUVASHIA
3. Smolensk	9. Belgorod	15. Ivanova	21. MARII-EL
4. Briansk	10. Lipetsk	16. Yaroslavi	22. Ulianovsk
5. Kaluga	11. Voronezh	17. Kostroma	23. TATARSTAN
6. Kursk	12. Tambov	18. Nizhnii	24. Krasnodar

25. ADYGEIA
26. KARACHAI-CHERKESSIA
27. Stavropol
28. KABARDA-BALKARIA
29. NORTH OSSETIA
30. INGUSHETIA and CHECHNYA*

* The boundary between Ingushetia and Chechnya has not yet been established.

Boundary of autonomous areas

NAME Autonomous regions

Name Non-autonomous regions

Figure 9–1   Administrative Divisions of the Russian Federation

143

the republics. The treaty delineated specific powers for the federal government, such as finance, protecting national minorities, and providing for the country's defense. The treaty also specified areas of joint jurisdiction between the federal government and the republics, including educational issues and the protection of human and civil rights. Finally, it declared the republics to "possess full state power on their territory, except for those powers that have been transferred to the jurisdiction of the federal bodies" (Article III.1). In a controversial section that foreshadowed the Chechen crisis, the treaty permitted the federal government to impose a state of emergency on a republic's territory without the republic's consent for the purpose of "stopping large-scale disturbances accompanied by violence" (Article III.4). This section in particular spurred Chechnya's and Tatarstan's refusal to sign the treaty.

The constitutional crisis between President Yeltsin and the parliament in the fall of 1993 provided an opening for a shift in center-periphery relations. Many of the regional governments took sides in the crisis, with regional executives (most appointed by Yeltsin) tending to support the president and with regional legislators (many holdovers from the Soviet-era government) showing sympathy for the parliament. After Yeltsin prevailed in his confrontation with the parliament, he decreed the nonautonomous regional legislatures dissolved. Their powers were temporarily transferred to the executives.

Russia's federative structure was refounded with the adoption of the Yeltsin Constitution in December 1993. The main provisions of the Federation Treaty were carried over with minor variations. A significant addition was a supremacy clause (Article 4), which proclaimed the priority of the federal Constitution and federal laws throughout the federation (Article VI.2). The gridlock that had derived from the "war of laws" between Moscow and the Soviet republics in the late Gorbachev period underscored the need for such a provision. (The Federation Treaty had simply referred interbranch disputes to the Constitutional Court.) Concessions to the nationalities were also included in the Yeltsin Constitution. Article 26, for example, guarantees to each individual a right to "determine and indicate his nationality"—a provision in direct contrast to the widely despised Soviet policy whereby a person's nationality was determined by the state and officially recorded on internal passports, among other places. Similarly, the new constitution guarantees the right to use one's native language.

Unlike the Federation Treaty and the aborted new Union Treaty, the Yeltsin Constitution does not rely on the voluntary accession of the country's component units. The constitutional referendum failed in 17 regions, eight of which were republics. Yet all 21 republics and 67 subrepublic regions are incorporated by name into the constitution (Article 65). The document makes no provision for secession—a right that had been afforded by the Federation Treaty. Still, the allocation of power between Moscow and the regions was very fluid at the time of the constitution's adoption. Some regions, such as

Primorsk krai, subsequently threatened to withhold taxes unless Moscow met its alleged obligations in other areas (such as making good on debts to the regions).

Even after the adoption of the Yeltsin Constitution in December 1993, various efforts have been undertaken to finesse the nationalities issue. At the end of 1995 the Nationalities Ministry prepared a "regional policy document" that would address the power relationship between Moscow and the nonautonomous regions. (In this sense it addressed the "nonfederative" parts of the Russian Federation.) The regional policy document nevertheless was rejected by First Deputy Prime Minister Oleg Soskovets a week after the December 17 parliamentary elections.

While a comprehensive regional policy document remained elusive, the federal government secured bilateral agreements with many of Russia's regional governments. In the winter of 1995–96, for example, Moscow signed power-sharing agreements with Krasnodar krai, the Komi republic, and the oblasts of Orenburg, Sverdlovsk (Ekaterinburg), and Kaliningrad. These treaties concerned such areas as economic and agricultural policy, trade, conversion of defense industries, control of natural resources, and foreign relations. Yeltsin also issued a decree on March 12 establishing the outlines for further power-sharing agreements between Moscow and regional authorities. Although his decree reiterated the supremacy of the federal constitution, it suggested that regions might be afforded greater latitude in policy-making. Within a few more months, Moscow had secured power-sharing agreements with more than two dozen regions. The Yeltsin government expressed its intention of eventually securing similar agreements with all 89 regions.

The Chechen Conflict

Chechnya's latest independence drive, which began shortly after Russian independence, illustrates the nightmare scenario concerning the interaction of ethnicity and federalism. Located along Russia's border with Georgia in the Caucasus mountains, Chechnya demonstrates the secessionist potential of peripheral republics in post-Soviet Russia. The Chechens trace their roots on this territory back 5,000 years—millennia before the Russians. From the time Ivan the Terrible extended Russian influence to the region in the sixteenth century, the Chechen people have resisted Russian rule. A costly and bloody 25-year war in the early nineteenth century subdued the Chechens, but mutual animosities remained.

The Soviet nationalities policy afforded the Chechens their own Chechen Autonomous Oblast in 1922. In 1934 the oblast was merged with the Ingush Autonomous Republic, whose titular nationality is ethnically similar to the Chechens. In 1936 the Chechen-Ingush region was granted the status of an autonomous republic. But Stalin, sensing Chechen disloyalty and betrayal in 1944, deported its half-million inhabitants to Central Asia. Only after Stalin's death in 1953 was the Chechen-Ingush republic restored and its titular peoples permitted to return.

Like the Tatars, the Chechens viewed the demise of the Soviet Union as an opportunity for liberation from Russia. A former Soviet Air Force general of Chechen blood, Dzokhar Dudaev, staged a coup and proclaimed Chechnya's independence on September 6, 1991—two weeks after the end of the attempted coup against Gorbachev. Neither the Russian government nor the West recognized Chechnya's independence, but the absence of international support did not dissuade Dudaev from taking provocative measures. In November 1991 he had himself elected president of the Republic of Chechnya in suspect elections and set about the business of creating a government. It will be recalled that the Russian parliament formalized the split of Chechnya-Ingushetia into separate Chechen and Ingush republics in 1992. But these new republics were meant to be autonomous, not sovereign. Thus Dudaev's concept of the Republic of Chechnya and Moscow's concept of the Chechen Republic differed on the degree of independence.

Chechnya functioned as a base for the Russian *mafiya* (see Chapter 10) and cooperated with other rebel groups in the region through the Confederation of Caucasus Nations (founded shortly after Chechnya's declaration of independence). The regime set up by Dudaev was understood to be exceedingly corrupt, and Chechnya became overrun with criminal gangs. For this Dudaev did not enjoy any significant degree of widespread popular support in his self-proclaimed country. Adding to the problems Chechnya caused for Moscow was the presence of three Russian oil and gas pipelines running through Chechen territory.

Events came to a head in the fall of 1994. In August Chechnya's newly established Provisional Council challenged Dudaev's rule. Umar Avturkhanov, the head of the council, claimed to be Chechnya's true leader. Dudaev dismissed the council as a puppet of Moscow. Chechnya's outlaw status grew as it became a center for counterfeiting, theft of pipeline oil, and bandit attacks on passing trains and other vehicles.

Finally, after months of speculation, Moscow launched a full-scale military attack against Dudaev's regime. Then–defense minister Pavel Grachev is widely perceived to have convinced Yeltsin of the need for the invasion. In an illustration of the hubris that frequently accompanies Russian military ventures, Grachev predicted that two paratroop regiments could pacify the Chechens in Grozny, the Chechen capital, within three hours.

Three hours, three months, and then a year passed, and Dudaev was still not defeated. Entire cities were destroyed and tens of thousands of people—Russian and Chechen, civilians and soldiers—were killed. (As many as 30,000 deaths were estimated to have been caused in the first year.) International and domestic criticism of Moscow's military operation mounted, earning Yeltsin's advisers and some government ministers the collective epithet "party of war." The operation also drained scarce resources. In 1995 alone Russia spent 6 trillion rubles (over $1 billion) on reconstruction in Chechnya, in addition to military outlays. Tentative abatement of the fighting brought occasional signs of hope and then disappointment. Federal forces managed to secure the Presidential Palace in Grozny in early 1995, but Dudaev had gone into hiding and guerrillas had taken up positions in the hills.

Chechen rebels in June 1995 seized hostages from a hospital in the southern Russian town of Budyonnovsk. Yeltsin was out of the country, and Prime Minister Viktor Chernomyrdin negotiated the release of the hostages, but only after a failed rescue attempt resulted in 140 deaths. Meanwhile the Organization for Security and Cooperation in Europe (OSCE) brokered talks between Moscow and Dudaev's regime. The OSCE attempted to secure Russian withdrawal and rebel disarmament through mutual concessions on the issue of Chechen independence. A cease-fire was implemented at the end of July 1995, but the settlement was widely ignored. Moscow was to withdraw troops and the Chechen rebels were to surrender their weapons, but disagreements over timing and charges of cheating prevented the fulfillment of these agreements. The cease-fire collapsed on December 14, 1995, when Chechens seized the Chechen town of Gudermes, about 40 kilometers east of Grozny.

Elections

The rebel action at Gudermes came three days before elections were to be held in Chechnya. Chechnya was to elect its representatives to the Russian parliament on December 17, along with the rest of the country. In addition, Moscow had arranged for the Chechen republic to elect its own president. Dudaev boycotted the elections, arguing somewhat convincingly that Russian occupation of the republic made free elections impossible. The republic's presidential election nevertheless took place as scheduled, although it was conducted only in those parts of the republic under Russian control. With Dudaev not participating, the election pitted Doku Zavgaev, who had served as the Soviet-era head of the Chechen Supreme Soviet and was subsequently appointed by Yeltsin governor of Chechnya, against Ruslan Khasbulatov, the ethnic Chechen who had been forcibly relieved of control of the Russian Supreme Soviet in the fall of 1993 (see Chapter 7). Zavgaev won handily.

Although Zavgaev could be considered a loyalist to Moscow, his powers within Chechnya were severely limited. The mere election of Zavgaev as president could not return Chechnya to the Russian fold, and the conflict wore on. Chechen rebels maintained bases in the countryside and continued to clash with Russian soldiers at checkpoints and around the perimeter of cities. A second hostage-taking in early 1996 underscored the determination of the

Chechen rebels and provoked the fury of the Russian government and military forces. This time, the Chechens took about 3,000 hostages in the town of Kizlyar (in the neighboring republic of Dagestan). Moscow negotiated their release, but apparent duplicity by both sides resulted in new hostages being seized in the village of Pervomaiskoe just across the Chechen border. At the same time, Chechen, Turkish, and Georgian supporters of Chechen independence seized a Turkish ferry on the Black Sea and threatened to kill the passengers. Confusion reigned, and in the end the ferry was released. Surviving hostages in Pervomaiskoe were also released, although the lives of 150 Chechens, 26 Russian soldiers, and an unknown number of hostages were lost. The town itself was flattened by Russian bombs.

Resolutions?

Prospects for a stable resolution to the Chechen conflict were bleak in the winter of 1996. Not only had Russia's bombing of Chechen civilians fostered widespread hatred against Moscow, but Yeltsin had also strengthened the hard-line elements of his administration with the appointment of Nikolai Yegorov as chief of staff in early 1996. Yegorov was considered an instigator of the original invasion of Chechnya in December 1994. Meanwhile, Chechen rebels renewed their efforts to wrest back Grozny from Russian troops in March 1996 with occasional successes and widespread Russian deaths. And although Russian citizens supported in the abstract efforts to maintain the country's territorial integrity, they increasingly opposed Yeltsin's use of force against the Chechens. Moscow's military actions earned the opprobrium of human rights advocates within Russia (including former Human Rights Commissioner Sergei Kovalev), as well as foreign governments (including the United States).

Then, on March 31, 1996, with presidential elections about 10 weeks away, Yeltsin announced a new plan to bring the Chechen war to a close. He promised a unilateral cease-fire and a phased withdrawal of Russian troops, and he called for the Duma to grant amnesty to the Chechen rebels. He also called for new Chechen parliamentary elections, given the dispute over those held in 1995. He indicated that, if negotiations went as he hoped they would, Chechnya could be granted a greater degree of autonomy than any other federal subject. Such a promise could not help but raise the expectations for other republics. But there were indications that once again Yeltsin's promises were hollow. Yeltsin maintained that the federal government would continue to battle "terrorism" in Chechnya, thus leaving the door open for further government fighting. And he stipulated that the proposed amnesty should exclude those "guilty of grave crimes."

In the following weeks, the federal government repeatedly violated its own unilateral cease-fire, and Chechen rebels showed little intention of accepting

Yeltsin's peace plan. An ambush on April 16 killed scores of Russian troops. Then the fundamentals of the conflict changed overnight with the killing of Dudaev in a rocket attack on April 21. Chechen Vice President Zelimkhan Yandarbiev assumed the Chechen presidency. A cease-fire agreement was signed between Chernomyrdin and Yandarbiev on May 27. And with Yandarbiev still in Moscow (perhaps as a de facto hostage), Yeltsin flew to Grozny for a photo opportunity as a peacemaker. Yet the cease-fire, which went into effect May 31, was violated almost immediately by the Chechens. The conflict resumed yet again.

The most dramatic breakthrough concerning the Chechnya crisis to date was facilitated by Yeltsin's August 1996 appointment of former General Aleksandr Lebed as the presidential representative in Chechnya. Lebed had been a frequent critic of the government's policy toward Chechnya, and within hours after his appointment he traveled to the republic to negotiate a settlement. Within three weeks Lebed and Chechen chief of staff Aslan Maskhadov signed an agreement which called for the withdrawal of Russian troops by October 20, the deferral of the question of Chechnya's independence for five years, and the creation of a joint commission to coordinate reconstruction of the republic. Lebed declared an end to the Chechen war.

Renewed fighting nevertheless erupted in mid-September. On October 19, the day before Russian troops were to be fully withdrawn from Chechnya, Yeltsin replaced Lebed with former Duma speaker Ivan Rybkin. The withdrawal of Russian troops was halted. Rybkin met with Chechen leaders in an attempt to resolve a range of issues, including reconstruction, the exchange of prisoners of war, and the pullout of Russian troops. The Russian troop pullout was finally completed on December 28, 1996. But the larger factor for the outcome of the conflict hinged on presidential and parliamentary elections in the republic, which were held on January 27, 1997. Maskhadov defeated Dudaev's successor, Zelimkhan Yandarbiev, and several other candidates for the post of president. OSCE observers declared the elections to be "legitimate and democratic." Although Moscow clearly viewed Maskhadov as a moderate Chechen leader with whom it could conduct constructive negotiations, Maskhadov continued to press for Chechnya's "independence," and there were indications that Yandarbiev's supporters and other Chechen factions might work to undermine Maskhadov's government.

Evaluation

The parallels between Chechnya's independence efforts and those of Russia are uncomfortable for the Yeltsin government. Moscow must balance the principle of self-determination, which it adopted in 1990 and which is supported in the 1993 Constitution, with the need to preserve the territorial integrity of the state. Some fear that the precedent of one secession would unleash other efforts—if not to secede outright, then to gain still greater autonomy. The Chechen debacle also illustrates the problems burdening the Russian military. Its poor performance against a relatively small group of rebels on Russian soil hardly lived up to the Red Army's reputation, which once inspired fear in an entire hemisphere.

Partly the army's poor performance reflected its poor resources (see Chapter 12). But also it may illustrate the limits of Russia's military power. While the military was able to secure major cities (such as Grozny) at high cost, it was unable to subdue the countryside. Rebels continued to attack Russian soldiers at remote outposts, and ethnic Russian civilians living in Chechnya became increasingly nervous. The lessons of Afghanistan might therefore be applicable to Chechnya, especially given the religious differences between Russians and Chechens. But as a part of Russia, Chechnya provides another lesson. It was Yeltsin who, in the midst of the Soviet right wing's efforts to forcibly prevent the Baltic republics from seceding, called on Russian soldiers not to use force against their own countrymen. This is precisely what happened in Chechnya. The loss of life, the low morale of the Russian soldiers, their all-night drinking, the lack of coordination between the Kremlin and the Defense Ministry and the field commanders—Chechnya is an expensive and distracting problem that Russia can ill afford.

Other Regional Trouble Spots

Although the level of center-periphery conflict in Chechnya is unique within Russia, ethnonational disputes plague other regions of the country as well. For example, conflict among the national groups within the Caucasus republic of North Ossetia has prompted military intervention by Moscow. Ethnic Ossetians comprise more than half of North Ossetia's population of 643,000. Another 30 percent are Russian, and 8 percent are Ingush. The Ingush historically had constituted a much larger proportion of the population, but Stalin accused them of wartime collaboration with the Nazis and deported the entire Ingush population to Kazakhstan. The collapse of the Soviet Union triggered a mass return of the Ingush to North Ossetia, which exacerbated conflict with the republic's Ossetians. The Ossetians opposed the Ingush's claims to property they held at the time of their deportation, but ethnic differences added to the friction. Sporadic fighting resulted in hundreds of deaths. Yeltsin imposed military rule and sent in Russian troops to control the conflict in November 1992.

Although the North Ossetian–Ingush conflict has not reached Chechen proportions, North Ossetia is further embroiled in a dispute with the former Soviet republic of Georgia, which is home to South Ossetia. The territory of North and South Ossetia together roughly corresponds to the historic kingdom of Ossetia, which had been incorporated into Russia in 1774. The Bolsheviks divided it into its northern and southern components in 1922 in an effort to dilute Georgian nationalism. After Georgia declared independence in 1990, the South Ossetians sought to secede from Georgia and unite with North Ossetia. A January 1992 referendum in South Ossetia revealed overwhelming support for unification. But like Russia with Chechnya, Georgia fought to prevent South Ossetia from seceding. And as it did with North Ossetia, Moscow has sent peacekeeping troops to South Ossetia.

The prospect of foreign regions trying to unite with Russia on the basis of their ethnic populations also applies to northern Kazakhstan, once part of the Soviet Union. Kazakhstan's government has even moved its capital northward, from Almaty to Akmola, to maintain greater vigilance over the territory, into which the Soviet government had once moved Russian farmers as part of Khrushchev's "virgin lands" campaign.

Although it is not constituted as an ethnic region, the oblast of Kaliningrad deserves special mention. Moscow seized this territory, which had been part of East Prussia, from Germany at the end of the Second World War. Sandwiched between Poland and Lithuania, Kaliningrad is not contiguous with the rest of the Russian Federation. Its discontiguousness was of little consequence when it was physically linked to Russia by Soviet territory. But after Lithuania's independence, Kaliningrad was physically cut free of the rest of Russia. Although the population remains overwhelmingly Russian, an increasing number of ethnic Germans have been resettling in this enclave, still known to Germans as Königsberg.

There have been some half-hearted calls for Kaliningrad's independence. But Russia has adamantly rejected such proposals, insisting in the words of former Foreign Minister Andrei Kozyrev that Kaliningrad is an "indivisible and undisputed part of Russia." Partly this has been a matter of pride for Russia, but Moscow has also jealously clung to the strategic value of the enclave, home to a sizable Russian military force. (Yeltsin indicated in 1996 that Russia will "strengthen" its military base in Kaliningrad.) With access to the Baltic Sea, Kaliningrad also facilitates Russian trade. But its location is something of a two-edged sword; Lithuania has also sought to exploit the enclave's location by demanding transportation payments for goods moving across Lithuanian territory.

Prospects

Five years after the collapse of the Soviet Union, the Russian Federation has failed to arrest the nationalist centrifugal forces that were partly responsible for Russia's independence in the first place. Russia's quasi-federal nature has placated some groups, but for others it has merely provided a basis for confrontational autonomy claims and independence drives. In all, the United Nations High Commission on Refugees has counted 164 ethnicity-based territorial disputes on the territory of the former Soviet Union.

The fundamental problem is that Russia is a multinational state without a tradition of civil societal relations. It was held together only by totalitarian power. The same forces that in the long term might be expected to create a civil society—increased communication, efficient transportation, integrated trade—in the short run are creating conflict. Just as Lenin in power had to scale back the revolutionary call for "all power to the Soviets!" Yeltsin has found it necessary to backpedal on his encouragement of national self-determination.

It is unrealistic to expect that resettlement—either voluntary or forced—will end regional conflicts. Indeed, the case of North Ossetia shows how resettlement can exacerbate interethnic frictions. Assimilation is also unlikely to occur quickly enough to significantly ease these conflicts in the medium term. Yet neither are secessionist efforts likely to succeed. Although the principle of self-determination might legitimately be invoked by various peoples within Russia, moral justification does not ensure practical success. The multinational makeup of most republics' populations would continue to threaten their own territorial integrity. As with North Ossetia, it is difficult to establish how far the progressive disintegration of territorial states should be permitted to proceed. Invoking claims of national self-determination risks tacitly endorsing similar claims by subnational groups.

This is not only a normative matter of identifying and evaluating competing claims of ethnonational self-determination within Russia's impossibly tangled population (a task complicated by the Soviets' efforts to divide the population against itself and by Stalin's deportation policies). In addition, there are practical considerations about the minimum size of a viable state. Most of Russia's would-be nation-states lack the wherewithal to survive independently the harsh and threatening environment faced by sovereign entities. A sovereign state must be able to sustain a domestic economy, provide for its own defense, maintain healthy trading relationships, and so forth. Few of Russia's ethnonational regions are capable of this. And aside from a few peripheral republics (such as Chechnya), most of Russia's ethnic concentrations are surrounded by Russians on Russian territory. It would be difficult for any of these to exist as states landlocked within Russia.

No simple answer to this puzzle is forthcoming. The political and demographic sins of the country's tsarist and Soviet past haunt modern Russia. Preserving the country's territorial integrity while dismantling the Communist Party's centralized structures makes for a difficult prescription, as the tasks that compose it work at cross purposes, at least in the short run.

The last part of Russia's ethnonational puzzle concerns Russian nationalism itself. Twenty-five million ethnic Russians live beyond the country's borders, creating a pretext for Russia's intervention in the Near Abroad. The alleged mistreatment of Russian minorities abroad has provided a potent issue for Russian nationalists who decry Gorbachev's poor stewardship of the Soviet Union and Yeltsin's purported selling out to the West. By a similar logic, Russian nationalists argue that Russian minorities in "ethnic" republics on Russian territory require special protection. As evidence of the urgency of their cause, they point to the hostage-takings at the hands of the Chechens in 1995–96. Those of the conservative nationalists who opposed the breakup of the Soviet Union can hardly be expected to take lightly any territorial concessions by the Russian Federation. Caught between ethnonational minorities demanding protections (often in the form of greater autonomy) and Russian nationalists insisting upon greater state cohesion, the government's options are not enviable.

Perhaps the most critical balms for Russia's ethnonational unrest are economic prosperity and political stability—both of which are in precious short supply. Ultranationalism feeds on discontent and wounded pride. Liberal pluralism can take root only where there is a reasonable expectation that one's individual needs can be satisfied under the aegis of existing governmental and societal institutions. When this confidence is finally achieved, ultranationalism's appeal will be largely neutralized. There are already some indications that secessionist tendencies might be abating. In the republic of Tatarstan, for example, economic growth in 1995 and 1996 weakened the nationalists' arguments about Russian exploitation. Further, the Ingush republic has not followed Chechnya's lead of secession, despite the geographical, religious, and ethnic similarities between the two republics. The fact that the Ingush republic receives special federal tax breaks and that it has enjoyed substantial outside investment suggests that economic conditions are a salve for nationalist agitation.

Five years after the demise of the Soviet Union, however, Russia's nationalities policy remains entangled in domestic politics. The 1995 parliamentary campaign, the presidential race in the summer of 1996, and especially the regional elections that continued until December 1996 all turned in some significant way upon the issues of center-periphery relations and ethnonational autonomy. For opponents of Yeltsin and those associated with him, the war in Chechnya served as a cudgel with which to beat the government's reputation. Yeltsin in turn blamed the Chechen debacle upon the military. In February 1996 he also blamed the 1993–95 parliament for adopting laws that he claimed exceeded the limits of federal jurisdiction—a clear effort to ameliorate the regions' hostility toward him in the run-up to the June 1996 presidential elections.

In the final analysis, center-periphery relations may prove to be the most critical issue for the Russian Federation's long-term development. The politics of center-periphery relations is not so much a geographical matter (as the term implies) but one of governmental hierarchy and relative autonomy. While the parliament and president in Moscow debate such matters as the pace of economic reform, appropriate responses to crime, and the country's relations with the West, power quietly slips from Moscow to the regions. Thus, the assessment of Victor Davidoff: "[T]he regions have gained more economic and political autonomy. What happens in Moscow doesn't mean anything to the person in Novosibirsk. His local governor is much more important to him than Yeltsin. Because the governor—he is god."[2]

A certain irony infuses Russia's ethnonational situation, as it does so many facets of life in the former Soviet Union. Russian nationalism played an important role in the breakup of the Soviet Union, and Yeltsin tapped into it as a key component of his power base. Yet Russian nationalism has been a fickle ally, eventually being co-opted by Vladimir Zhirinovsky and far-right opponents of Yeltsin's reformist policies. It remains an open question whether democratic pluralism can take root in such an environment.

Suggested Readings

Carrére d'Encausse, Hélène. *The End of the Soviet Empire: The Triumph of the Nations.* New York: Basic Books, 1993.

Chinn, Jef, and Robert Kaiser. *Russians as the New Minority: Ethnicity and Nationalism in the Soviet Successor States.* Boulder: Westview, 1996.

Hajda, Lubomyr, and Mark Beissinger, eds. *The Nationalities Factor in Soviet Politics and Society.* Boulder: Westview, 1990.

Rywkin, Michael. *Moscow's Lost Empire.* Armonk, N.Y.: M. E. Sharpe, 1994.

Smith, Graham, ed. *The Nationalities Question in the Post-Soviet States.* 2d edition. London and New York: Longman, 1996.

---

2. "Regional Press Fights Political Control," *Transition* 6 (October 1995): 66.

10

Law and Order

"**R**ussia is large, and the tsar is far away." This venerable Russian proverb underscores the difficulty of maintaining a governmental presence—law and order—throughout the Russian empire. The tsars had never fully managed the lives of their subjects; it is doubtful they desired to. But the Communist Party of the Soviet Union took a different approach. The Soviet regime achieved unprecedented success in making its presence felt throughout the territory of the USSR. The rigid constraints of censorship, central planning, and forced labor imposed a crude order upon many facets of life. Now the post-Soviet leaders of Russia have taken on the unenviable task of refounding Russia's societal and political order upon the rule of law.

The Rule of Law

There is a critical distinction between a state that uses laws and a state governed by the rule of law. In tsarist Russia the regime promulgated laws, but it was the tsar's absolutism, not any principles embedded in law, which set the standard for governmental action. Neither could the Soviet Union be classified as a law-governed state. (Indeed, the very principle—*pravovoe gosudarstvo*—was

155

derided in Marxist-Leninist ideology.) The constitutional structure of the Soviet Union was especially important to this determination. Despite its self-professed claims to the contrary, the Soviet Constitution (in all three of its incarnations) did not truly circumscribe the government's powers. The constitution served not as the source of governmental authority, but as a facade of democracy that obscured the unfettered power wielded by the Communist Party. The various provisions of the constitution were repeatedly ignored with impunity. And with the regime showing disdain for its own constitution, the myriad lesser laws could hardly maintain independent force of their own. Indeed, the Bolsheviks initially rejected the need to create code law at all, moonstruck as they were by the Marxist-Leninist promise of human perfectibility.

It is doubtful that Soviet law as a whole could have been genuinely enforced even if the authorities wanted to. The statutes, regulations, five-year plans, and other formal templates for expected behavior were fashioned from the idealized doctrine of Marxism-Leninism, a doctrine that arguably misunderstood fundamental elements of human nature. For the system to actually operate—for goods to be produced, families to be fed, armies to be equipped, money to be exchanged—the regime's idealistic, unrealistic rules and laws had to be violated.

Many of the day-to-day violations of law were necessitated by the shortcomings (mostly congenital flaws) of the command economy. There developed alongside the command economy a black market for goods and services. The common term for this market, the "second economy," properly evokes the image of two parallel economic systems—one official and serving the state, the other unofficial (often illegal) and satisfying human needs. Within the second economy entrepreneurs sold scarce goods, which sometimes were stolen from state warehouses and stores. Service providers, employed by the state, moonlighted for barter or for money under the table, providing services not readily available through the "first" economy without waiting for weeks and in some cases years. Factory managers falsified production reports to create the illusion of meeting state-mandated (and frequently unattainable) quotas. Employees covered for their fellows who had to spend hours of the workday standing in line to obtain consumer goods. Others simply stole state goods from work.

The command economy was not the only progenitor of widespread lawbreaking. Many other aspects of daily life required that the people violate regulations as a matter of course and that the state turn a blind eye to the practice. The Soviet Union's perennial housing shortage required that the state's already modest occupancy standards be ignored. It also provided the impetus for complex apartment-trading schemes to circumvent the state's bureaucratic regulations and permit requirements. Pollution-control regulations similarly were ignored when they would otherwise constrain the already inefficient Soviet industries. The democratic principles voiced in the constitution and the electoral laws passed by the legislature had to be violated as a matter of procedure, lest the Party surely lose its control of the government. Courts were pressed into the service of the Party and therefore could not be bound by the narrow pursuit of blind justice. The Soviets used the court system as a tool for controlling the society; judges were indirectly and directly influenced by local party officials. Hence the applicability of another Russian proverb, "Where a court is, truth is absent."

Of course, this litany of official and private violations of law should not be interpreted to mean that the Soviet Union was devoid of any meaningful law; it is not to say that the country was anarchic. Certainly there were laws that were promulgated, generally observed by the population, and rather consistently enforced by the regime. But the point of a law-governed state is not simply that it has working laws, but that in the final analysis, it is laws, and not politics or naked power, that regulate the actions of society and the government. Law in the Soviet Union was subordinate to the regime.

The case of the Soviet Union demonstrates that some degree of order is possible without the rule of law. Yet such an arrangement is not without its costs. The order created in the Soviet Union was purchased at the expense of justice and was facilitated by widespread, institutionalized corruption. It ingrained in the society a set of attitudes and mores that were in many ways antithetical to the beliefs that must undergird a law-governed state: that the law will be fairly applied, consistently enforced, and widely respected. It becomes evident, therefore, that achieving Yeltsin's 1991 inaugural goal of transforming the Russian Federation into a "prosperous, peace-loving, law-governed and sovereign state" requires not merely legal reforms but also a transformation of social attitudes. The first five years of Russia's independence revealed that these tasks would be harder than Yeltsin had initially suggested.

Legal Reform

The Yeltsin leadership set itself upon the task of reforming the legal system with the same ambition, and perhaps the same lack of preparation, as it did reforming the economic and political systems. Few legal procedures and institutions were left untouched by the reform program. Some of the reforms simply applied international norms to the Russian legal system; for example, there was a requirement that all laws be published. Others filled large voids that the Soviet legal system had never had reason to address—consumer protection requirements and laws protecting intellectual property, for example. But the most important reforms concerned limitations on state power.

One of the most important bulwarks of a law-governed state is an independent supreme court. Through the 1993 Constitution Yeltsin sought to recast the Russian Constitutional Court as such a body. The Russian Constitution grants to the Constitutional Court the power of judicial review: to determine whether laws and governmental actions conform to the constitution. The Court also decides questions of competence between central governmental bodies. It also is charged with resolving disputes between the central and the regional governments. On paper the Constitutional Court indeed appears as an important guardian of the constitution. The Court did not become operational, however, until February 1995, when the Duma had finally approved all 19 of its justices and the Court elected its chairman. That chairman, Vladimir Tumanov, was himself involved in the writing of the 1993 Constitution and therefore was perhaps uniquely suited for the job. Tumanov reached mandatory retirement age (70) in 1997, and was replaced by Marat Baglai.

But a Constitutional Court is only as powerful as the rest of the government allows it to be. Many wondered how much judicial independence would be tolerated by President Yeltsin, who had suspended the last Constitutional Court after it ruled unconstitutional his dissolution of the Supreme Soviet in September 1993. The powers of the Justice Ministry and the prosecutor general would also be critical.

To help isolate the courts from political pressure, judges in Russia are immune from criminal prosecution. This provision was upheld by the Constitutional Court itself in March 1996. It is a difficult and important provision, given the Party's co-optation of the courts in the Soviet period and also the incidents of bribery and other forms of corruption in the post-Soviet court system. In 1995 alone some 54 judges were removed from the bench for misconduct. Such removal is carried out by boards of judicial peers and is considered distinct from criminal prosecution.

Punishment

Historically, Russia has been a land of cruel, merciless punishment at the hands of the regime. For its part, the Soviets did not shrink from meting out punishment as a form of control and retribution. Capital punishment (usually administered with bullets) was carried out with staggering frequency. Although the line between official execution of criminals and the state-sanctioned murder of political opposition was frequently blurred, the Soviet regime appeared to have executed criminals about 20 times more frequently per capita than the United States. In post-Soviet Russia the practice dramatically dropped off. In 1993 only three persons were executed, and four more were executed in 1994. The number of state executions again reached double digits in 1995 and 1996, but the number remains lower than in the United States, which had 101 executions in those two years.

Still, Russia has come under increasing international criticism for not banning the death penalty. Responding to this criticism, Duma Security Committee Chairman Viktor Ilyukhin unconvincingly argued that his country's limited capacity to keep prisoners with life terms makes terminating the death penalty impractical. And Foreign Minister Yevgeny Primakov argued that the Russian public would not accept a complete and immediate cessation of capital punishment. Nevertheless, Russia's admission to the Council of Europe in 1996 requires that the country eliminate the death penalty by 1999.

Death penalty or no, Russia's prisons are overcrowded. The slowness of the new judicial system, the increase in crime, and the shortage of funds to build new facilities have created severe overcrowding in jails and prisons throughout Russia. The Butyrka prison in Moscow, for example, is holding up to 100 people in cells designed to hold a quarter that number. Prisoners are forced to sleep in shifts, and epidemics are common. The situation is exacerbated by the prisons' meager budgets for food, medicine, and maintenance.

Upon seizing power, the Bolsheviks abolished the jury system and imposed a magistrate system. In 1994 jury trials began to be reintroduced in Russia, though only in a few of the country's 89 regions. Today's Russian judges are supposed to be independent, but their low salaries keep them susceptible to the influence of other local officials, including prosecutors, who control their access to services such as phones and housing. Hence another of Russia's proverbs about law: "Law and money flow from the same spring." The role of prosecutors is poorly defined in the Russian Constitution. Compared with the West, prosecutors in Russia wield greater powers. Prosecutor's offices typically run their own "general surveillance" divisions, which conduct "routine" information-gathering activities upon the public. These practices appear to violate the constitution. Further, the Russian legal system suffers from a severe shortage of lawyers (a problem for which American observers have felt little empathy).

Federal Law-Enforcement Agencies

In 1991 the Soviet KGB was replaced by two major Russian organizations. The Ministry of Security became Russia's primary domestic investigatory and law-enforcement body. A separate Foreign Intelligence Service (SVR) was created to carry out foreign security operations. On paper the division of operations was akin to the United States' functional distinction between the FBI and the CIA.

Several days after the December 1993 parliamentary elections, Yeltsin dissolved the Ministry of Security and replaced it with the Federal Security Service (FSB). It was understood that Yeltsin was motivated by the Ministry of Security's insufficient opposition against parliamentary Speaker Ruslan Khasbulatov's forces during the October "events." Since that time, the FSB has operated as a fairly nonpoliticized law-enforcement body (by historical Russian standards).

The Russian Federation also has an Interior Ministry concerned with domestic order and security. Overall, the various responsibilities that had been held by the KGB have been assumed not only by these organizations (FSB, SVR, and the Interior Ministry), but also by the Procuracy, the Economics Ministry, the Justice Ministry, and other agencies. As the country's largest city and a major venue for crime, Moscow has created its own Moscow Regional Agency for Combating Organized Crime, which is modeled after the U.S. Federal Bureau of Investigation.

Order and Liberty

In the chaos of contemporary Russian politics and society, it is not uncommon to hear people recalling the Soviet period with wistfulness and nostalgia. Just as the Fascist dictator Benito Mussolini is credited with making the Italian trains run on time, the Soviet regime, and certainly Josef Stalin, managed to impose strict order upon Russian society. Police states, after all, tend to be well-policed. Or so today's Russian conservatives would have one believe.

Theoretical considerations of lawmaking and enforcement commonly presume an inverse relationship between liberty and order. Achieving a high measure of societal order and stability requires a reining in of individual liberties. Conversely, a free society must be willing to tolerate a lesser degree of conformity and equality. By this logic, the Soviet Union could achieve the equality promised in Party doctrine only through strict governmental control. It has already been observed that equality in the Soviet Union, to the extent it existed, was manifested in the equal impoverishment of the people. The privileged status of party *apparatchiki* did further violence to the Communist ideal of equality.

But nostalgia tends to gloss over the warts, even the congenital defects, of that which it recalls. This might explain the Communists' renaissance not only in Russia, but also in other former Soviet republics and East European countries. The perceived failure of Yeltsin's government to maintain an adequate level of law and order in post-Soviet Russia contributed to the success of Communist and nationalistic parties in the 1993 and 1995 Duma elections. These parties have struck a chord with large segments of the population by appealing to their desire for order. They argue that the societal and economic problems Russians face can be ameliorated only with stronger governmental action, even coercion.

Other factors certainly contributed to the conservatives' political success, including the reformists' own disorganization and their association with the West. But the public's flirtation with parties and politicians promising a return to the old ways—even a reconstruction of the Soviet Union itself—suggests that the reformers have not adequately responded to Russians' need for order.

This poses a dilemma: until a conducive political culture can support a law-governed state, the reformers must be willing to rein in liberty to keep reforms on course. This logic has gotten Yeltsin and his lieutenants in trouble more than once.

Crime in Russia

There is no question that various forms of crime have increased dramatically in post-Soviet Russia. Worsening crime statistics have dogged Yeltsin since Russian independence. Data from the Interior Ministry's Main Administration for Criminal Investigations revealed 31,500 homicides and attempted homicides in 1995, more than double the 1990 total of 15,500. The 1995 figure amounted to about 22 homicides per 100,000 people per year, which is more than twice America's rate. In 1995 other violent crimes were up from 1990, including 61,700 cases of grievous assault and 12,500 rapes. These figures reflected about a 10 percent drop from 1994, however. The official number of various lesser crimes, including robbery and drug trafficking, have skyrocketed since the last years of Brezhnev's rule in the late 1970s and early 1980s. Still, instances of especially brash crimes, such as the theft of over a quarter-mile of railroad track from Primorsk krai in April 1996, indicated a brazenness seldom encountered in the Soviet period.

More broadly, the phenomenon of increasing crime is the continuation of a trend that began with Gorbachev's glasnost and perestroika, which granted freedoms to a society that lacked a strong sense of civic values. But the Russian public has been unwilling to simply shrug off increasing crime as the price of independence. Neither can much solace be drawn from the frequently overlooked fact that crime and corruption existed in the Soviet period.

Crime is an ugly and constant reality in Russia, made more visible by the relatively free press and the campaign speeches of opposition political groups. The causes are varied, including the exacerbation of the moral vacuum initially fostered by the Soviets (see Chapter 11) and the absence of a supportive political culture (see Chapter 6). But there are also more concrete causes. Easy access to weapons is especially problematic. After seizing power, the Bolsheviks somewhat understandably banned the personal possession of most guns. In Yeltsin's Russia the ban was revoked, and the legal possession of guns has proliferated (although numerous restrictions remain). Their illegal possession has posed an even greater problem. Some 150,000 automatic weapons were stolen (or illegally sold) from government armories in 1994. Russian Army soldiers, who after the collapse of the Soviet Union have endured chronically low morale and poor living conditions, commonly sell their rifles or barter them for other goods. Any number of other types of military hardware, including even artillery pieces, are available on the black market.

Some argue that high unemployment triggered by Russia's economic turmoil, coupled with Russia's traditional discrimination against women, have
pushed large numbers of women into the criminal class. To be sure, women
live disproportionately in poverty, and crimes among women are certainly
increasing. Some 238,000 crimes committed by women were recorded in
1995, compared with 142,000 in 1993. But considering that a total of
2,750,000 crimes were recorded in 1995, it is premature to declare a "femini-
zation of crime."

Another structural contributor to Russian crime is its post-Communist
economy. Russia's economic system has been largely freed of centralized state
control, but no "market" as it is known in the West has yet developed to
impose discipline upon economic transactions. In 1992 a Russian official described his country's economic culture as "wild capitalism." Wild capitalism
can be distinguished from its "tame" Western variant: "In a desperate embrace of Western economic practices, the marketplace in Russia now knows
no boundaries. Everything and everyone is for sale. There are no reference
points for prices, no rules for deals, no grounding for economic theories."[1]
Such an environment breeds corruption, exploitation, and crime. The market
is speculative and parasitic, rather than productive and disciplining.

Some of the less heinous crimes in Russia perhaps can be discounted as a
manifestation of the unfamiliarity with market principles and a temporary in-
dulgence in get-rich-quick schemes. Such activities as reselling state-subsidized
goods purchased from state stores is more of a response to the confusion
within the Russian economy than a manifestation of moral depravity. Many
so-called environmental crimes (such as illegal hunting, logging, and fishing)
that have been growing in number may also reflect a clash of the old notion
of public ownership with the new opportunities for profit. Similarly, the old
Soviet *apparatchiki* have found their connections and knowledge helpful for
recreating small empires within the new system. While of dubious ethical
standing, these private empires are not intrinsically criminal.

But much of the Russian economy is. A study conducted for the Yeltsin government in late 1993 found that organized crime was linked to at least 70 percent
of Russia's commercial banks and recently privatized enterprises.[2] Criminals prey
upon the Russian economy with protection rackets, extortion schemes, investor
scams, and "business killings." In 1996 about 450 successful contract killings
were recorded. One particularly loathsome scheme illustrates the evil side of wild
capitalism: A con man offers to purchase an apartment from its elderly owner,
but agrees not to take possession until the owner dies. This allows the elderly

---

1. Bruce Stokes, "Wild Capitalism," *National Journal,* January 11, 1992: 76.

2. *Izvestiia,* January 26, 1994: 1.

owner to tap into the apartment's "equity" without losing the apartment. In this scam, however, once a contract is signed the owner is killed.

Attacks against the nouveaux riches are epidemic. Some criminals, finding the temptation presented by flaunted wealth irresistible, steal jewelry directly off the person of its owner. Others have engaged in kidnapping to extort ransom money. In response to this increasingly common risk, many wealthy families send their college-age children to study abroad. But the rich have also experienced artless, violent attacks to themselves and their property. Crimes lacking an economic motive point to other troubles in Russian society. Hate crimes, crimes of passion, vandalism, and other expressions of societal dysfunction have proliferated. Drunken fights, public brawls, and attacks on women after dark have become commonplace in many of Russia's cities.

Organized Crime

The criminal opportunities afforded by the transitional economy and corrupt and inefficient law enforcement create ideal conditions for organized crime. Russians commonly refer to the criminal gangs that plague them as the *Mafiya* because of the similarity to the entrenched criminal syndicates in Italy. In fact, the major Italian Mafia families have established a presence in Russia. In 1996 Russia's Chief Directorate of Organized Crime counted a total of 5,000 gangs in Russia, of which about 100 had international operations.

But it is the Chechen Mafiya that has achieved the most notoriety in Russia. Even before Yeltsin's government launched its attack against the breakaway republic in December 1994, the Chechens were considered by Russians to be untrustworthy and corrupt. Dzokhar Dudaev's Chechnya was frequently compared to 1920s Chicago, "but without the city services."[3] The republic serves as a base for criminal gangs that operate throughout the former Soviet Union, and especially in Moscow and St. Petersburg. (St. Petersburg had the country's highest crime rate in 1995.) The airport in Grozny is a major entry point for drugs entering Russia. Printing presses in the republic produce counterfeit currency.

Official Corruption

Despite the Chechen regime's reputation for crime, however, the very governmental authorities in Moscow that fight the Chechens are themselves infected with the taint of corruption. In 1993 Defense Minister Pavel Grachev, who later would justify the Chechen operation partly on grounds of Chechen

---

3. David Remnick, "In Stalin's Wake," *The New Yorker*, July 24, 1995: 53.

lawlessness, admitted that 46 top Russian military officers, including generals, would be court-martialed in answer to corruption charges. Grachev himself fell from grace amid vague allegations of coup plotting in the summer of 1996. As of the fall, criminal proceedings were under way against about 100 high-ranking officers, including 15 generals and admirals.

Official corruption was not limited to the military. In Yeltsin's Russia, numerous government, parliamentary, and law-enforcement officials also would be caught in corruption scandals. In his 1996 state of the nation speech, Yeltsin acknowledged the extent of corruption within the government. According to his own figures, 1,200 state officials were charged in 1995. Worse, more than 100 of these worked for the Prosecutor General's Office—the agency charged with weeding out corruption. Corruption has appeared even closer to the Kremlin. For example, Yeltsin adviser Sergei Stankevich, who had also been a Duma deputy, disappeared when a warrant was issued for his arrest on corruption charges in February 1996. Even a former acting prosecutor general, Aleksei Ilyushenko, was imprisoned for taking bribes and other crimes.

Official corruption extends to the regional and local levels. Local officials commonly require bribes for the provision of basic services. Widespread corruption within law-enforcement agencies has dealt a serious blow to the public trust that is needed to undergird a law-governed state. Just as business owners find themselves having to pay "protection" money to racketeers, criminal gangs routinely budget funds to bribe law-enforcement personnel. The Interior Ministry itself estimates that half the earnings of criminal gangs are used to bribe judges, journalists, and other officials. In 1996 an official at Moscow's Butyrka prison revealed that only one of the 14 "thieves in law" (members of the criminal elite) arrested since 1994 had been booked and put through the courts. The 13 others managed to avoid the legal process through bribes and threats.

In politics corruption has reached the level of assassination. The State Duma, which was established only in December 1993, saw at least four of its deputies slain by 1996. A number of candidates in the 1995 Duma elections were also killed. Politicians aren't always innocent, however. A candidate in Tatarstan's March 1996 election was arrested in January in connection with a murder case.

Other occupations have become potentially deadly. In 1994 and 1995 there were dozens of attempts on the lives of bankers. In early 1996 several gunshots were fired at the home of the Russian Central Bank chairman—the highest-ranking Russian government official to be physically threatened by violence. Authorities speculate that the attacks on bankers arise from the heavy involvement of criminal gangs in the banking industry. Investigative journalists following stories of governmental and business corruption also are frequently threatened, attacked, and sometimes slain. The 1995 killing of a popular television journalist, Vladislav Listev, was a particularly high-profile example of the spectre of partisan violence against the media. Business leaders in Russia's military-industrial complex have been frequent targets as well. The 1996 slaying of Deputy Justice Minister Anatoly Stepanov at his home underscored that in the "war on crime," criminals were not afraid to fight back. And the shooting death of a U.S. businessman in November 1996 emphasized the dangers the foreign business community faces doing business in Russia.

Nuclear Crime

Perhaps the most frightening aspect of Russian crime concerns the country's nuclear stockpiles. Russia inherited most of the Soviet Union's nuclear weapons and many of its nuclear production facilities and reactors. Security at the facilities is dangerously lax. U.S. Deputy Secretary of Energy Charles Curtis calls Russia's security measures little more than "guards, guns, and gates." None of Russia's storage facilities for nuclear waste has electric perimeter safeguards, and at some nothing more than a padlock stands in the way of thieves. The problem is compounded almost daily, as the decommissioning of Soviet nuclear weapons in accordance with nuclear arms reduction treaties produces additional nuclear waste. A storage facility for such materials is not scheduled to be complete until 1998, and funding for it is in jeopardy.

Small quantities of nuclear material have simply disappeared. Record-keeping is so bad that precise figures are impossible to come by. Particularly worrisome is the involvement of organized crime. The *mafiya* was widely blamed for the theft of radioactive beryllium from a Russian nuclear laboratory in 1993. In August 1994 German authorities seized a small quantity (360 grams) of plutonium that they claimed was stolen from a Russian research reactor. In November 1995 a Chechen rebel commander buried radioactive material in a Moscow park. (Russia still has bomb-grade nuclear material stored in Chechnya.) In April 1996 the Federal Security Service arrested a scientist who had allegedly smuggled over a kilogram of bomb-grade radioactive material out of the country. As of the summer of 1996, Russian authorities had recorded seven incidents of nuclear theft.

The Russian nuclear regulatory agency, Gosatomnadzor, has reacted with some urgency to reports of deteriorating safety at its plants. But a lack of adequate funding has stood in the way of comprehensive measures.

The United States and other Western countries have expressed serious concern about the security dangers posed by the former Soviet Union's nuclear technology and materials. The United States alone has committed hundreds of millions of dollars for security measures for the former Soviet Union. The United States has also established research institutes that hire former Soviet nuclear scientists, mitigating the incentive to sell their nuclear know-how to America's enemies. Further, the U.S. Department of Energy provides technical assistance for improving the safety and security of nuclear plants in the former Soviet Union. More direct involvement has also taken place. With the cooperation of the Kazakhstan government, the United States launched Project Sapphire, which spirited nuclear material out of Kazakhstan in 1995 after it had been determined that the safety of that material could not be ensured where it was. The action provoked protests by some nationalist groups in the former Soviet Union who saw Project Sapphire as more proof of American meddling in their security affairs. Still, in the fall of 1996, the U.S. Central Intelligence Agency reported increasing concern about the lack of adequate safeguards for Russia's tactical nuclear weapons.

Anticorruption and Anticrime Efforts

There has been no shortage of measures to combat corruption and crime in Russia. In the spring of 1994 the Russian Security Council prepared a wide-ranging program to adopt new criminal codes on organized crime and corruption; crack down on money laundering, illegal immigration, and gun- and drug-running; improve control and inspection of exporting operations; strengthen criminal rehabilitation programs; improve capabilities for monitoring illegal activities; and facilitate cooperation with international law-enforcement organizations. The program came under some criticism for its alleged violation of human rights, including a provision allowing the detention without charges of suspects up to 30 days. (The constitution limits such detention to 48 hours.) Despite various criticisms and political battles, the parliament and president approved a comprehensive criminal code to take effect January 1, 1997. The new code focuses on crimes against individuals, as distinct from the emphasis on crimes against the state, which characterized Soviet law.

The government also continued to battle official corruption. Anatoly Kulikov, appointed interior minister in 1995, launched a "Clean Hands" campaign against corruption within law-enforcement agencies. Interior Ministry officials tested the honesty of various officials, at one point driving a truckload of vodka through highway checkpoints. The overall operation netted some major figures, including four generals and Moscow's deputy police chief, who were charged with extortion and taking bribes. Kulikov said he was shocked by the extent of corruption in the government, including his own ministry.

Periodic outrages have brought new calls for governmental action. When Russia's popular television director Vladislav Listev was assassinated in March 1995, it was widely assumed to be the work of Russia's *Mafiya*. Listev's death galvanized public and governmental resolve to more vigorously weed out criminal gangs. Yeltsin blamed lax law enforcement and argued that Russian officials had been afraid to attack criminals and "bandits" because they feared being accused of "turning Russia into a police state." The Russian Security

Council promptly took up the issue of increased anticrime efforts, and Yeltsin called on the Duma to pass an organized-crime bill.

In the days before his successful runoff election against Communist Gennady Zyuganov, Yeltsin appointed Aleksandr Lebed to the posts of national security adviser and head of the Security Council. In these bodies, "national security" is construed largely as domestic security; this provided Lebed with an opportunity to translate his tough law-and-order rhetoric into action.[4] But Lebed only lasted about three months in those positions, ultimately falling victim to the whirlwind of corruption charges that were traded between governmental factions. Interior Minister Anatoly Kulikov accused Lebed of coup plotting and Lebed was unceremoniously removed by Yeltsin. He was replaced by former Duma speaker Ivan Rybkin. It is worth noting that Lebed had come to power by charging his longtime rival Pavel Grachev with planning a coup. As a result of these charges, Grachev was removed from his post as defense minister.

There is no question that law enforcement in post-Soviet Russia is ineffective. The militia (as the Russian police are called) are generally underpaid and poorly equipped. Corruption is rampant. Lacking proper training, resources, and numbers, the militia in many parts of the country is an unreliable law-enforcement institution. Even more than in countries without a history of "communalism," theft of personal and state property in Russia has become commonplace. Daylight homicides are increasingly common in the cities. The courts are so overworked as to make the swift administration of justice impossible. And even when court decisions are obtained, over half of these are not implemented.

The market has responded to the government's perceived inability to provide reliable law enforcement. The perceived necessity of making private arrangements for basic security is expressed in the slang term *krysha* ("roof" in Russian). "Buying a roof" means purchasing private security, a throwback to feudal societies. Increasingly private businesses and citizens are taking over law-enforcement tasks that they feel the state has been unable to provide. The proliferation of private security firms dramatically illustrates this. These firms draw heavily upon veterans of the Soviet Union's security agencies. The elites of this group worked for the KGB's Ninth Directorate, which used to provide protection for Soviet government officials. Since the demise of the Soviet government, these security agents have been forced to find new employment. And in the security business, the private sector pays better than the government. Businessmen and bankers increasingly have resorted to hiring security

---

4. Although Article 83 of the Russian Constitution specifies that the role of the Security Council should be established by federal law, no such law had been passed when Lebed assumed the chairmanship.

guards for their businesses and bodyguards for themselves. It is only prudent, as contract killing of business rivals has become a not uncommon response to market competition. Technically, private guards may legally be hired only to protect property, not persons. But this provision is easily circumvented by hiring a guard to protect a piece of jewelry worn by the employer.

Private security details are also hired to enforce contracts and collect payments. In an economy infested with organized crime, collections is not a job for a pin-striped banker. Many of the purveyors of *krysha* are themselves part of the criminal class, at once making them more effective and more dangerous. Larger firms have built what amount to small private armies.

Although private security firms fill a market niche, heavy reliance upon them signals that the ideal of a law-governed state has not been achieved. Allowing basic security and law enforcement to be a service purchased through the market leaves the poor unprotected. Moreover, the security firms have little accountability, choosing their own methods and even objectives without concern for legality. The highly publicized arrest on bribery charges of the head of the Academy of Economic Security, a private security firm, drove this point home in the spring of 1996. Indeed, the widespread dependence on these private firms for law enforcement destroys the concept of "law" altogether.

Prospects

As Thomas Hobbes wrote in the seventeenth century, governments are created for the maintenance of "peace and common defense."[5] The other tasks that have been adopted by governments—redistributing wealth, maintaining infrastructure, providing education, regulating cable television—are subordinate to the basic necessity of establishing order.

It is unclear whether Yeltsin's victory over Zyuganov in the 1996 presidential election reflected popular acceptance of the Yeltsin campaign's argument that Communist-imposed order was worse than no order at all. Alternatively, Yeltsin's victory might have reflected the population's belief that increased material benefits were more likely under Yeltsin's leadership. In either event, it seems certain that the majority of Russian voters rejected Zyuganov's argument that only the Communists could reimpose a salubrious order upon Russia.

Russia's dilemma is that the post-Soviet government's legitimacy rests on the three pillars of popular consent, individual freedoms, and societal stability. Maintaining all three requires constant effort by even the most successful law-

---

5. *Leviathan*, Part II, Chapter 17.

governed state. But for Russia, with neither a tradition of rule of law nor a firmly rooted political system, the simultaneous efforts to maintain any two of the pillars may well jeopardize the third.

Suggested Readings

Barry, Donald D., ed. *Toward the "Rule of Law" in Russia? Political and Legal Reform in the Transition Period.* New York: M. E. Sharpe, 1992.

Chalidze, Valery. *Criminal Russia: Essays on Crime in the Soviet Union.* New York: Random House, 1977.

Clark, William A. *Crime and Punishment in Soviet Officialdom: Combating Corruption in the Political Elite, 1965–1990.* Armonk, N.Y.: M. E. Sharpe, 1993.

Grossman, Gregory. *Second Economy: Boon or Bane?* Berkeley: University of California Press, 1987.

Handelman, Stephen. *Comrade Criminal: Russia's New Mafiya.* New Haven and London: Yale University Press, 1995.

Smith, Bruce L. R. and Gennady M. Danilenko, eds. *Law and Democracy in the New Russia.* Washington, D.C.: The Brookings Institution, 1993.

Waller, Michael J. *Secret Empire: The KGB in Russia Today.* Boulder: Westview, 1994.

11

Religion

Russia is inseparable from religion. The Russian Orthodox Church and the tsar were closely linked, and Russian laws have traditionally been based upon, or at least justified by, Orthodox values and principles. Religious identity colored diplomacy and foreign policy, helping to define enemies (the Islamic Ottomans) and allies (the Orthodox Serbs). Perhaps this is so with most countries.

But Russia's connection with religion is more organic than in many nations. Not only are the values and politics of the Russian people influenced by religion, but in addition the very definition of Russia as a nation hinges upon its religious identity. This could help explain the Soviets' inability to extirpate religion in Russia. As Leonid Kishkovsky, a priest in the Orthodox Church of America, wrote, "the only way to make Russia truly godless would be to destroy all Russian literature, architecture, music and art. Despite the communists' brutal campaign against religion, even at its totalitarian worst it proved incapable of destroying everything authentic in Russian literature."[1]

---

1. Kishkovsky, "Russian Orthodoxy: Out of Bondage, Into the Wilderness," *The Christian Century*, October 6, 1993: 936.

From Cathedrals to Warehouses

For over a thousand years Russia has been linked to Christianity. The tradition goes back to 988, when Vladimir I received Christian baptism and married the sister of Basil II, the emperor of Byzantium. Vladimir had chosen his faith and his spouse with a savvy, perhaps Machiavellian shrewdness. Legend holds that he had dispatched envoys to collect information on various world religions: Islam, Judaism, and Christianity in its Roman and Byzantine variants. After the envoys made their reports, Vladimir weighed their respective merits. Islam he rejected outright, certain that its proscription of alcoholic drink made it anathema to the people of Rus. (Centuries later the philosopher L. A. Feuerbach would call alcohol "the substance of Russia's religion.") But the grandeur of Byzantine Christianity's liturgy, and the submission to authority required by its doctrine, were qualities that Vladimir realized could be useful in a state religion.

Whether the foregoing is true or not, Vladimir did in fact establish Russia's state religion according to the Byzantine model. The link between Russian Orthodoxy and Byzantine Christianity was strengthened further when Vladimir's son, Yaroslav the Wise, took the leadership of Constantinople. By these events, Russian Orthodoxy took root as part of the country's spiritual identity.

Tsarist Russia

By the 15th and 16th centuries, the Russian tsars were claiming that their right to rule came from God, and the Church thus took on a more formal link with the Crown. The Church came to be placed more firmly under the state's control in 1443, when the Church in Moscow declared its independence from the patriarch in Constantinople. The Russian Orthodox Church came to conceive of Moscow as the "Third Rome" (coming after the "heretical" first Rome and the fallen second "Rome" of Constantinople.) As the third and final "Rome," Moscow claimed to be the new center of Orthodoxy. In 1589 a "Patriarch for Moscow and all Russia" was established. Thereafter, the patriarch was subordinate to the tsar and the Church was more firmly established as a tool of the state. And just as the Church had been brought up with the Russian tsars, it would be brought down with them.

The Soviet Period

The Marxist doctrine that allegedly drove Bolshevik policy was hostile to religion, which Marx had derided as the opiate of the masses. After seizing power in 1917, the Bolsheviks moved against the churches, nationalizing their property and restricting their activities. The 1918 decree that authorized the actions against the Church bore the Orwellian title "Decree of the Separation of Church and State." With a vicious relish the regime converted churches into stables, cathedrals into warehouses. Some church facilities would be spared this degree of insult, assigned instead to become museums or, much less frequently, being permitted to remain a house of worship. Some, such as Kazan cathedral, were converted into museums for atheism and religion, with the former subject receiving more approving treatment.

Under Soviet rule, clerics and believers were harassed, persecuted, and arrested as "counterrevolutionaries." Émigrés and refugees escaping the Russian civil war and the Bolshevik regime itself established a Russian Orthodox Church Abroad, which presumably would keep the faith alive beyond the reach of the Soviets. To add to the confusion, about this time the Soviet state created a puppet "Renovationist Church," which was intended to siphon believers away from the Orthodox Church.

Within a few years the new regime had largely subjugated the Russian Orthodox Church, having arrested, co-opted, or executed many of its leaders. One of the regime's major triumphs along these lines was securing Russian Patriarch Tikhon's profession of loyalty to the Soviet government. (He had been arrested in 1923.) Tikhon died, perhaps by the hands of an assassin, in 1925, and was replaced by Metropolitan Sergi. In 1927 Sergi formally acknowledged the Church's subordination to the government in all "temporal" matters, and the regime's domination of the Church was complete. This spurred the creation of yet another pretender to the official leadership of Russian Orthodoxy, the True Orthodox Church. An illegal, underground operation, this church was established by Orthodox Christians who could not accept the Church leadership's cooperation with the Soviet regime.

After Sergi's bow to the state in 1927, the Russian Orthodox Church survived, sometimes only barely, by acknowledging the state's authority. Even then the Church was subject to varying degrees of official harassment and persecution. These became especially hostile during Stalin's reign. In 1929 the Law on Religious Associations prohibited almost all religious activity except worship at state-approved facilities. Such facilities were scarce, since the regime had closed most of the remaining operating churches, as well as every monastery and seminary. Stalin eased these anti-religious pogroms during the Second World War as part of his larger effort to resurrect Russian patriotism toward "Mother Russia." But Khrushchev renewed the attack in the late 1950s, reclosing many of the religious buildings that Stalin had allowed to reopen. Religion enjoyed a reprieve—by Soviet standards, a renaissance—under Brezhnev in the late 1960s and 1970s. A new Law on Religious Associations in 1975 granted several additional rights and freedoms to religious organizations, and the government permitted a greater number of clerics to be trained.

The experience of the Russian Orthodox Church was not shared by all of the religious groups in the Soviet Union. Jews, who comprised slightly less than 2 percent of the Soviet population, were granted their own Jewish Autonomous Republic within Russia. This did not, however, prevent their persecution by the regime. Muslim peoples in Central Asia and the Transcaucasus comprised a significant portion (about a sixth) of the USSR's total population, and the regime permitted some Islamic religious activity. But again, the Islamic Muftiates were controlled from without by the Soviet government and from within by collaborators and KGB infiltrators. Notwithstanding these meager concessions to nominal religious activity, the Soviet authorities actively promoted atheism through the schools, the media, and the Party. To the extent they allowed religious organizations to exist, they did so with the intent of co-opting cultural institutions.

Moscow's policies toward religion in the early Soviet period may well have struck the most effective balance between oppression and toleration, managing to destroy the religious base of tsarism without causing the remaining believers to become a potent anti-regime force. Marxist-Leninist ideology served as a substitute for religion—at least superficially.[2] It was a system of belief with its own set of values and its own guidelines for behavior; it was a dogma with its own liturgy. The holy trinity was not even entirely forsaken, reincarnated in the forms of Marx, Engels, and Lenin. The regime's policies were successful by a number of measures. Even if the masses were not thoroughly filled with the spirit of Soviet Communism, many were at least guided away from theistic religion. Although the veracity of official statistics from the period is always suspect, most estimates place the number of believers at the time of Gorbachev's ascension in 1985 at 30–40 percent of the population. The proportion of the population brought up in the Russian Orthodox Church had fallen to about one in 10 by that time.

Religious Revival

Despite persecution and state atheism, Russian Orthodoxy endured. Through underground church networks, secret ceremonies, smuggled Bibles, and various other illegal means, the Church survived the harshest of the state's anti-religious policies. When Gorbachev's glasnost permitted the greatest religious freedom ever in the history of the Soviet state, the Church was able to draw upon scattered clerics and believers, carefully preserved liturgy, and unextinguished beliefs. Long-abandoned and converted church buildings were

---

2. An early and cogent expression of the analogy between Communism and religion was made by Nikolai Berdiaev in *The Russian Revolution: Two Essays on Its Implications in Religion and Psychology* (London: Sheed & Ward, 1931).

consecrated once again; worship services and baptisms returned to their sanc-
tuaries; marriage ceremonies regained their religious grounding. At the time
of the Soviet Union's collapse, made possible largely by the widespread repu-
diation of the discredited Communist doctrine, theistic religion offered a new
basis for belief.

Analysts of post-Soviet Russian society almost invariably refer to the
"moral vacuum" that supposedly resulted from the widespread abandonment
of Marxist-Leninist ideology. But that analogy can be misleading. Given the
haste with which many Russians disavowed Communists and Communism, it
is hard to argue that that doctrine could have been very firmly rooted in the
society. People do not abandon basic values and moral beliefs lightly. Rather
than provide through Communist doctrine a moral compass that substituted
for religion, the Soviet regime created a social order designed to obviate moral
choice. And to the extent the state limited individual choice, it eliminated
personal responsibility. The collapse of the regime and its doctrine therefore
did not create a moral vacuum; it merely cast a harsh light upon the moral
vacuum that had been created decades earlier.

Suddenly burdened with the responsibilities that accompany freedom,
many in post-Communist Russia sought divine guidance. A 1991 survey found
between 47 and 74 percent of Russians believing in God, depending on how
the question was phrased. More tellingly, 22 percent of the population had
converted from atheism to theism. That figure was even higher for younger
Russians.[3] Yet the newly exposed moral vacuum has not driven all of Russia
to the established, theistic religions. Some have turned to New Age quasi-
religions and the more secular doctrines of philosophers and moralists. Some
politicians and business leaders are reportedly turning to those who claim to
practice witchcraft and sorcery for guidance.[4] And, initially at least, a visible
minority has apparently foregone moral guidance and has taken advantage
of its new freedom and society's confusion to bribe, cheat, steal, rob, and
otherwise prey.

The Russian Orthodox Church in the Russian Federation

Standing alongside the inchoate political institutions and amorphous moral
fabric of newly independent Russia, the Russian Orthodox Church offers a

---

3. See Andrew Greeley, "A Religious Revival in Russia?" *Journal for the Scientific Study of Religion* 33:3 (1994): 253–272.

4. Andrei Kolesnikov, "Wizards, Fight Fair!" *Moscow News* (U.S. ed.) 50 (December 22–28, 1995): 13.

sense of stability and legitimacy. It is trusted considerably more than the other national institutions (such as political parties, the government, and the universities). The Church patriarch, Aleksii II, in particular enjoys a popular following. This did not escape the notice of Boris Yeltsin, who arranged for the patriarch to officiate at his inauguration as president in 1991 and 1996. The symbolic connection between Yeltsin's inauguration and the coronation of his tsarist predecessors could not have been lost on the Russian people. Yeltsin clearly hoped some of the public's trust and goodwill toward the Church would be extended to the presidency. The restoration of the Church at the side of the state was further illustrated in the fall of 1992, when Yeltsin transferred to the Church authority over the Kremlin's cathedrals.

Many of Russia's political parties court the Russian Orthodox Church as a way of tapping into the symbols of the past and the loyalty of the masses. At a conference organized by the Church shortly before the 1995 Duma elections, the leaders of 18 electoral blocs made appearances. Most pledged general support for religion in general and the Russian Orthodox Church in particular. Liberal Democratic Party leader Vladimir Zhirinovsky went so far as to call for the re-establishment of Russian Orthodoxy as Russia's sole state-recognized religion. The Communists also sought to demonstrate their new-found support for Christianity. Several months earlier, Gennady Zyuganov went on record as calling Jesus Christ the world's first Communist, "because he wanted justice in this earthly life and sacrificed his life . . . to atone for other people's sins." In a campaign speech he also promised to defend religion as president. At other appearances Zyuganov has been flanked by tapestries bearing images of Jesus and the Virgin Mary. Most church leaders nevertheless did not especially welcome the courtship of the LDP and the Communist Party.

By virtue of its role as the country's spiritual center for almost a millennium before the arrival of Communism, the Church acts as a unifying force and a source of national identity for the Russian Federation. For many, the persecution of the Church in the twentieth century bolsters its moral standing through martyrdom. Membership in the Church has almost doubled, accounting for about 18 percent of the Russian population in 1994. The rebirth of Orthodoxy was also demonstrated symbolically, as with the rebuilding of Moscow's Cathedral of Christ the Savior, which had been destroyed by the Soviets in 1931. In 1996 Yeltsin used his attendance at Easter Mass (presided over by Patriarch Aleksii II) in the cathedral to show his support for the Russian Orthodox Church. The reconstruction was timed to (almost) coincide with Moscow's 850th anniversary in 1997.

At the same time, however, the position of the Church has drawn some criticism. Although the Church now enjoys an autonomy not experienced for centuries, if ever, there lingers a sense that its position comes at the cost of political subordination. Aleksii's officiating at Yeltsin's inauguration suggested a collaboration between church and state that made some feel nervous. This was repeated when Aleksii took sides against the coup plotters in August 1991. Rather than serving as a reminder of Russia's glory days under the tsars, for some the patriarch's support of the political leadership recalled the Soviet period. The Church's reputation has never fully recovered from Patriarch Tikhon's profession of allegiance to the Soviet regime and Sergi's acceptance of state superiority in the 1920s.

With the collapse of the Soviet Union, a widening rift has developed between two camps: conservatives who want the Church to reclaim its influence and identity with the Russian nation, and reformers who believe the Church must first own up to its venal, but still perhaps venial, abdication of moral responsibility during the Soviet period. The conservatives call for religious leadership, while the reformers seek ecclesiastical repentance. The reformist camp has been especially active in the country's politics. A prominent name among the reformers is Gleb Yakunin, a Russian Orthodox priest who had been imprisoned by the Communists. He later became a member of the Russian Duma and co-chairman of the Democratic Russia party. A potential martyr for the reformist cause is Father Aleksandr Men, called "the C. S. Lewis of Russia," who was slain with an axe in 1990.

The Church is also haunted by a lingering connection with anti-Semitism, prevalent today in the Church's authoritarian wing. Until his death in the fall of 1995, St. Petersburg Metropolitan Ioann served as a disturbing example of open anti-Semitism. It was not immediately evident whether his successor, Metropolitan Vladimir of Rostov and Novocherkassk, would distance himself from these tendencies.

The Church's various shortcomings have provided openings for its growing host of challengers. The two breakaway sects of the Russian Orthodox Church, the True Orthodox Church and the Russian Orthodox Church Abroad, still question Aleksii II's legitimacy and challenge his authority. (He had been made a bishop during Khrushchev's rule in 1961 and was made patriarch during Yeltsin's and Gorbachev's rule in 1990.) Battles have ensued over doctrine, liturgy, and hierarchy. A recent illustration of these sectarian conflicts concerns the Russian Orthodox Church Abroad's efforts to conduct a long-delayed funeral for Nicholas II, the last tsar. Bones excavated from a field near Yekaterinburg in 1991 were eventually shown by forensic tests to be those of Nicholas II and most of his family. The Church Abroad, always more conservative than the Russian Orthodox Church, has hoped to have the bones buried in the Romanovs' crypt in St. Petersburg.

The Russian Orthodox Church also serves to institutionally and spiritually link Russians living abroad with Moscow. In carrying out this function, the Russian Orthodox Church finds itself competing with the Ukrainian Autocephalous Orthodox Church, the Roman Catholic Church, the Greek Orthodox Church, and various Protestant denominations for political influence and the souls of the Russian people abroad. Tensions were illustrated in a much-publicized schism in the spring of 1996 between Constantinople and Moscow, both of which claimed jurisdiction over the Estonian Orthodox Church. (About a third of Estonia's population is ethnic Russian.)

Foreign churches also have proselytized within Russia's borders. There remains a widespread concern that Russia has become a hunting ground for evangelical religions and cults. Expressing sentiments analogous to the complaints about foreign capitalists taking advantage of Russians' economic neophytism, concerned Russians express worry about foreign missionaries preying upon spiritually weakened Russians. In response, conservatives within the Russian Orthodox Church sponsored legislation that would have severely restricted the ability of foreign-based religious organizations to conduct missionary work in Russia. The Supreme Soviet passed such a bill in 1993, but Yeltsin refused to sign it. Shortly thereafter the Supreme Soviet was defeated in its battle with Yeltsin during the October events, and the issue was at least temporarily sidelined.

Some still question whether Russia is prepared for religious pluralism. If not, it faces some very difficult challenges. Christian fundamentalist organizations (sometimes derided as purveyors of "English-speaking Christianity"), the Salvation Army, Hare Krishnas, Scientologists, and Japan's Aum Shinrikyo sect have established a substantial presence in Russian cities.

The Green Peril?

Although Russians professing a religious faith are overwhelmingly Russian Orthodox, the Islamic faithful constitute significant pluralities and even majorities in some regions. The republics of Bashkorstan, Chechnya, Kalmykia, Tatarstan, and Yakutia are especially important Muslim strongholds. The sheer existence of this national minority of 11 million persons (about 9 percent of the Russian population) has led some to protest the government's close association with the Russian Orthodox Church. After all, the 1993 constitution proclaims a separation of church and state and guarantees religious equality. Russian Orthodoxy, it is argued, should not be treated as a state religion.

As Russia's second-largest religious group, Muslims can wield significant political influence. In practice, however, their potential clout has not been realized. Two Muslim groups were established to participate in the 1995 Duma elections. The Union of Muslims failed to secure enough signatures to appear on the ballot. The Muslim Public Movement (NUR, meaning "light") did qualify, but obtained fewer than 400,000 votes (0.57 percent). Consequently, no specifically Muslim groups were represented in the 1996–99 Duma. Nonetheless, Muslim groups, of which there are more than 2,000 in Russia, continue to press local and regional governments for concessions to their religion and culture. There is a growing demand that Muslim interests be acknowledged and promoted by the governments of Russia. Their political strength was expected to increase with the creation of the Russian Muslim Union in 1996. The union was formed by NUR and the Union of Muslims, who called upon all other Muslim organizations to join it.

More immediately threatening to Moscow than the insistence of some Muslims that they should have an equal claim to Russian citizenship is the claim by other Muslims that they should not. That is, some groups—notably the Chechens—have sought outright secession from Russia. Further, the affinity between Muslims living in Russia and the Islamic countries to Russia's south worries Russian authorities. Shortly after the demise of the Soviet Union, the Islamic Renaissance Party in Russia sought to unite Muslims of the former Soviet Union into a pan-Islamic organization. Although the various ethnic Muslim peoples of the USSR have resisted political integration, the scattered incidents of radical Islamic movements in the region and the world unsettled the Russian leadership. A particularly worrisome scenario envisioned by Russian authorities is the potential co-optation of Russia's ethnic Muslims with Russia's historic Muslim adversaries such as Iran and Afghanistan. In the mid-1990s Russia's two major religions were especially divided on the country's foreign policy concerning Bosnia, where Muslims and Orthodox Serbs were carrying on bloody fighting.

Prospects

By definition religion appeals to loyalties higher than patriotic devotion to the state. By linking the monarchy to the Church the tsars were able to secure the compliance of the masses even where feelings of patriotism were absent. Alternatively, pluralistic societies such as the United States have found it expedient to enforce a distinction between religious and state authority; they decline to establish a state religion lest the government lose the support of those who adhere to nonstate religions. Yet even secular governments can become embroiled in religious conflicts, as Turkey, Iran, and Egypt have illustrated in recent decades.

Yeltsin's government cannot afford to completely separate itself from the Orthodox Church, whose reputation and history far outweigh those of the state. And yet neither can Yeltsin's government alienate adherents of other religions without exacerbating the cleavages that divide the diverse population of the Russian Federation. In the long run the government must associate itself with universal Russian values that are consistent with Orthodoxy but that also transcend religious differences. In the United States such a set of values has often been defined as Judeo-Christian. It is unclear whether an analogous lowest common denominator of quasi-religious values even exists in contemporary Russia.

Suggested Readings

Anderson, John. *Religion, State, and Politics in the Soviet Union and Successor States.* Cambridge: Cambridge University Press, 1994.

Davis, Nathanial. *A Long Walk to Church: A Contemporary History of Russian Orthodoxy.* Boulder: Westview, 1995.

Neilsen, Neils C., Jr., ed. *Christianity after Communism: Social, Political, and Cultural Struggle in Russia.* Boulder: Westview, 1994.

Preobrazhensky, Alexander, ed. *The Russian Orthodox Church: 10th to 20th Centuries.* Moscow: Progress Publishers, 1988.

Ellis, Jane. *The Russian Orthodox Church: A Contemporary History.* Bloomington and Indianapolis: Indiana University Press, 1986.

Part V

Russia and the World

12

Russian Foreign Policy

After the sudden conclusion of the Cold War during the final years of Gorbachev's rule—comprising in part the reduction and even elimination of entire classes of nuclear weapons; the unification of Germany and the withdrawal of all foreign troops from Berlin; the dissolution of the Warsaw Treaty Organization and the redefinition of the North Atlantic Treaty Organization as an organization without specified adversaries; and the accession of Moscow to the American-led coalition against Iraq—after all this, it would have seemed churlish for the West to have exploited the logical, though unanticipated, disintegration of the Soviet Union itself in 1991. Instead, the West, led by the United States, sought to create a nonthreatening environment for the dismantling of Russia's 74-year-old Communist empire. Through a combination of official pronouncements and largely symbolic military reconfigurations, the new American strategy of accommodation in essence reassured the Soviet regime and then the post-Soviet leadership that the West harbored no hard feelings from the Cold War, that so long as Moscow had forgone its military and ideological hostility toward the West, the United States would treat it without prejudice.

Russia's foreign policy during its first months as an independent state in many ways exceeded the West's expectations for post-Soviet repentance. Russian cooperation where once there had been Soviet confrontation facilitated a second strategic arms treaty, a united front against North Korea's nuclear program, a rejuvenated and restructured European security organization, and other signs of what American President George Bush called a "new world order." Domestically, Russian economic and political reform efforts, though uneven, suggested that the Yeltsin government was committed to overcoming the legacy of Communist rule.

By 1994, however, the bloom already was off Bush's new world order. In the Balkans, in the Persian Gulf, and in Eastern Europe, Russian and Western policies and stated interests clashed. Russian military actions in the territory of its neighbors raised concerns about a renewal of Russian imperialism. Russian arms sales to Iran and other "pariah" countries raised fears of a new arms race. And Moscow's voice in the UN Security Council began once again to obstruct Western-initiated proposals.

Although these and other actions quickly eroded the Russian Federation's image as a rehabilitated member of the international community, they did not indicate the inevitable "reverting to type" of a hopelessly imperialist, anti-Western Russia. Rather, the discontinuities in Russian foreign policy in the mid-1990s reflected a clash of forces struggling to define Russia itself. It is the outcome of that domestic struggle which will most influence the orientation of Russian foreign policy at the dawning of the new millennium.

Systemic Collapse

The attenuation of Russian amity in the international sphere might be explained by what amounts to a Russian identity crisis. Whereas Americans perhaps can feel a sense of closure for having prevailed in the Cold War and can turn their attention back to the regular business of being Americans, Russians must reconstruct an international role and even a self-image for their country. They now find the ideological shibboleths that served, however awkwardly and imperfectly, as a surrogate raison d'être for most of this century, discredited and abandoned. The cohesion of the Russian people has been further diluted, as the fragmentation of the Soviet Union instantly caused one-seventh of the Russian population to become foreigners in newly created (or re-created) countries. Virtually all of Moscow's confederates in the Cold War have severed their ideological and military ties with Russia and redirected their attention westward. And today, for the first time in most of their lives, Russians find that their country is not an especially influential player in world affairs. It therefore should come as no surprise that the relatively restrained foreign policy of post-Soviet Russia's first years should come under domestic fire.

Nor should the consequent change in Russia's official foreign policy orientation be surprising. The rapidity of the changes in the late 1980s and early 1990s should have taught the West how suddenly change can come to even so firm an international order as the bipolar system of postwar Europe. But as public opinion polls indicate, Americans have not resisted the temptation to accept the first outlines of the post–Cold War world as essentially fixed—the "end of history," as it were. Such thinking misses an important point, particularly regarding Russia: The collapse of the bipolar order neither exorcised all Russia's motives nor eviscerated all its powers for opposing the West, any more than the 1917 Revolution precluded alliance with the Americans during the Second World War. Instead, by destroying the ideological and institutional frameworks through which Soviet Russia conducted its foreign relations, the demise of the Cold War imposed on Russia the need to fashion a new modus vivendi with the West, with the East, and even with parts of the newly dismantled Soviet Union itself. The nature of those new relationships is neither yet stable nor predictable. Russia, like the world order itself, is still reeling from the blows of 1989–1991.

Reorientation

The unsettled nature of Russia's international orientation rises not only from international turbulence, but also from internal disorder. Without the coordinating function of the Communist Party of the Soviet Union, post-Soviet Russia found itself without an apparatus for making coherent foreign policy.

The Foreign-Policy Apparatus

Russia's Foreign Ministry naturally held a significant claim for foreign-policy-making responsibilities. But the exigencies of domestic politics brought challenges in the form of other institutional actors. The Supreme Soviet, and later the State Duma, increasingly challenged the Foreign Ministry's policies and actions, generally opposing what was perceived to be Foreign Minister Andrei Kozyrev's obsequiousness toward the West.

Meanwhile, other institutions solidified their claims on Russia's foreign policy making process. These pressures increased until the opposition's strength in the Duma was renewed in the December 1995 elections, after which Yeltsin relented and replaced Kozyrev with Yevgeny Primakov. In October 1991 the KGB was broken into two parts, with one, the Foreign Intelligence Service (SVR), responsible for gathering intelligence. Moscow established a Russian Defense Ministry and an independent Russian army in May 1992, marking the end of Moscow's hope that defense of the former Soviet republics could be coordinated through the Commonwealth of Independent States. In July

1996 Yeltsin added an 18 member Defense Council to help draft military policy. In addition to the various legislative committees, government ministries, and presidential councils associated with foreign policy, a variety of non-governmental and quasi-governmental foreign-policy think tanks also arose, including the high-profile Council for Foreign and Defense Policy. Several of these directly opposed the government's official foreign policies.

In an effort to coordinate foreign-policy making processes and bodies, an Inter-departmental Foreign Policy Commission (IFPC) was established within Russia's Security Council in December 1992. In effect, however, the IFPC merely became another actor in a crowded field of foreign-policy bodies. Eventually frustrated by the unsatisfactory implementation of his foreign-policy objectives, Boris Yeltsin in late 1995 created the Presidential Foreign Policy Council, which attempted (yet again) to coordinate foreign policy from the president's office. The council was to draw together the ministers of defense, foreign affairs, CIS affairs, and finance, as well as the heads of the intelligence and security agencies.

Besides dealing with the day to day business of maintaining Russia's relations with the outside world, the various institutions of the country's foreign-policy apparatus sought to develop more cohesive, broader expressions of Russian interests. Along these lines the Council on Foreign and Defense Policy released its Strategy for Russia in the summer of 1992, offering an alternative conception of Russia's international orientation. The Foreign Ministry developed its Foreign Policy Concept in early 1993, and this was subsequently modified before approval by the Security Council. The Defense Ministry, for its part, drafted a military doctrine shortly after its creation in 1992, and the doctrine was approved with modifications in November 1993. In the fall of 1996 Prime Minister Viktor Chernomyrdin called for a new military doctrine to facilitate fundamental restructuring of the armed forces. Together, these and other expressions of Russian interests in the post–Cold War world illustrate the amorphous and conflicting nature of elite perceptions and values. They also illustrate the degree to which a consensus on Russia's external orientation is prevented by political conflicts among governmental institutions. After its first five years as an independent state, Russia still had not established a coherent *mirovozzrenie* (worldview) on which to base its policy.

Those who try to understand the emerging identity and nascent foreign policy of contemporary Russia can do more than shrug and retreat into a pessimistic (mis-) interpretation of Churchill's "riddle/mystery/enigma" comment. Although the making of Russian foreign policy traverses a vaguer path and involves a broader range of actors than in the Soviet period, the discussion of foreign policy is freer and franker than during the Cold War. A first step, therefore, is to identify the primary orientations visible among Russian elite.

Debate in Three Dimensions

Observing cleavages in Russian foreign policy orientations has a long, if perhaps not distinguished, history. Analysts have traditionally distinguished between "Westernizers" and "Slavophiles" in Russia. But the questions surrounding Russia's place in the world are more complex than this dichotomy suggests. Instead, one can identify at least three primary cleavages in Russian attitudes about their country's foreign policy orientation.

Civilization Linkages   Foremost in Russia's debate over foreign policy is the question of the country's linkage with broadly-defined civilizations. This debate is most closely related to the Westernizer/Slavophile dichotomy. Although this distinction has been defined in various ways, it essentially arises from Russia's somewhat ambivalent existence on the border of two civilizations: the Western and the Slavic.[1] Questions about Russia's membership in either or both of these civilizations were especially salient during the reforms of Peter the Great, the rise of the Enlightenment, and the construction of the Soviet empire. Most recently, the Westernizer/Slavophile dichotomy has been made salient by the efforts of Gorbachev, Yeltsin, and other Soviet and Russian leaders to adopt Western political and economic systems, and otherwise to promote values associated with the West. Russia today has been called a "torn country," divided between two civilizations.[2] The Westernizers see Russia as a European country desiring to adopt Western values and emulate Western society. By contrast, the Slavophiles emphasize Russia's Slavic heritage, viewing their country as spiritually, ethnically, and historically distinct from the West. Developing a consensus on Russia's civilization ties is especially relevant as a prerequisite for a proper discussion of foreign policy: Self-knowledge should precede the identification of friends and enemies.

In the mid-1990s a number of foreign policy issues hinged upon how Russia viewed its civilization ties. Its relations with Germany, long a product of ambivalent attitudes, partly depended on whether Russia saw itself as Western. So did the matter of Russia's participation in international institutions such as the International Monetary Fund and the World Trade Organization, which long had been perceived as Western-dominated organizations. International sanctions on the Serb-dominated rump Yugoslavia stuck in the craw of Russian Slavophiles who felt Russians should defend their Slavic brethren. The matter of Russia's economic and political ties with Belarus and Ukraine, both Slavic countries, similarly turned on this issue.

---

1. See Samuel Huntington, "A Clash of Civilizations?" *Foreign Affairs*, 72:3 (Summer 1993): 22–49.
2. Ibid, pp. 43–44.

The civilization debate does not, however, capture all, or even the most important, aspects of the current efforts to redefine Russia's place in the world. Although the distinction between Westernizers and Slavophiles demarcates a primary fissure in conceptions of Russian identity, other dichotomies— or, in the language of pluralism, "cross-cutting cleavages"— further divide Russian foreign-policy orientations.

Geographical Scope of Interests   Distinct from the strict question of civilization linkage, but related, is the matter of the geographical scope of Russian interests. The debate in this dimension concerns Russia's Great Power status. In simple terms, the debate pits those who see Russia as a regional power against those who retain a sense of Russia's global role. Those persons adopting the latter orientation typically wish Russia to retain the global interests and policies developed during the Soviet period. Although few cling to the Cold War terminology of "superpowers," the champions of Russia's global interests speak of Russia as a "special" power in the same category as the United States. On the other hand, many Russians partly blame the Soviet Union's collapse on overextended interests— "imperial overstretch," to use historian Paul Kennedy's famous phrase.[3] They see Russian interests as properly confined to a limited sphere of influence.

Although Russia generally continued Gorbachev's gradual contraction of Moscow's global military operations, the question of defining the geographical scope of Russia's legitimate interests remains. This question has manifested itself in Russia's attempt to find a role for itself in the Middle East peace process, in the Bosnian conflict, and in relations with South Africa. The issue infuses the debates about Russia's position within the CIS and the protection of Russian minorities living abroad. In addition, the issue colors Moscow's attitude toward arms control and the activities of the Organization for Security and Cooperation in Europe (OSCE), the United Nations, and other international organizations.

Level of External Threats   A third dimension of the fundamental debates that underlie efforts to define Russia's place in the world concerns perceptions of outside threats to Russia. Notwithstanding George Bush's new-world-order paradigm, the international sphere remains conflictual. As must all countries, Russia must evaluate the nature and extent of threats to its interests. The most obvious of these threats is, of course, the United States' nuclear arsenal. Despite arms reduction agreements and a de-escalation of

---

3. Paul Kennedy. *The Rise and Fall of the Great Powers: Economic Change and Military Conflict from 1500 to 2000.* (New York: Random House, 1987.)

tensions, the United States and Russia retain nuclear forces capable of anni-hilating each other. Other countries, including China, also possess substantial nuclear forces.

There are numerous less dramatic potential threats to Russian territory and interests. Islamic fundamentalism in Central Asia, in the Middle East, and even within Russia itself is a frequent worry. Factional fighting in Bosnia and in the former Soviet republics also gives cause for Russian anxiety. Even the expansion of the European Union and the development of new World Trade Organization regulations are held up as potential threats to Russia's economic and trade interests. Most of all, Russians are preoccupied with the expansion of NATO as a potential threat to their country's interests.

Significant disagreement exists among Russians as to the nature and level of these potential threats. Certainly Russia's foreign-policy orientation depends fundamentally on the perceived threat emanating from beyond Russia's borders. Until Russia's political elites develop some basic consensus on this issue, Russian foreign policy will remain somewhat tentative.

Overall, the three cross-cutting dimensions of Russia's foreign-policy debate provide for a broad range of foreign-policy doctrines. If each dimension is treated as a dichotomy, eight possible foreign-policy orientations can be identified (see Figure 12–1). Each of the eight categories probably is not equally represented among Russian elite, but the existence of these cross-cutting cleavages suggests an important insight: Two persons with similar views in one dimension will not necessarily share the same opinions in other dimensions. Indeed, this could explain both the rifts within the "reformist" and "hardline" ranks, and the unexpected hardening of Russia's rhetoric toward the West. In the case of coalition rifts, Yeltsin may have been losing support from erstwhile allies, not for abandoning the Westernizer course to which he was putatively committed, but because he and they parted ways at a second or third dimension of the foreign-policy debate. Regarding Russia's relations with the West, Yeltsin and his supporters may well remain committed Westernizers. They may even be committed to a less globalist interpretation of Russian interests (although these remain debatable points). However, in the mid-1990s Yeltsin and his advisers seemed to be edging toward a more nationalistic rhetoric designed to placate those who saw the international order as hostile to Russia and its legitimate interests.

Heeding Nationalism

The nationalists' grievances had grown increasingly vocal in the mid-1990s. Yeltsin and his foreign minister until 1996, Andrei Kozyrev, were accused of selling short the Russian people in an effort to obtain Western aid. The nationalists found humiliating what they perceived as the Yeltsin

CIVILIZATION LINKAGE

		Western		Slavic	
		SCOPE OF INTERESTS		**SCOPE OF INTERESTS**	
		Global	Regional	Global	Regional
PERCEIVED EXTERNAL THREAT	Low				
	High				

Figure 12–1   Three dichotomies underlying Russian foreign policy debates

administration's pandering to the West. They chafed at what they described as Russia's role as a "junior partner," which "only says 'Yes,' silently swallowing affronts and even insults."[4]

In the mid-1990s, while maintaining a commitment to a Western foreign-policy orientation, Yeltsin and his spokesmen adopted many of the nationalists' themes and even some of their terminology. It was a somewhat defensive theme, sometimes heard by foreign governments as a threat, that Russia must be treated by the West, and by the United States in particular, as a great power. Although Yeltsin took up this argument with some urgency shortly before and after the 1995 Duma elections, he had never neglected it completely. In October 1992, for example, Yeltsin criticized his own Foreign Ministry for its alleged lack of well-defined foreign policy, especially with regard to the interests of Russians living abroad and to the preservation of Russia's Great Power status. But as the Communists, Liberal Democrats, and other forces of the Red-Brown opposition gained political power in the mid-1990s, Yeltsin and his foreign minister adopted more nationalistic tones. When this failed to prevent the Red-Brown victory in the December 1995 Duma elections, Yeltsin

---

4. *Izvestiya*, October 28, 1993, cited in John Lough, "The Place of the 'Near Abroad' in Russian Foreign Policy," *RFE/RL Research Report*, 2:11 (March 12, 1993): 28.

replaced Kozyrev with Yevgeny Primakov, who was less susceptible to charges of ignoring Russia's national interests.

Policies and Relationships

Notwithstanding political rhetoric, how have the competing views within the Russian foreign-policy debate played out in foreign-policy actions? In the Russian Federation's first five years, Russia remained somewhat restrained in its international behavior. While the Kremlin made loud noises in opposition to the expansion of NATO, and vociferously protested NATO air strikes against the Bosnian Serbs in 1995 and U.S. attacks on Iraq in 1996, Russia took few provocative actions outside the former Soviet Union.

The "mellowing" of Moscow's international behavior (to use George Kennan's term), which began under Mikhail Gorbachev, had been motivated largely by economic considerations. Gorbachev sought to reduce the costs of empire and of the arms race, and to earn the West's good will, financial assistance, and trade benefits. Much of this logic still applied to post-Soviet Russia. Although no longer as contrite as it had been in the final years of Gorbachev's rule, Moscow still recognized that it could ill afford the adventurism that had characterized much of Soviet foreign policy. Perhaps the Russian political and military leadership still felt wary after the Red Army's de facto defeat in Afghanistan by the rebel *mujahideen*. Perhaps Moscow retained a posture more in search of stability than of geostrategic advantage, choosing Lenin's doctrine of *peredyshka* ("breathing space") over Leon Trotsky's "permanent revolution" or even Andrei Zhdanov's "two camps." Certainly the Russian Federation's international position in the 1990s bore similarities to post–World War I Soviet Russia. Not only had it recently removed itself from an international war it could not win, but it also found itself partially surrounded by hostile armies (this time by Chinese troops). It is one of history's ironies that post-Soviet Russia would be burdened with a Communist threat at its southern border.

Russian diplomacy in the first half of the 1990s generally sought to normalize its international relationships which had been either exacerbated by the Cold War or thrown into turmoil by the collapse of the bipolar order. In January 1992 Moscow and Washington signed the START II Treaty, which committed both countries to further reductions in their strategic nuclear arsenals. Russian-American cooperation was further enhanced through such symbolic actions as joint military maneuvers and a joint space program. In addition, Russia applied for membership in various international organizations that once had been associated with the West: the General Agreement on Tariffs and Trade (later the World Trade Organization), the International Monetary Fund, the Council of Europe, the Group of Seven, the Organization for Economic Cooperation and Development, and even NATO's Partnership for Peace. In 1993 the Russian Federation and Japan issued the Tokyo Declaration, which committed the two countries to a prompt settlement of their long-running dispute over the Kuril Islands. In all these ways Russia gradually moved itself into the international mainstream.

Being in the mainstream has not guaranteed harmony of interests, of course. Indeed, Russia's relations with the Western powers frequently are tested by conflicting positions on issues. Despite the Tokyo Declaration, a resolution of the Kuril Islands dispute continued to evade Moscow and Tokyo three years later. And four years after the signing of START II, the Duma continued to hold up ratification of the treaty. (The United States Senate ratified it only in 1996.) Meanwhile, the Russian parliament threatened to renounce the 1990 Conventional Forces in Europe (CFE) Treaty, unless the treaty were revised to accommodate Moscow's post-Soviet situation. On top of this, the discovery of highly-placed Russian spies in Britain and the United States in late 1996 spoke against Russia's declared "partnership" with the West. It has nevertheless generally been taken as a sign of international stability that Russia and the West can clash over their different interests without returning to the Cold War.

The Russian-German Axis

From amidst Russia's reconciliation with various Cold War adversaries emerged a special relationship between Germany and Russia. Diplomatic relations between the Soviet Union and the Federal Republic of Germany during the Cold War had been formalized in the 1970s, under the umbrella of détente and Bonn's "new Ostpolitik." Still, the relationship was one of grudging cooperation, ambivalent motives, and (especially for Moscow) cynical manipulation. Today, with both Russia and Germany experiencing economic and social challenges, as well as shared concern about political instability in Eastern Europe and the former Soviet Union, Bonn and Moscow have apparently found that their problems require shared solutions. Or, to put it differently, that their political and economic interests intersect.

Certainly Chancellor Helmut Kohl's Germany recognizes that logic. Bonn has called improving relations with Russia a cornerstone of its foreign policy. It was among the first major powers to lend recognition and support to Yeltsin's leadership, both during and after Russia's separation from the Soviet Union, through cooperative agreements and treaties.[5] Germany has provided

---

5. A 12-page Russian-German cooperation agreement was signed on Yeltsin's trip to Bonn a few months before the demise of the Soviet Union. In April 1992 Germany and Russia agreed to a mutual cancellation of debts.

hundreds of billions of Deutsche marks to Russia in aid (including debt for-giveness and funding for the withdrawal of Russian troops from its territory), amounting to more than half of all Western aid to Russia combined. The Kohl leadership is one of Russia's most enthusiastic boosters in such multilateral organizations as the European Union, the IMF, and the G-7. German support for Yeltsin's Russia also extends beyond financial assistance. In a way reminiscent of the governments of Peter the Great and Catherine the Great, some German nationals today hold official positions as advisers to Russia's government. As their Petrine predecessors did, many Russian officials now welcome the infusion of German expertise. Perhaps even more significantly, Kohl made it his mission in 1995 and 1996 to stump for Yeltsin before Russia's June 1996 presidential election. To a large extent the special relationship between Russia and Germany was supported by the personal relationship between Yeltsin and Kohl.

Some observers (not least of which were those in Warsaw) viewed the warming relationship between post-Soviet Russia and reunited Germany with anxiety. The rise of rightist elements in Germany and Russia spurred speculation about a confluence of reactionary agendas in the two countries. It became fashionable to observe that, in Alexei Pushkov's words, "There are striking similarities between Russia today and the rise of Nazism in Germany."[6] A variety of developments played on those fears, including Zhirinovsky's calls for a redrawing of European boundaries to the benefit of Germany and Russia. Yet worries of a new Rapallo or, more darkly, a new Molotov-Ribbentrop Pact, appear to be unfounded. Bonn has scrupulously denounced rightist elements in both countries, even denying an entry visa to Zhirinovsky after his election to parliament in the fall of 1993. Even after Kohl's government is eventually replaced, Germany's postwar democratic institutions and its integration with the West place the reins of government beyond the extremists' grasp. Further, there are signs that the warming of German-Russian relations have reached their limit. In the mid-1990s Germany was showing little patience for Russia's demands for further economic aid and its opposition to NATO expansion. Finally, Russia was simply too preoccupied with the stabilization of the territories of the former Soviet Union to dream of a grand alliance with Germany to dominate Europe.

Indeed, even Eastern Europe has slipped from Moscow's primary foreign-policy focus. It is true that Russian foreign-policy statements have described Eastern Europe as part of "Russia's historical sphere of interests." And Russia has repeatedly expressed concern about the Partnership for Peace, insofar as it extends the American-led alliance closer to the borders of Russia. Nevertheless, Russian policy concerning Eastern Europe has been largely reactive;

---

6. "Is Yeltsin Becoming a Dictator?" *The Christian Science Monitor,* December 31, 1993: 19.

Yeltsin's Russia (like Gorbachev's Soviet Union before it) was surprisingly willing to virtually abandon Moscow's postwar sphere of influence in Eastern Europe. Russia's pullout of former Red Army troops from the region was conducted with little hesitation. And although Moscow protested alleged discrimination against Serbia in United Nations actions in former Yugoslavia, the Russians generally abided by UN sanctions and other decisions concerning the country. The projection of Russia's military power instead has been generally confined much closer to home.

The Near Abroad

The foreign-policy actions of the Russian Federation in its first five years suggested that Moscow's historical preoccupation with Eastern Europe had taken a back seat to its new border countries—that is, the Near Abroad. The very phrase "Near Abroad," which crept into Russian policy statements in early 1992, reflects a particular foreign-policy orientation. That countries as diverse politically, geographically, and economically as Estonia, Ukraine, and Turkmenistan could be treated as politically similar targets of a particular Russian policy orientation suggests Russia's stubborn adherence to the notion of empire. Other evidence of this accumulated as the years went on.

The Commonwealth of Independent States (CIS) had been established in December 1991 as a way of coordinating the trade, security, and foreign policy of most former Soviet republics. Structurally the CIS was rather amorphous, with ad hoc bodies and vague mandates. Over time, however, Russia has repeatedly tried to deepen the integration of the CIS countries. It has proposed and implemented "ruble zones" and customs unions that link the members' economic systems. It has worked toward the creation of a common air defense system for the CIS members. It has sought to establish permanent decision-making bodies for the CIS that would exercise real power. Moscow's integration efforts became especially earnest in 1995, as Yeltsin announced that further expansion of NATO would leave Russia with no choice but to transform the CIS into a genuine military and political alliance along the lines of the Warsaw Treaty Organization. But as of the mid-1990s, most of these efforts had accomplished little in the way of reestablishing a functional equivalent of the Soviet Union.

Even without formal integration, Russia soon managed to use the CIS as a framework for projecting, or at least as a fig leaf for obscuring, its influence in the former Soviet Union. In the mid-1990s Moscow had troops or "military specialists" stationed in every CIS state. In many of those countries, such as Moldova, Georgia, Belarus, and Tajikistan, the Russian presence was substantial. Some of these troops Russia deployed to quell civil wars on the territory of CIS members. (It is widely believed that Moscow had been behind the initial causes of some of those civil wars, particularly in Georgia.) For some of these operations, Russia has requested and received UN endorsement, although Russian troops were denied the status of UN peacekeepers. Russian troops also have been deployed to protect CIS "exterior" borders between Belarus and Poland and between Tajikstan and Afghanistan.

From these and other actions emerged a Russian Monroe Doctrine, or a Yeltsin Doctrine, in which Yeltsin ascribed to Russia the "peacekeeping burden in the territory of the former Soviet Union." Increasingly, Russia has become more direct about its need to maintain its sphere of influence. Official statements speak of "ensuring the stability and military security on the entire territory of the former Soviet Union." They define Russia as the "guarantor of the stability of relations among the states which used to make up the Soviet Union." They express the desire "to achieve the greatest possible degree of integration among the former Union republics in all spheres of their vital activities." They proclaim the importance of the "security of the Commonwealth's external borders," and they emphasize that the "internal borders" between the former Soviet republics "were never intended to be real borders." And they identify "instability in the CIS" as the greatest external threat to Russia.[7]

At the same time, Moscow was working on a more piecemeal basis to bind the wayward republics of the former Soviet Union to Russia. In the spring of 1996, for example, the presidents of Russia, Belarus, Kazakhstan, and Kyrgistan signed the Treaty on Deepening Integration in Economic and Humanitarian Spheres, which called for a common market and other coordinating institutions. The presidents also agreed to establish an Inter-government Council, an Integration Committee, and an Inter-Parliamentary Committee. Other CIS states were invited to join these bodies.

Since Belarus gained independence from the Soviet Union, its depressed economy has conspired with its close cultural ties with Russia to push the country toward a renewed union. In May 1995, for example, Russia and Belarus formed a customs union. A year later the two countries moved still closer to integration by signing the Treaty on Forming a Community. While confirming the two countries' "sovereignty and equality," the treaty creates a joint Supreme Council to direct economic and political integration. Yeltsin and Belarus President Aleksandr Lukashenka suggested the treaty would lead to a single currency and perhaps even a single constitution by the end of 1997. The fact that both countries declared the April 2 signing date an annual public holiday may underscore the intended importance of the treaty. The augmented powers granted to Lukashenka in a November 1996 referendum increased the chances that his integrationist goals would be realized.

---

7. These statements are drawn from Russia's Foreign Policy Concept and from Yeltsin's spring 1996 "National Security Message" to the Federal Assembly.

Significantly, a deepening of integration with the former Soviet Union's third Slavic country, Ukraine, has eluded Moscow. The countries remain embroiled in disputes arising from the collapse of the Soviet Union. Especially contentious has been the basing of the Black Sea Fleet, which itself has been a subject of ownership disputes between the two countries. The problem extends to the status of the Crimean peninsula, which had once been Russian, but which Khrushchev had transferred to Ukraine in the 1950s. The transfer did not matter much at the time, given that republican ownership was superseded by Soviet unity. After the collapse of the Soviet Union, however, the Crimea's large ethnic Russian population has called for the return of their territory to Russia.

Disagreements between Russia and Ukraine also developed with regard to the former Soviet nuclear arsenal. The Soviets had deployed their nuclear weapons in four republics: Russia, Ukraine, Belarus, and Kazakhstan. Although the four countries signed an agreement in 1992 to consolidate all tactical nuclear weapons on Russian soil, the matter of strategic weapons took longer. Ukraine hesitated to give up its strategic nuclear missiles, claiming that it required security guarantees from the West before it could give up this important defense against Russia. Five years after the independence of Ukraine and Russia, the two countries had made little progress in resolving the issues that divide them. Yeltsin nevertheless pledged at the G-7 summit in April 1996 that all remaining Soviet strategic warheads would be on Russian soil by the end of the year. They were not. (ICBMs remained in Belarus as well, with Lukashenka insisting they were necessary as a hedge against NATO deployments in Eastern Europe.)

The political resonance of the idea of restoring the Soviet Union was most dramatically illustrated by the State Duma on March 15, 1996. On that day a Communist-led majority passed a resolution declaring the 1991 dissolution of the Soviet Union (the so-called Belavezha Accords) to have been illegal, and thus void. Although the referendum had little practical influence upon the independence of the former Soviet republics, it demonstrated the lingering nostalgia for the Soviet Union and the collective strength of the hard-liners in the Duma. Two days later the Communist Party of the Russian Federation announced the "voluntary" restoration of the Soviet Union as a plank of its presidential platform. The Duma has also taken other symbolic actions in support of the Soviet Union, such as condemning desecration of the Soviet flag (a not uncommon activity in post-Soviet Russia). Not to be outdone on the emotional topic of the Soviet flag, Yeltsin issued a decree restoring the flag as an official symbol for ceremonies connected with the Second World War. A few weeks later, presidential candidate Gennady Zyuganov also got in on the act, promising that, if elected, he would call a referendum to make the Soviet flag the official flag of the Russian Federation.

For the moment Russian actions and statements are largely inconsistent. Whether Russia really intends to reestablish an empire, particularly in the face of strong Western opposition (were it to materialize), is impossible to know. This is not due so much to secrecy on Russia's part as it is to the absence of cohesive goals among Russian policy elite. Distinguishing statements and even actions meant for domestic consumption from those that are truly strategic will require considerable study, analysis, and especially the passage of time.

Prospects

Those who would hope to understand the future of Russian foreign policy are frustrated by the country's apparent lack of a cohesive new Russian identity, an established process for making foreign policy, and a predominant ideological bloc. There is, in short, little solid ground from which to project a consistent foreign-policy orientation. And yet, although we cannot know how the mix of Russian interests and policies will come to be defined, we can at least estimate the viability of the primary foreign-policy orientations. And in assessing Russia's ability to carry out its various options, we would do well to recall that the Soviet Union collapsed.

Mikhail Gorbachev spent seven years attempting to address his country's economic, political, and societal problems, which he believed had crept in during the "stagnation" of the Brezhnev years but which, it turned out, resulted from congenital defects within the system itself. Not only did the collapse of the Soviet Union reflect and exacerbate the economic problems that prevented the country from maintaining its position in the arms race, and not only did the collapse of the Soviet Union dismantle the empire the Communist Party had created for military and economic gain, but it more importantly stripped away the façade with which the Kremlin had projected its image as a superpower. The events of the late 1980s and early 1990s revealed the myth of Soviet superiority for what it was. Superpowerdom is more than nuclear weapons and empires. It is more than winning Olympic gold medals and reaching the moon. A key requirement for a superpower—even a "great power"—is having the ability to command respect and, perhaps, admiration. The Soviet Union achieved its visible measures of superpowerdom, such as Sputnik and its empire in Eastern Europe, at the cost of the dignity, freedom, and even the lives of its and other people. It bought its industrial achievements at the cost of its environment, as witnessed at Chernobyl and Magnitogorsk. It founded its image as a "proletarian state" upon subterfuge, lies, and hypocrisy. The calls one hears in Russia for a return to the Soviet Union's past glory therefore ring hollow, hearkening as they do to a past that never was.

Beyond the loss of the superpower image, Russia is still saddled with much of the economic, political, societal, and environmental crises that had beset Gorbachev's Soviet Union. There is little reason to believe that these problems were suddenly expunged by cutting loose the periphery of the Soviet empire and changing the political structures through which the same group of elites govern. The causes of the Soviet crisis did not evaporate with the demise of the Soviet Union itself.

Creating and maintaining an empire is a costly proposition. For the Soviet Union it became an unaffordable task, at least given the particular economic, military, and political resources available to the Kremlin. It amounted to a demonstration of Paul Kennedy's "imperial overstretch," although Kennedy evidently expected to see it in the United States before observing it in the Soviet Union.[8] Why would Russia now want to acquire the same albatross of empire?

Heeding the more imperialistic foreign-policy orientations would ensure that post-Soviet Russia remains saddled with the fundamental problems encountered and mishandled by Gorbachev. Imperialism would prevent Russia from returning to great power status. It well could promote a further disintegration of the Russian Federation. Today, it is Chechnya. Will Tatarstan be next? Parts of Siberia?

The Russians have been granted a reprieve. The Soviet Union was on a collision course with the West for four decades after the Second World War. The global war that both sides feared and prepared for never materialized, and many, including Gorbachev, deserve praise for averting it. As George Kennan anticipated in 1947, the Soviet Union did in fact break up. It now is up to Russia to complete its transformation, to heal the self-inflicted wounds of the Soviet period. Russia is a large country with a proud people and many historic achievements. It doubtless has foreign-policy interests connected with its worthy characteristics that most of the rest of the international community can appreciate. If Russia can transform itself to emphasize those positive aspects, while at the same time putting to rest the myths created by the Soviets, then Russia can be a great power indeed.

Suggested Readings

Blackwill, Robert D., Rodric Braithwaite, and Akihiko Tanaka. *Engaging Russia*. New York: Trilateral Commission, 1995.

Kennedy-Pipe, Caroline. *Stalin's Cold War: Soviet Strategies in Europe, 1943–56*. Manchester: Manchester University Press, 1995.

---

8. Kennedy, op cit.

Kolstoe, Paul. *Russians in the Former Soviet Republics.* Bloomington: Indiana University Press, 1995.

Malcolm, Neil and Alex Pravda. *International Factors in Russian Foreign Policy.* New York: Oxford University Press, 1996.

Odom, William E. and Robert Dujarric. *Commonwealth or Empire? Russia, Central Asia, and the Transcaucasus.* Indianapolis: Hudson Institute, 1995.

Ra'anan, Uri and Kate Martin, eds. *Russia: A Return to Imperialism?* New York: St. Martin's Press, 1995.

Rumer, Eugene B. *Russian National Security and Foreign Policy in Transition.* Santa Monica: RAND, 1995.

Shearman, Peter, ed. *Russian Foreign Policy Since 1990.* Boulder: Westview Press, 1995.

Wallander, Celeste A., ed. *The Sources of Russian Foreign Policy After the Cold War.* Boulder: Westview Press, 1996.

Webber, Mark. *The International Politics of Russia and the Successor States.* Manchester: Manchester University Press, 1996.

13

Russia at the Twenty-First Century

For Russia will certainly inherit the future.

— D. H. Lawrence

Russia is one of the world's most resilient countries. Well over a millennium has passed since the founding of Kievan Rus in the ninth century. Since that time, Russia's history has been marked by disruptive and sometimes cataclysmic epochs. It suffered under the Mongol yoke for two centuries; it was ruled by the House of Romanov for 300 years; it expanded its frontiers through continual imperial conquest; it was overrun by the armies of Napoleon and Hitler, and it repulsed both at enormous cost; it was stifled by the totalitarian control of the Communists for most of this century. Given such a history, Russia's half-dozen years as an independent post-Soviet state can hardly be viewed as definitive. The accumulated weight of Russia's past fosters an inertia that is not easily overcome.

And yet there is cause for hope that in its most recent incarnation Russia may succeed in finally bringing to its people a measure of liberty, security, and prosperity. Unlike all of its predecessors, the Russian Federation places ultimate political power in the hands of the people. This has not merely been a formality. The expression of the people's will via elections has been heeded by all political contenders—no small feat for an infant democracy. This, more than any of the myriad other changes Russia has undergone during the final decade of the twentieth century, has radically altered the course of Russia's development. The making of public policy now is limited by the tolerance of public opinion. Whereas the Communist Party of the Soviet Union claimed that its policies were by definition in the interests of the people, the actions of today's Russian leaders must meet the standard of public acceptance. Whereas the Soviet Union's leadership was assembled through the *nomenklatura* system, the Russian Federation's leadership is chosen through the marketplace of political ideas.

As noted in Chapter 6, Russia's procedural democracy should not yet be equated with the type of established democracy found in the West. History has shown that fledging democracies have frequently failed, giving way to coups, dictatorships, and civil wars. Such a fate still may await the Russian Federation. But several events in the mid-1990s helped to improve the chances for democracy's survival. The quality of life for most Russians, though still unacceptably low by Western standards, had begun to rise in a number of important categories. The national economy had ended its free fall and was slowly rising, as shown by a reduction in the country's unemployment and inflation rates. Russia's electoral laws were being expanded and refined, and a number of international organizations had expressed confidence in the basic fairness of its electoral system.

A watershed in Russia's democratic development continued with the presidential elections in June and July of 1996. The election was important at three levels. Most importantly, it marked a further institutionalization of democratic mechanisms. The losers in both rounds of voting accepted the electorate's verdict, and the ultimate winner—Boris Yeltsin—seemed to understand the nature of his mandate.

Secondly, the elections expressed the people's unwillingness to succumb to the Communists' appeals for a reinstitutionalization of Soviet values. It was highly ironic that Yeltsin, who had commonly been labeled as a populist as he challenged Mikhail Gorbachev's leadership, found himself in the position of fending off Communist Gennady Zyuganov's populist appeals. It now was Yeltsin who urged the electorate to stay the course, to support the slow but steady transition to market economics and an expansion of personal responsibility. In the end, the voters did indeed resist the Communists' message of revisionist nostalgia. Yet the voters' rejection of Zyuganov was distinct from a wholehearted endorsement of Yeltsin's policies, as illustrated in the first round of voting, in which Yeltsin garnered barely one of every three votes. It was only with the second round's starker choice of Yeltsin or Zyuganov that the electorate consolidated around Yeltsin.

Hence the third level of significance to the 1996 presidential elections: it provided continuity in the form of Yeltsin's and centrist Viktor Chernomyrdin's leadership. What this leadership lacked in comparison to the democratic ideal was at least partly compensated by the virtue of leadership stability in tumultuous times. And most of the other personnel changes Yeltsin made in his administration—notably the return of economic adviser Anatoly Chubais, this time as Yeltsin's chief of staff—seemed to place Russia's presidential leadership more firmly in the reformist camp.

The next major milestone in the institutionalization of Russian democracy should occur with the scheduled presidential election in 2000. Because the constitution limits Yeltsin to two consecutive terms, a new president must be chosen at the next election. At the latest, therefore, Russia should experience its first democratic transfer of executive power at that time. And the precarious nature of Yeltsin's health, even after a successful cardiac bypass operation in November 1996, made it a strong possibility that he would not see his 69th birthday in 2000, thus necessitating an earlier transfer of power. Either through term limits or physical incapacitation, a transfer of executive power will do much to separate the institution of Russia's presidency from the dominance of a single personality.

Whoever leads Russia into the twenty-first century will face many of the same issues that have sapped Yeltsin's energies: center-periphery relations, balancing individual liberties with societal responsibility, integrating Russia within the community of nations. The end of this decade may see the resolution of some current manifestations of these issues—Chechnya, denationalization, and membership in the Organization for Economic Cooperation and Development, for example—but surely Yeltin's legacy will include numerous other unresolved aspects of these long-lived challenges. It is not, as some given to hyperbole have argued, a matter of life or death for Russia. Whatever the successes and failures of the government's policies, Russia will endure. The more relevant question concerns what kind of Russia will develop from the ruins of the failed Soviet experiment. The leadership's handling of the challenges that face it, and the population's evaluation of those efforts, will help to dissipate the amorphousness that characterizes post-Soviet Russia. Matters as central as Russia's territorial boundaries and population are still subject to redefinition.

Most of all, Russia's development at the twenty-first century will continue to turn on the question of national identity. Other questions concerning the Church, state-society relations, economic and political development, and foreign relations are subordinate to the definition of Russian national identity. Yet at the same time, national identity is not a biological characteristic that is objectively "discovered," but rather it is a cultural feature that is constantly subject to redefinition. National identity is more a matter of public consensus than of destiny. And thus at a time of social and political turbulence, the definition of a nation's identity is highly uncertain. It is formed and reformed by a range of influences, both historical and contemporary, both internal and external.

As so it is that the West should consider its policies concerning Russia carefully. The country is not only politically weak; it also is highly malleable. This does not mean that outside powers, including the Cold War's victors, have the power to direct Russia's development. The complex amalgam of pride and humiliation, of nationalism and cosmopolitanism, of opportunity and denial, of nostalgia and hope—of all these paradoxes that are Russia—cannot easily be directed by its government, let alone orchestrated by outsiders. Their interaction is susceptible to any number of unforeseeable consequences.

The West has already had a tremendous influence upon Russia's development. America's containment policy undeniably contributed to the collapse of the Soviet bloc and of the Soviet Union itself, thereby freeing Russia from the 74-year grip of Soviet Communism and four decades of the stultifying Cold War. Containment was vindicated by the disintegration of the Warsaw Pact, the reunification of Germany, and the liberation of Eastern Europe, in addition to the "non-event" of preventing a westward expansion of Soviet power. But the successful application of Western power and ideas should not be interpreted as a sign of Western omnipotence. It is one thing to protect one's sphere of influence and to defeat an adversary; it is another to remake that defeated adversary in one's own image.

This is not to argue that the West must now sit on the sidelines and watch anxiously as the collapse of Communism plays itself out in the former Soviet Union. In addition to the "negative" objective of preventing Soviet expansion, America's containment doctrine also included a more positive, frequently overlooked, element that called for the West to win the hearts and minds of the peoples behind the iron curtain by force of example. Surely this positive element of containment was at play in East Berlin in 1953, in Hungary in 1956, in Czechoslovakia in 1968, in Poland in the early 1980s, and throughout the Eastern Bloc in 1989. Just as surely it continues to play a role today.

The more passive elements of the West's policy toward Russia might therefore be most effective in encouraging the country's transformation in a more benign direction. In addition to demonstrating the virtues and dividends of an unflinching commitment to such precepts as liberty and rule of law, the West is well advised to afford Russia open access to its markets and capital, to continue to provide technical assistance as needed, and to solicit a wider Russian presence in international organizations and summits. Although the West must forcefully promote its security interests, particularly with regard to such critical matters as the expansion of NATO, security decisions like these cannot ignore the effect they can have upon Russian politics. The imprimatur of elegant foreign policy, after all, is in achieving one's objectives without creating unnecessary conflict.

Russia at the twenty-first century will choose for itself its relationship with the emerging post–Cold War international system. Its options are limited, however. It cannot be a superpower, if for no other reason than the era of superpowers has passed. The post–Cold War international system is too interdependent, too deideologized, and too dangerous for a return to bipolar superpower dominance. Instead, Russia may seek to be a regional hegemon. Or it may seek membership in the Western-oriented world. Or it may retreat into isolation or descend into civil war.

Far from being the "end of history," the dawn of the twenty-first century is the beginning of a new era. Russia's greatest hope, as that of all countries, lies with global engagement and a commitment to the universal human values in whose name the Soviet state was toppled. Only then will Russia finally "inherit the future."

Index